Rebearths

Conversations with a World Ensouled

Edited by Craig Chalquist

World Soul Books
654 Center Street
Walnut Creek, CA 94595

Printed in the United States of America
ISBN 978-0-9826279-1-4

Cover photograph by Katrina Martin Davenport. Spiral image design by Robb Castaneda.

Visit the editor's web site at Chalquist.com.

Contents

DEDICATION

For Earth and all who bow to listen to you.

ACKNOWLEDGMENTS

The editor thanks all the contributors for their soulful writing and many moments of labor to fashion chapters for this book. Thanks also to Lola McCrary (http://www.LolaCanHelp.com/) for her supportive critical feedback.

Introduction:
Coming Deeply Home

Craig Chalquist

In the past when people asked me what my doctoral work involved, or why I spent so much time exploring and writing about California, I told them I was tracking "the spirit or soul of place." When they assumed I meant something metaphysical, as do those "energy" or "vibe" explanations that tend to conceal more than they reveal, I tried this: "I'm interested in how the features of the geographical sites where we live worm their way into our psyches." Did I mean, then, how local air temperature affects mood, or the impact of crowding on emotional development?

What I'm really talking about is a capacity for deep relationship.

Back when I was a troubled young college student, long before my fascination for place, I met a professor who became for me a role model of what a wise, strong, self-related man was like. I felt fully visible to him and understood by him. His influence on me? Profound. This influence could not be grasped, however, in terms of how many minutes we spent talking, the length of his glance upon me, the books he suggested I read, or the effect of the gray and blue sweaters he wore on my mood, self-image, or self-efficacy.

Why not? Because as everyone but the occasional research psychologist knows, the relationship between two people cannot be reduced to its contents or parts. Quantify the details as you will, you still miss the transformative essence, its felt sense, the byplay of conscious and unconscious influences, the very soul or spirit of the encounter. What the relationship means and symbolizes, how much unstated emotional resonance it channels back and forth, and how deeply it reaches into the mind and heart remain out of reach. The reason is simple: a relationship will always present something more once its visible details have been added up. What ties us together runs deeper than empiricism can know, however scientifically informative its limited applications as it peers in from outside.

So it is with our relationship with the living reality of place and nature and Earth.

Unfortunately, most of us miss such complexities because centuries of religion and industry have conditioned us to think of the land and its elements as unintelligent and insensitive, mere dumb resources to be exploited on the road to somewhere else. In fact, some of our scientists now tell us that consciousness is a purely human prerogative even though they can't define or quantify it. Because of this anthropocentric prejudice, ethologists realized only recently that dolphins and elephants can recognize themselves in mirrors, that ravens stage what seem like funerals for dead loved ones, that chimps and otters use tools, that octopuses carry quick-assembly shelters, and that whales sing in languages so complex that their songs compare favorably in information content with human symphonies.

Even so, the idea that Earth itself might possess a kind of primal intelligence, sensitivity, and reactivity has remained excluded from serious study...until now.

In 2007 I published *Terrapsychology: Reengaging the Soul of Place* (Spring Journal Books) to present examples of these remarkable qualities of earthly sentience. Such examples include:

- A graduate student realizing that the writing style of her master's thesis—half concentrated and anecdotal and half linear and expansive—closely paralleled civic history and recent land development in the city she was studying.

- The Devil's Tower, or *Mato Tipila* ("Bear Lodge" in Sioux), where climbers armed with hand and foot spikes come to Wyoming to unconsciously repeat the local Native myth of ascending bears scoring the sides of the igneous butte.

- San Diego and other places showing up in dreams as dream characters who speak accurately about themselves.

- The Garden of Eden imagery playing out in Sebastopol, California, where a dream figure named Evie (Eve) addressed me, a gardener soon to move on, as Cain.

- The numbers **911** decanted from the New York Lottery on September 11, 2002.

- Spring Street, originally named *"Primavera"* (First View), site of these and many other Los Angeles firsts: first multi-story building, first public school, first tall hotel housing the first mechanical elevator, first nightclub, first place motion picture contracts were signed, first City Hall, first city jail, first brewery, first beer garden...as though the street itself contained some invisible but persistent personality trait of "firstness."

- "Kings" in Memphis, Tennessee, a city named after Egypt's royal capital: B.B. King, Martin Luther King Jr. (who died there), Elvis "the King" Presley, the Royal Court of Carnival, Johnny Cash ("king of country"), King Curtis...

- Matthew Cochran's discovery of petroglyphs resembling jets and bombs inscribed long ago at what is now a gunnery range in Three Rivers, New Mexico. Local tales describe Three Rivers as the house of the mythic Thunderbird (see his chapter in this book).

- Inadvertent "continuities" in London (see Peter Ackroyd, *London: The Biography*), where the Public Cleansing Department was unknowingly built on the site of an old public privy, where Whittington Hospital stands over the healing wells at Barnet, and where a sauna on Endell Street echoes an ancient bath. Road courses and curves often correspond to ancient Roman counterparts unmapped, invisible, and discovered only later.

- A question: Do animals "speak" an unconscious symbolic language, as when a grizzly bear enters a hospital emergency room around the time a conservationist describes his species as entering the "emergency room" phase of its existence? Did the family of skunks invading a black tie party in San Francisco parody the human doings there? Does more than chance operate when gangs of rodents immobilize smog-spewing automobiles by chewing up their electrical connections?

- Another question: Do even storms and earthquakes gesture or parody, like Hurricane Katrina invading one oil-rich gulf while American troops invaded another? Is it mere chance or nonhuman intention that the name of refinery-threatening Hurricane Wilma means "Determined Protector"?

- When alchemists of old fashioned exquisite woodcuts and elaborate charts to reflect reactions observed during painstaking experimentation, were these early researchers projecting their own psychological dynamics into matter, as C.G. Jung initially thought, or were they actually revealing what matter looks like to *itself* when screened through states of experimental reverie?

Since the publication of *Terrapsychology*, and in some cases with no previous awareness of the book, more than two dozen beautifully deep approaches to understanding the powerful psychical presence of places, creatures, and things have demonstrated so much originality and creativity that a collection of the most prominent became an obvious necessity.

As the contributors' biographies reveal, the people who work in this "terrapsychological" field come from many backgrounds. My own includes former work in psychotherapy, certification as a Master Gardener through the University of California Cooperative Extension, sustainable landscape design training, a certificate in permaculture design, a doctoral degree in depth psychology (the clinical and research tradition built on the work of Pierre Janet, William James, Sigmund Freud, Alfred Adler, and C.G. Jung), and my own Californian investigations, which began along the coast from San Diego to Sonoma and have since extended into the Great Central Valley. Some chapters herein saw their initial composition as papers for graduate courses I teach at John F. Kennedy University and at the California Institute of Integral Studies.

What is terrapsychology? I first defined it as the study of the presence or "soul" of place. As the pre-Socratic philosopher Thales expressed it long ago, "Place is the greatest thing, as it contains all things." Indigenous and contemporary naturalism, depth psychology, ecopsychology, deep ecology, Systems Theory, panexperientialism, Goethean phenomenology, embodied realism, permaculture's interest in nature's patterns: these and other fields offer insights to light our terrapsychological work.

The deep exploration of our tangled, resonant, and often unconscious relationships with specific geographical locales remains a key aspect of our work and of Terrapsychological Inquiry, an exploratory research methodology proposed by me and expanded by Sarah Rankin and other dedicated investigators (see the Methods section in this book) who understand that the pioneering nose of research should never be confused with its fact-consolidating rear. Terrapsychological work now deals not only with place, however, but with interpreting the metaphoric language of animal behavior, weather, and even supposedly nonliving matter as it *moves beyond facts, units, and quantities by uncovering their underlying forms, images, and reconnective motifs.* In this we owe direction to Jung's practice of "amplification," to Hillman's of "seeing through," and to the seasoned sensitivity to symbol and metaphor that informs the best of the humanities.

Nor do our efforts confine themselves to graduate-level study. Terrapsychology has evolved as a genre, as the following chapters reflect, one that summons forth evocative, post-positivist, non-academic language—"wild speech" Laura Mitchell named it in her dissertation—to illuminate the strength and profundity of our ties to the subtle intelligence of Earth. We need such language to open realms of earthly encounter normally relegated to the margins of consciousness and culture. We need it to compose new stories about why we humans are here and how we should live here—stories that encompass more contextualized variables than simple, linear research will ever be able to handle. And we need it to mature our collectively dismal relations with environments under siege and species threatened, as ours now is, with extinction.

Whether employed as genre, research tool set, psychocartography for mapping the world in depth, or gnosis of place and planet, *terrapsychology is the deep study of our largely unconscious (because disregarded) connections to and interdependencies with the multileveled presence of our living Earth, including specific places, creatures, and materials.* "Deep" because what links us to places and animals and elements travels along bridges of symbol, metaphor, image, and even dream. To say it differently, *terrapsychology explores how the patterns, shapes, features, and motifs at play in the nonhuman world sculpt our ideas, our habits, our relationships, culture, and sense of self.* Whether we know it or not, we speak all the time in the discourse of nature, terrain, and place, their jagged places roughening our turns of phrase, rivers carrying our endeavors onward, skyscrapers tempting us to irresponsible heights, polluted bays polluting our moods, corridors of wildlife preserving our pathways of sanity.

Several contributors to this anthology avail themselves of a mythological lens through which to study the topic that has captured them. As Janet, Freud, Jung, Campbell, Bachelard, a host of poets, and more recently Hillman and Lakoff have shown, our "higher" cognitive operations always rest on a substratum of image, fantasy, and metaphor. When the structures of these operations reveal collective themes and plots, we can identify them as the structures also revealed in myth. To the mythic eye, for example, the preoccupation of Philosophy (from "love of Sophia") of Mind with zombies, automatons, and dead materiality recalls the fall of Sophia into the darkness of matter unconsciously related to. Little wonder deep seeking so often feels like hunting for sparks in the shadows, or as Hermann Hesse put it, gathering flowers in the center of hell.

Very often, however, a depth-psychological analysis stops at the myth or motif "behind" or "below" the surface of the topic of study, as when impressions of a landscape are filed in the Great Mother Archetype category. Terrapsychology closes the circle of inquiry by looking still deeper for the place, creature, world, or thing that hosts the archetypal figure. Seeing in Saint Barbara a Christian variation on fallen Sophia, in brilliant Barbara's case imprisonment and a descent from her high tower, we could interpret Santa Barbara mythologically as a site or altar of Wisdom and leave it at that, but we would leave important questions unaddressed. For example, what tangibilities—geography, soils, minerals, airs—make nearby Summerland an Otherworld, Point Concepcion the Chumash portal to the Beyond, and Carpinteria a kind of *Tir na Nog* or Eternal Land of Youth? What are the implications of this persistent myth for deep education in this county? Because the story will not stay in story-books, we might expect local pedagogy to seesaw between the material and the ethereal, the castles and the lowlands, across many levels inside and outside the academy.

Terrapsychological work—whether writing, research, poetry, art, wisdom practice or some other way into the animate field—grounds itself in four crucial observations:

Facts of environment translate into motifs operative within the human mind and body. Depth psychology taught us long ago that from the perspective of unconscious psychic life, everything around us shimmers as potential symbol. Your home has a front door, and one fine day it flies open and can't be shut. What in your life can't be kept outside any longer? What if we interpreted "outer" facts and events like images in our dreams? Metals would then be metalphors, landscapes inscapes, crowded parking lots holding up our drive, meandering tributaries tributarrying through our moods.

Movements of mind and body parallel movements of nature, surround, and place. Moods and dramas, symptoms, conflicts, and troubles often, perhaps always, reflect those going on all around us: bulging waistlines and urban sprawl, congested conversations and congested freeways, spiritual epiphanies and panormamic sites. Not only do we harbor within us the same earthly patterns that twist and curve around us, we think, feel, live, and die by them as well.

Ignoring these connections between self and world pathologizes them and us. Although we now possess piles of research evidence that chronic disconnection from the natural world makes us physically, socially, and psychologically ill, we are only beginning to explore even subtler disturbances resulting from what we ignore around us. Broken cities and barren rainforests wreak havoc right down in our depths, diminishing us below and beyond the range of measurable illness as interiorized droughts and deserts encroach upon what remains of oases of human sanity.

Working conscientiously with deep connections between self and world heals the split driving environmental crisis and collective self-alienation and invites new delight in the complexity of our ties to nature, place, creatures, and things. So much of the modernist moaning about the separateness, randomness, and "thrownness" of life fades out when we realize how deeply we belong to this lively world and to the cosmos glittering all around it.

Just how this deep work shows up reflects all the diversity of its doers, from online projects like the Powers of Place Initiative and Katrina Martin Davenport's deft management of TerraPlaces, which teaches the public how to connect inner and outer as seasons go by, to startlingly animated presentations such as Marna Hauk's evocative parallels between bridges in Portland, Oregon and intelligent cell membranes, to my own "Earthrise: Decoding the Speech of the Planet," a research paper written with a grant from OPUS Archives.

The collection before you has been organized along six dimensions of embodied encounter with earthly presence:

Elements: encounters among the four primal "substances" herein revealed as living processes.

Places: accounts of how deeply the locales where we live reach into us.

Bodies: our very flesh as a doorway into nature, place, matter, and world.

Things: examples of how everyday items speak to us.

Methods: disciplined ways of studying, wandering over, or ritualizing our relationship with the animate Earth.

Ethicks: toward the need for a new ethic "thick" (William James) enough to hold our solid sense of connection and relation to things, beings, and planetary soul.

No words can approach my pride and satisfaction at beholding the richness and beauty of the work on display in this anthology. Reaching across a wide range of regions, cultures, ethnic backgrounds, and spiritual orientations, Earth has called out to every one of these authors—called out in voices tantalizing and urgent, but also startling, life-changing, sometimes dangerous to hear but more dangerous to repress and ignore. The responses reflect a very high level of courage, self-inquiry, and fidelity to the inner bonds joining us to the world that gave birth to us. It remains relevant, then, that this blossoming genre evokes straightaway the name of mighty Terra, the Roman goddess of our irrepressibly expressive planet, as we continue our diverse interpretations of what Earth speaks to us through the uniqueness of her places and their creatures, ecologies, and materials.

Who knows but that Terra hopes in her own mysterious way for reconciliation as her wayward children struggle towards responsible adulthood, foregoing neglect and regression alike to turn our travel-weathered faces finally homeward.

elements

Compass

for Marcel

I am scanning the skies
for signs of birds
opening my ears
to catch the sounds
of drumbeats on the winds
standing ready at the door
my satchel near
with a journey's worth of food
and my flute

some days ago
I thought I heard the sound
of passing footsteps
I thought there was a soft knocking
at my door
but when I rose myself
thick with slumber
to open it
there was only the night

in the days since
I have not slept
some part of me has followed the trail
of that mysterious guest
who did not stay
long enough to be known
and the rest of me
left behind
has felt hollow
and uneasy
with restless feet

so I have made myself ready
studied the stars
remembered all the wise things
I have been told
I can feel my departure
coming to meet me

but how will I know the way?
do I follow the leaves
as they are turning?
the bends in the grass?
the clawprints in the dust?
there are so many signs
all of them beautiful
which one is for me?

and as soon as this question leaves my lips
offered up to the sun
with a genuine heart
I hear again
the faintest suggestion of footsteps
drawing nearer

and I find
to my amazement
that I have been walking
this whole time

—Catherine Baumgartner

Catherine Baumgartner fell in love with poetry when she realized its capacity to communicate on deep levels that lie beyond everyday language. Her work in poetry, collaborative performance, and installation art seeks to explore the ways in which individuals and cultures organize sensory experience into worlds of meaning. She currently lives in the San Francisco Bay area, where she is completing a master's degree in Transformative Arts at John F. Kennedy University. For more of her poetry please visit www.wingbone.net.

A Personal History of Dirt

Laura Vogel

"Dirt has always been important to me. Walking the rain saturated slope of the property we now inhabit and on which we are building a home, I've come to appreciate the layers of the earth in an entirely new way. Yesterday as we built a live-edge wood shed on the fragile moss, I moved a family of salamanders who had crawled under some wood we had stacked temporarily. A small one had been unintentionally trapped halfway under my partner's foot before we saw her. I awoke before first light, deeply troubled, unable to get the small creature out of my mind. People in my profession would say I was overidentifying with her pain and displacement because of my past history of displacement trauma. But I've yet to conclude whether this overidentification is a bad thing."

This is what is the matter with us: we are bleeding at the roots because we are cut off from the earth and sun and stars. Love has become a grinning mockery because, poor blossom, we plucked it from its stem on the Tree of Life and expected it to keep on blooming in our civilized vase on the table.
— D.H. Lawrence

My father, every bit a man of his time, did not know how hope and absence chased him; he simply followed what everyone else was following: that bruised and tattered promise of a place that would at last rise up to meet his fantasy of perfection, a place washed clean of his past, pristine as the innocent dream and the fresh children he had spilled by accident into the world.

Each time my father uprooted our family it was for what he thought were good reasons. He would draw long on his pipe, then look thoughtful and tell us the move meant more money, a better position, or a preferable climate. But we dragged with us, among the Atlas Van moving stickers and thrice labeled boxes, a sense of discontent that no place ever eased. As if the movers had unwittingly grabbed a bottle or two of this discontent, we would get to our new place and find it among our dishes and clothes, carefully wrapped and waiting for us. I have come to call this displacement "severed belonging." Severed belonging was not the fault of any place we were in. It was in part our own fault—our own inability to connect with the places we inhabited.

And it is how culture, power, and sometimes nature eject humans and other creatures from connection to place and land through disaster, war, disease, violence, greed, and agricultural practices. It is now the basic condition under which many endure life.

If, as some other cultures and indigenous people believe, my soul is rooted in a place, I have at times wondered if I am a ghost, walking around without a soul, without a sense of belonging. Like the uprooted plant, am I severed from what might sustain me? Does this severance grow a hungry ghost, a bloated consumer who will attempt to fill the empty spaces with every sort of corn-sweetened product or latest online game? Or a discouraged activist, who lashes out in violence and anger? Is this severance the root from which so many of our labeled pathologies grow? Depression? Anxiety? Attention-Deficit Disorder?

As a very young child in New Mexico, where I was born, I tasted the dirt. I collected it from the backyard and sprinkled it on Saltine crackers and ate it. I later learned this was a disorder called pica (probably related to anemia), but on a deeper level, I longed to taste the earth and take into myself the place in which I was living. My child palette unconsciously knew to seek minerals and connection to earth, and spontaneously sought healing for this deficiency.

Traveling through wine country some years back, I was told of monks who once had so much sensitivity and intimate contact with soil that they could sip wine and tell you about the place where the grapes were grown. The French have a name for the taste of the earth. *Goût de terroir* refers to how regional differences of a place or soil express themselves through what is grown in a particular location, usually wine, but sometimes tea or cocoa beans. A controversy among wine-makers today is whether, after the mechanized and industrial practices of modern vinery, does the wine continue to have *terroir?* When the wine is shipped about and mixed with other wines, does it lose its *terroir?*

And what about us—aren't we made up of the places we inhabit? If I am made up of the places of earth, if my body has a *terroir,* it must be confused by many moves, by spending so many years of my life encased in square buildings, automobiles, and educational institutions. Has the mechanization of the modern, industrialized world destroyed my *terroir?* Can I resurrect it and create it again from the dirt of this place? My fear is that I am severed irreparably from my ancestral roots, from what a friend of mine calls my bone country.

Bone country, my English friend says, is a place where most of one's ancestors are buried. I like the sound of it, and wish I too, had a bone country. Her ancestors have been buried for a thousand years in England, and I wonder how many Euro-Americans have bone countries. In thinking about where mine might be, I trace my father's bones to Nevada, where his ashes were recently scattered. His immediate ancestors are buried in New York, and before them, a few in Wisconsin, having come from Switzerland and England. I don't know if Switzerland is my bone country, or England, or the Netherlands, where half of my mother's family comes from. Or Germany, where the other half lies.

Like my father's remains scattered in the desert, my bone country is scattered over the continents of Europe and North America. Sometimes I think I want to go and trace this history, visit each place and find the gravestones and the old houses, if any of them still exist. I search European history looking for clues. Why did my father's ancestors leave Appenzell? Why did they go to another, more remote canton? From what religion or practice did they convert in the 1500s to Christianity?

An Acoma pot from the state of my birth perches on the windowsill. A round and stylized eye stares at me from within a triangle. I wonder what the symbols mean. They could be a ridge of mountains, thunder and rain, or leaves erupting. I recall the smell of clay pots and leather from the dirt-floored Indian shops where my family stopped when I was a child on our way from New Mexico to Kansas, of bins abundant with nesting dolls, moccasins, bull whips, and woven rugs. I remember fingering each hand-crafted toy— inhaling the spicy, earth-laden fragrances.

I pick up the pot and put my face into its opening. Covered in glaze, perfect, ringing pleasantly as I tap it, the pungent scent of earth is no longer there. Beneath the glaze is dirt, clay that passed between the fingers of someone named D. Chino on the Acoma mesa. The smell of terracotta is clear and distinct only in my memory. And I realize, in piecing together this disparate past, that where I live now is the present, the aroma of clay beneath my feet. This place is my home, and this place's history must be sewn together with the fragments of my past.

My partner and I have come here, to this island in the Pacific Northwest, with a similar mission to the one my father had. We, too, hope for a pristine beginning, to ground ourselves and set down roots—something that I have been unable to do for various circumstances for the better part of my life, and can do now only because of a series of unforeseen and fortuitous events.

From the window of our rental house I contemplate our imminent move from Useless watershed over to the Maxwelton watershed, to a place called the Chinook lands on Whidbey Island. The Chinook people, situated south of here, are said to have disappeared from this more northern area as a result of smallpox long before ever meeting a Spaniard or European, and the more recent inhabitants of this place were the migrating Salish tribe. The land we will soon move to bears a tribal name because of a warm wind that blows through the valley, a Chinook wind.

From where I write, I see black crows perch at some distance across the farm fields in a golden leaved tree. Spaced evenly and fluttering to change positions, I watch the pattern of crows, noticing how they move in community. I've learned that they remember my face for years, and they are fierce and loyal to each other. I don't know where they nest. Like the many birds now within my view, they inhabit the earth in a way I do not. Starlings, invasive European imports like me, dot the neighbor's metal roof, and then leave all at once. Against a hillside dark with trees, a flock of seabirds turns, brightens, turns away, disappears.

I miss the earth. My desire now is to know the place, to become intimate here, to allow the patterns of my brain to form around local smells, textures, moods and rhythms. My exploration begins with the smell of the ground, with the soil, the roots, and the geology of this little region to which chance has brought me. And to the many voices of this place, I add my voice.

Out walking again; the Chinook earth springs like a firm mattress under my feet. Detritus from the thick stands of trees and the violent winds of fall have shed maple leaves so numerous the trail has disappeared. Ground and water mix here in ways that are complicated and strange. Glacial till combines with old lava and uprisings of granite and other minerals, and is then covered by thousands of years of plant and tree debris. Who knows how deep it goes beneath my feet, the thick coating of this world over the rocks? And then the rain comes, comes in buckets and torrents and months of drizzle, but it comes. A heavy, wet musty thing, the earth of this place, exuding the musk of leaf mold. Dig deep enough, and the mud we make with machinery and boots is slippery and full of clay. But it will grow nearly anything that knows how to make use of the scant forest sunlight.

Later I arrive at and listen to a presentation at the watershed stewards training. I try to understand how the apple can come from a family of roses, how native willow competes with invasive plants, how canary grass slices the fingers and clogs up the streams needed for the salmon. I learn how the salmon swim through the rivulets and riffles, their bodies violently spasming, their drive to complete the furrowing and spawning made more and more difficult by our fences and property rights.

Well before my ancestors came to the east coast of this country with their bright hopes of starting over, displacement of the people who had long inhabited these lands in a more balanced (albeit involved) way had begun. Invasive seeds brought in by crops were spreading over the prairie. The camas that the natives relied on for starchy tubers were displaced by scotch broom. Early settlers began to struggle with the rhizomous bracken fern to clear land for wheat and oats, taking away another native food source. Having killed off their only other predator, the wolf, the settler's cows and pigs were over-populating and running amok. The elk disappeared. The food supply of the native peoples largely diminished, and already they had sustained the loss of many members because of foreign diseases. Places were re-named by surveyors and explorers, often only gazing from ships, having little if any relationship to the land. Leshootseed (the local language) place names such as *TSEHT-skluhks*, or "ragged nose," for what is now known as Sandy Point, and *D'GWAD'wk*, or "lots of certain species of crabs" for Cultus Bay, were nearly forgotten.

Unable to further explore my own history, I drive over to Sandy Point looking for remnants of the long houses of the native people. I'm not sure why I'm doing this. I can scarcely believe there is no trace of their lives here, only a brief mention in an obscure history book, and a place name reference on a government website. I'm startled when I drive into Sandy Point and signs greet me: "Members Only." I'm not even allowed to park anywhere. Across Saratoga passage is Camano Point, another site used by the first inhabitants. Driving out of Sandy Point, I notice archways made of driftwood, with metal lifts for those who cannot scramble up and down the sides of the embankment. Gates and houses block the rest of the view. I see no one.

The impermeable signs disturb me. All around is evidence of caretaking, tending, and opulence, but no lights are on in the houses. An occasional BMW or Lexus speeds by, but no one is out walking. I think of those vast and perfect vacant lawns created out of forests once crawling with wildlife, or those golf courses in Arizona where saguaro, chollo cacti, and rabbit brush used to be with their many skittery lizards doing territorial push-ups. Now, within the windows of the dark houses here, I occasionally see a glowing screen, but many of the houses belong to part-time residents who are absent.

The connection I sense between my past and the past of the first inhabitants is displacement. We have been displaced by powers we could not fight or foresee, and we have both been compensated somewhat for our losses—the white race far more than the First Nations. However, I don't think my race understands how damaging separation from land and place is. Still, with regard to land and roots and ancestry, native and non-native might join in understanding how our uprootedness is a common ground that we share. \

I walk up to the Chinook lands again, and sit on a knoll in the rare sun. I'm engaged in a study of the Heart Sutra, a sutra recited in many forms in many Buddhist practices around the world. Opening to a page in Thich Nhat Hanh's book *The Heart of Understanding*, I read a story about Buddha embracing the demon Mara, who comes to visit after a long absence. Hanh is trying to illustrate that when we push away our darkness, we are pushing a big part of ourselves away. We are connected to the darkness, and cannot be in the light without it. Evil depends on good as much as good depends on evil. Even though I may feel isolated and cut-off, nothing is truly separate, and I am inter-related with all beings. It is when I lose sight of this that I suffer and create harm.

As if to illustrate this, I listen later as the director of a large organization tells a gathering about her severance from her home, and the meaning she has begun to make of it. She realizes her strength is in not belonging, and in not knowing the stories. She embraces her Mara, her sense of separation, for how her fresh perspective helps her not get mired in a past that clings in hurtful ways, one that could limit the vision of the organization she now runs.

A day or two after, as my partner and I stand looking at the site where we will make a home and build trails for meditation and walking, a leaf falls from a tall alder, in slow motion, wagging back and forth in its descent, light and airy from having hung on so late into the season. The ways in which I do belong begin to clarify. I appreciate the miracle that anything, the earth, the sky, the tree, the leaf, formed out of the strange imbalance of cosmic forces that created our big bang—that I came to be at all, that I have consciousness of this life lived here now, that I am able to parse my history from yellowed sheets of paper found in my father's file drawers and the history I find on the many pages of the internet.

Ernest Hemingway famously wrote that the world breaks every one, and afterward many are strong at the broken places. I don't really have any answers about how or why one person becomes strong at the broken places, or why another weakens and quits. The tenacious seed will take root in poor soil, and the tenacious plant will cling to life regardless of its perilous existence on a rocky outcropping. And given fertile soil and ample nutrients, a weak seed will take root, grow and do just fine. Yet, weak or strong, every one of these seeds, and every one of us, travels here from an immense distance, down a long historical path. All of history conspired for us, in whatever circumstance we happen to be in, to arrive in this here and this now, this present moment. Imbalances, imperfection and severance were all necessary conditions for what is exactly now.

And so how do we make sense and heal in the face of great planetary turmoil? The globe warms, and the air fills with coal dust, and dioxins spill out of our breast milk and into infant mouths. History also conspired to bring these things here to this moment, where we meet them, puzzle over them, and attempt to save ourselves from their caustic effects. This is our story, my story. My own father engineered parts of atom bombs while in New Mexico. His father before him drank, beat his wife and womanized. His father before him helped runaway slaves escape along the Underground Railroad. It's hard for me to make sense out of the conflicting impulses running through my family and through me.

Meditation practice helps me. I belong to a tradition that connects me to an ancestral lineage going all the way back to Buddha. It is literally thought of as a bloodline. And strangely enough, this tether to an ancient practice has been a source of freedom for me in the here and now, its particular *terroir* imbuing me with the scents of connection and rebirth at the same time. When I sit, I recite a purification chant, and with this chant I let go of how my negative thoughts and chatter want to tell me about who I am. I return to the moment, to here and now, and to my body.

One might mistakenly believe I'm trying to get rid of my past by doing this, but I'm not. I'm simply clarifying and feeling my condition. There's no static past to get rid of, only the past's effects in the here and now, and this past is always changing. Fascinating revisionist stories, for instance, tell how some of the first settlers in our country starved themselves to death because they planted every inch of arable land with tobacco and neglected to grow food crops. Or about how much the first native peoples manipulated land for food they needed by burning forests and propagating their favorite edibles. Recently a book about Zen women ancestors, so seldom heard about in the tradition, was published, helping to fill in a deep vacancy left in Buddhist history. As my awareness and knowledge grows, the past actually changes. Nothing is as solid and certain as it seems.

And this is liberating, because if all that remains are my stories, then I get to start out new and fresh every day. I do the best I can with what is in front of me now, and I don't fret about the past or the future. This view doesn't mean I shut out the damage that is going on, or remain blind to the suffering in and of the world, or to history and what it means. In fact, I am generally more aware of what is actually going on. I see with fresh eyes, with interest, and with real curiosity. If today is a new story, what does this toxic effluent going into the river really mean? Who do I talk to about it? Imagine, if I approach the party responsible for polluting the river not with outrage, but with curiosity and wonder, as if he is a part of myself I am baffled by and want to understand, will that make a difference in our interaction? If I invite him for tea, will that create an opening my sense of outrage would have shut off had I treated him as a separate and undesirable person?

As an activist interested in saving the earth, I sometimes feel isolated and alone in my efforts. This perception of separation creates problems with my energy and commitment. Effort on behalf of the earth is essential, and I must act. Strong feelings often create further polarization around difficult issues. But if I see those who do harm to the earth as myself, and find an attitude of compassion in the midst of my strong feelings rather than acting out of hurt and anger, maybe my actions will have more impact. Maybe not—it doesn't always work out this way. But I find there's a lot more energy available to me when I embrace rather than shut out the darkness. And I know that every day, when I go to my meditation cushion, I have the opportunity to tell a better story, and this I includes the "we," the corporation that is creating nuclear waste and the people who have eradicated homelessness in Vancouver, British Columbia. I'm not separate from either of them.

And the story can change in any moment of any day, not just in meditation practice. Each time I stop for a cup of tea, or pause to do dishes, this opportunity unfolds, and I come back to myself, recreating my life in a more sustainable, earth-friendly, and loving way from this moment on. So I can approach you with new eyes, not through my projections, and you have room to change and be who you really are. And I can come to a new place, even while embracing my whole history and lineages, and take its soil in my hand, smell it, breathe it in, and know that a universal and shared *terroir* is also here, in this soil, and here, within my body, and this is the most authentic intimacy available to me—this piece of earth at this piece of time in this piece of space—something utterly unrepeatable. The *terroir* of the present moment.

Laurel Vogel, MA practices as an ecotherapist with her partner, conducting Nature Therapy Retreats on Whidbey Island (visit naturetherapyretreats.com). In addition to being a poet and working on a place-based novel, she conducts workshops on Sacred Writing. She is precepted into the Everyday Zen lineage and is currently creating an Edible Forest Gardening practice that she plans to incorporate into her retreats and healing work with those suffering from trauma and recovering from addiction.

Evanescent Dewdrops and Wildflowers:
Keys to Our Survival

Janet Bubar Rich

As people devote increasingly more attention to cell phone calls, text messaging, Twitter, Facebook, and streaming video, and less on participating in the natural world with its evanescent dewdrops and colorful wildflowers, will they become oblivious to the earth's wonders and consume its resources with total disregard for the ecosphere? Or can appreciating the dewdrops and wildflowers elevate our sensibilities about our earth and psyche enough to give us a chance for survival?

To appreciate nature's marvels, from delicate rainbows reflected on dewdrops to kaleidoscopic expanses of wildflowers in bloom, one must leave cozy computer nooks and take outings in the natural world. Some of us do venture out into the natural world beyond the virtual realities that are downloadable from Internet-enabled devices. At such moments we catch, and are even inspired by, fleeting spectacles of natural phenomena.

But for the few of us who make the occasional effort, many more do not. What the latter miss is the authenticity of nature's wonders: not only evaporating dew and colorful wildflowers blanketing hillsides, but deep connections with the earth, our home.

Images of dew and its symbolism appear in a wide range of mythologies and legends, particularly from ancient times when people lived closer to nature than they do today. These myths and legends help shed light on the human desire to interpret, understand, and appreciate natural phenomena like dew. According to Tamra Andrews in *A Dictionary of Nature Myths*, "Dew is moisture that renews the earth. Condensed from the air, it falls in droplets and covers the grass and plant life, seemingly like magic, during the night."[1] With its sparkle and magical dispensation, people of long ago believed dew to be of celestial origins; it "healed like rain, cooled like snow, and therefore represented water from some heavenly force."[2]

Many attribute dew to sky forces. Some associate it with the cold and watery moon, with *moon dew* a silvery liquid sent by lunar gods to nourish the crops; others, with the night and thunder. In some Chinese and Japanese myths, dew drips from the stars; in some Scandinavian myths, from the bit of the celestial horse that brings night. In an Iroquois legend, dew falls from the wings of Oshadagea, the Big Eagle of Dew who assists the thunder god by carrying a lake of dew on his back to refresh the earth after fire depletes its vegetation. In a wide range of classical myths, dew represents the tears of gods and goddesses who lament their loved ones: tears fall to the earth as water imbued with restorative heavenly powers.

Although highly symbolic and even poetic, the reality of dew can easily be missed by those who are too preoccupied to take notice. In *The Penguin Dictionary of Symbols*, Jean Chevalier and Alain Gheerbrant suggest that dew's symbolic meaning is much like that of rain, but its influence is subtler: "As the expression of heavenly blessing, it is essentially life-giving grace,"[3] a pure water with generative powers. The ancient Greeks associate dew with fertility myths, especially those pertaining to love gods and goddesses. In Buddhist thought, the "world of dew" is that of appearances and represents the ephemeral nature of material things and of life's brevity.[4] In *An Illustrated Encyclopaedia of Traditional Symbols*, J.C. Cooper reveals that dew is symbolic of "the light of dawn; spiritual refreshment; sweet dew is peace and prosperity" and can represent change and illusion.[5]

Encountering Wildflowers

Years ago while in a contemplative mood, I took a leisurely walk in the semi-natural world on a cool, cloudy day in Berkeley, California, and was struck by the utter magnificence of some wild-flowers that poked their way through cracks in the cement sidewalk, almost as if to emerge so they could absorb and greet the soft sunlight with full presence. As I was delighting in the variety of their colors and dance-like movements corresponding to the sway of the gentle breezes, I was awe-struck by their untamed beauty, particularly as it created a vivid contrast to the stale cement's grayness and illusion of stillness—*illusion* because of the gradual shift and decay in the blocks' stability that opened the cracks from which the flowers emerged.

While enveloped in the cool breezes and the intensity of the flowers' colorful brilliance, I suddenly caught sight of a person up ahead who had stopped and picked a flower. Zoom! My attention could not disconnect from that moment. I felt horrified, as if the act were a direct assault on the planet. My own sense that the flower deserved to live out its life without human intervention and disturbance and reach maturity and full bloom until, in its own time, it could gracefully wilt, die, and fall to the earth to integrate or reintegrate into the rich soil received a shattering blow.

Feeling disheartened and devastated, I wondered about the impetus behind that flower-picking as I continued on my walk next to Berkeley Peoples' Park, for decades the site of struggles, protests, and riots between residents who want the lot preserved as a park and those who want to develop the land; the site now has a mythology surrounding it, one that carries the voice of local radical culture. Was the flower picked to appreciate its beauty, or as a mindless act of pick and toss, with a lack of respect and honor for its life? Was the flower picked to fulfill a need to acquire and possess it, a need expressed in the plaintive cries at urban shopping malls: *Give me, give me!;* from the gestures of consumers who learn from a culture in disharmony with its natural roots that satisfaction derives from acquisition? The moment is still alive within me as a disturbance that perhaps connects with complexes in the depths of my own psyche; I am possessed by the need to fight for the rights of the flower. In *The Spell of the Sensuous*, David Abram raises the issue that each flower "is an *experiencing* form, an entity with its own predilections and sensations."[6] What, then, would be its sense of a hand that swoops down and snatches it? I am left in the pursuit of truth about that flower.

I wonder, too, about the correlation between the disregard of dew, the abuse of the wildflower, and the depletion of our planet's natural resources. Abram states that "our culture's relation to the earthly biosphere can in no way be considered a reciprocal or balanced one."[7] Further,

> Caught up in a mass of abstractions, our attention hypnotized by a host of human-made technologies that only reflect us back to ourselves, it is all too easy for us to forget our carnal inheritance in a more-than-human matrix of sensations and sensibilities.[8]

If people lose interest in the natural world, with its evanescent dewdrops and colorful wildflowers, and no longer behold these presences with awe, will we evolve into oblivious consumers of the earth's natural resources? When we no longer turn to natural phenomena with a sense of wonder, nor appreciate and live in accord with nature, will we act in ways that harm the natural world and threaten the species for which our planet is home?

Earth-cultivating Myths

The ancients revered their nature gods in part because they feared their power, just as they feared neglecting any power strong enough to control the destiny of the world. Their worship of nature involved a reverence for natural events as animated, conscious forces: living beings analogous to people but with more power, as demonstrated by thunder's tremendous roars during storms, and lovely dewdrop's evaporation under the sun's heat. Phenomena now explained by science were mysteries in the ancient world. Back then, people created myths to help them understand the inexplicable, using the best tools available to them: experience and imagination. Andrews affirms, "Nature was revealed to them in symbols."[9]

Carl Gustav Jung's insights help derive important inner truths about modern peoples' relationship with dewdrops and wildflowers. In *The Earth Has a Soul: The Nature Writings of C.G. Jung* edited by Meredith Sabini, Jung suggests that within each individual is the power to imagine a life lived in harmony with nature. This is consistent with our development as a species on a particular planet that evolved under specific conditions. To live in disharmony with nature takes work; to live in harmony is easy but runs counter to the mass culture. Therefore, the individual, much like the mythic hero, must break away from an absorption in virtual realities to lead the way back to a connection with the earth. As Jung puts it, "A fundamental change of attitude (*metanoia*) is required, a real recognition of the whole [individual],"[10] a far-reaching metamorphosis that comes not from outside but from inside the individual, or the "bearer" of life.[11] To reconnect with nature, individuals must face "the present condition of the world"[12] as well as their own souls. That is, to unveil the original patterns and reestablish humankind's initial bridge to nature, one must remove the extraneous historical layers and connect with their own "nature within" at the animal level that is not conscious.[13] Now individuals, much like mythic heroes, must set themselves apart from others in the wasteland and extricate themselves from the extraneous to respond to their own inner nature at the animal level. Abolishing the break between humankind and nature reveals the "truth, but a truth which [one] cannot prove."[14] The truth is that humans, no matter how civilized, urbanized, and technologized, all live together on earth, our organic home. We need to attend to our inner nature and take care of ourselves and our home, the earth, if human life is to continue for generations to come.

The ancient Greeks were aware of the importance of their relationship to the earth. In their mythology they tell stories of Hestia, Goddess of the Hearth, center of the earthly sphere and terrestrial surface. This goddess signifies the household, city, and interior of the earth containing our planet's fire.[15] Hestia also represents one's steady core and inner fire as well as the stable, unyielding, feminine nature within human beings. Hestia reigns over the hearth, where the spiritual realm is embodied in the activities of daily life. A loss of a connection to the earth is thus a loss of one's place, center, self, and soul. To restore these requires breaks from the daily grind, disconnection from Internet-enabled devices, and walking in the woods, listening to birdsong, and reengaging in the natural wonders beyond the virtual pleasures derived from technology.

Jung observes that too much emphasis has been placed on the development of that technology, the uses of which are determined by people's states of mind. Through wisdom from dreams we can find our way back to humane organic existence.[16] As Thomas Berry offers, perhaps through the wisdom of the "dream of the earth" humans can find their way back to their bio-spiritual ground as well.[17]

Joseph Campbell relates the Pygmy legend of the little boy who finds the bird with the sweet song and brings it home:

> He asks his father to bring food for the bird, and the father doesn't want to feed a mere bird, so he kills it. And...with the bird he killed the song, and with the song, himself. He dropped dead, completely dead, and was dead forever.[18]

Campbell concludes that when we destroy our environment, we destroy our own nature as well as the song. He reveals that "mythology is the song...of the imagination, inspired by the energies of the body," and adds, "The only mythology that is valid today is the mythology of the planet—and we don't have such a mythology."[19] Campbell also believes that the same powers that animate people also animate the life of the world. The ideal is not to dominate, subjugate, or control nature, but to live in careful accord with it. [20]

A Pawnee story tells us that "in the beginning of all things, wisdom and knowledge were with the animal" because the One Above sent certain animals to let humans know that the divine shows itself through the animal, the sun, the moon, and the stars: from these, humans need to learn how to live here.[21] When Native Americans received horses from the Spaniards and learned to take part in the great hunt, their "mythology transform[ed] from a vegetarian mythology to a buffalo mythology."[22] From this, Campbell concludes that myth is alive, and able to inspire us to mythologize the living world.

Permeating Aesthetic Depths

Some poets venture into the natural world and share their impressions in their work as they record the world's aesthetic depths. William Wordsworth and Emily Dickinson did not live in today's America with the "incessant drone of motors that shut out the...winds;...air 'conditioners' that hide the seasons;...and shopping malls that finally obviate any need to step outside the purely human world at all."[23] The fleeting beauty of natural phenomena touched these poets instead.

Two hundred years ago an English poet, William Wordsworth, knew the ephemeral nature of dew and, in a poem entitled "To H. C., Six Years Old," used dew as a metaphor to reflect on painfully transient aspects of human life, such as youth:

Thou art a dewdrop, which the morn brings forth...
A gem that glitters while it lives,
[Then] slips in a moment out of life.[24]

In New England, Emily Dickinson wrote a poem, "Nature: XCIX," in which she cast light on dew's ability to satisfy a leaf in the act of its self-fulfillment and perhaps to reflect on our human condition with its inherent brevity within a larger temporal context:
A Dew sufficed itself
And satisfied a Leaf,
And felt, "how vast a destiny!
How trivial is Life!
The Sun went out to work,
The day went out to play,
But not again that dew was seen,
By Physiognomy."[25]

These are two among the many poets who not only observe and appreciate natural phenomena, but perceive them as a bridge for deepening our understanding of ourselves and our time.

Today, if we can make an effort to see the wonderment in nature and allow it to awaken our imagination, then perhaps we will imagine and embrace myths about "earth-cultivating" humans,[26] myths that inspire us into lifestyles that accord with nature and champion the protection of the environment and therefore the continuation of human life. In this historic hour, the destiny of the human species and of many others on this earth could hinge on a small shift in our perspectives on dewdrops and wildflowers.

Endnotes

1 Andrews, Tamra. *Dictionary of Nature Myths*. Oxford: Oxford UP, 1998, p. 56.

2 Ibid.

3 Chevalier, Jean and Alain Gheerbrant. *The Penguin Dictionary of Symbols*. Trans. John Buchanan-Brown. New York: Penguin Books, 1996, p. 289.

4 Ibid.

5 Cooper, J. C. *An Illustrated Encyclopaedia of Traditional Symbols*. New York: Thames and Hudson, Inc., 1979, p. 50.

6 Abram, David. *The Spell of the Sensuous*. New York: Vintage Books, 1996, p. 10.

7 Ibid., 22.

8 Ibid.

9 Andrews, p. xii.

10 Sabini, Meredith. *The Earth Has a Soul: The Nature Writings of C. G. Jung*. Berkeley: North Atlantic, 2002, p. 167.

11 Ibid., p. 168.

12 Ibid.

13 Ibid., p. 172.

14 Ibid.

15 Paris, Ginette. *Pagan Meditations, The Worlds of Aphrodite, Artimis and Hestia*. Trans. G. Moore. Woodstock,, Connecticut. Spring Publications, 1986. p. 167.

16 Sabini, *Earth,* p. 175-177.

17 Berry, Thomas. *The Dream of the Earth*. San Francisco: Sierra Club Books, 1988, p. 223.

18 Ibid., p. 117.

19 Campbell, Joseph. *The Power of Myth with Bill Moyers*. Ed. Betty Sue Flowers. New York: Broadway Books, 2001, p. 22.

20 Ibid., p. 22-24.

21 Ibid., p. 79.

22 Ibid., p. 85.

23 Abram, p. 28.

24 Wordsworth, William. "To H. C., Six Years Old." *Major British Writers, Enlarged Edition II*. Ed. G. B. Harrison. New York: Harcourt, Brace and World, 1959, p. 93.

25 Dickinson, Emily. "Nature: XCIX." *The Collected Poems of Emily Dickenson*. Ed. George Stade. New York: Barnes and Noble Classics, 2003, p. 141.

26 Campbell, p. 23.

A writer and speaker living in Southern California, Janet Bubar Rich explores mythologies with a focus on the contemporary concerns of our world. She has a BA in English from the University of California at Berkeley, MEd from the University of Massachusetts, and PhD in Mythological Studies with an Emphasis in Depth Psychology from Pacifica Graduate Institute.

Embodying the Power of the Storm

Katrina Martin Davenport

In 2005 Hurricane Katrina barreled into New Orleans, taking away lives and livelihoods. At the same time, in another state, author Katrina Martin Davenport faced difficult personal events and grappled with the grief of sharing a name with the killer storm. Eventually, she came to terms with Hurricane Katrina and other significant storms that impacted her throughout her life.

My family vacationed in Cancún for spring break when I was eighteen. We went on a three-hour tour (and *Gilligan's Island* jokes abounded) to snorkel the waters off Cozumel. However, the weather took a rapid turn for the worse. Although all the other boats returned to shore, ours remained on the water. Eventually the captain forced us to jump off the boat and swim for shore. He said he was worried the boat would capsize.

My self-inflatable life preserver wouldn't inflate. I didn't know how to snorkel; I was on this trip to learn. No one told me to take off my snorkel mask and flippers for swimming. It all happened so fast that no one really helped anyone else. I jumped in the water last and no one was in sight—I was utterly alone. Although we had made a pact to swim in together, no one remembered that once they hit the water.

My mother couldn't swim, so I worried about her safety as I looked after my own. I struggled to swim in the fifteen-foot waves, trying to breathe before water shot down the tube of my snorkel mask. All I could see was a canyon of water below me and a wall of water in front of me. Once in a while I caught a glimpse of my brother's body on the crest of a distance wave. The enormity of the ocean made me feel like a tiny speck, and my heart ached. Why had everyone left me behind? Why didn't my family at least stick together? Why had the captain abandoned us? I didn't know where the shore was, but I kicked for my life. Finally I saw the beach in the distance.

When I tried to walk onto the beach, I tripped and fell, my legs giving out under me. It felt like the final insult. I called for help and the tour guide came to assist me. Eventually my father came over to tell me he had watched me swim in to make sure I made it.

Many stories flood my brain when I think of this moment, stories of mothers doing everything in their power to save their children, stories of fathers performing death-defying feats to make sure their children survive. None of that occurred for me that day. The storm uncovered for me the inner workings of our family dynamics and the depth of my abandonment wound.

The events of that March afternoon in Cozumel illustrate how storms show up in my life. But, astonishingly, that storm did not have the biggest impact on me. Instead, a more well-known storm holds that honor: Hurricane Katrina. A powerful, deadly storm that bore my name. A storm that changed the face of this country and ripped the veil off of our denial. These two storms, one intimately experienced, the other intimately associated, changed my life, and by exploring the meaning of storms within my life, I began to understand why.

Water, Water Everywhere...

My inquiry into storms led me first to examine water's symbolism and its presence in my life. I began with my astrological sign Pisces: two fish swimming in a circle. Pisces represents unity, imagination, intuition, the arts, the redeemer, the death and rebirth cycle, compassion, and empathy. Neptune the sea god rules Pisces, and he too has powerful influence in my life.

Imbued with salt, Neptune's waters purify. Here I found a direct link to my name: Katrina means "pure." How does that connect with Hurricane Katrina? Her salty water purified the land, wiping out oil rigs whose product pollutes the Earth. The storm sent us a message: purify our actions or face destruction. The same message holds meaning for me: I must purify my body and my actions or face illness and distress.

It's not just my first name that connects to water. Both my maiden name, Martin, and my married name, Davenport, hold its essence: in Old English, Martin means "settlement by a lake," and Davenport refers to a port or town by the river Dan or Daven. Even an alternative name my parents considered for me connects to water: Greta comes from the name Margaret, meaning "pearl," a treasure a mollusk creates while purifying its inner environment. It surprised me how this trail led again and again to purification, highlighting that I must bring light to the shadow in order to cleanse and transmute it.

Beyond my birth chart and names, significant memories featuring water abound in my life. I remember with great fondness a trip up Rist Canyon in Colorado which included a picnic alongside the Cache La Poudre River. My family explored the area where my great-grandparents had lived. I was around nine years old. After our riverside picnic, we spread out and spent time alone. I wandered to the river and sat on a rock; immersed myself in the sounds of the rushing river, the wind shaking the tree branches, and melodic birdsong. Suddenly, I knew intuitively that something greater than me operates in the world. Everything took on a mystical glow and new meaning. I never spoke of this revelation with my family, but it impacted me tremendously. When I hear wind blowing through pine trees this memory rushes back and goose bumps form on my arms.

It was also at age nine that I first met the ocean on a family trip to California. On a beach near Los Angeles the ocean waters' power and immensity captivated me and set up camp inside my heart. Since then I feel torn between the grace of the Cache La Poudre, Big Thompson, and Yampa River waters of my youth and the power of the Pacific ocean. This conflict caused me to move back and forth between Colorado and California three times since age eighteen. I have settled near the Pacific, but I often hear the rivers calling me and I am not sure how long I can be away from them.

Since water constitutes a significant part of my psyche, it is not surprising that my art strongly connects with water. One of my best-selling photographs features the Big Sur coastline. Another customer favorite captures the sky's reflection in a lake at Denver's Washington Park. I am often drawn to water when on photography excursions, its reflective and mysterious surface showing me pieces of myself that in turn reflect natural events.

Water is restorative, life-giving, and powerful. It is often my first connection to nature, and it appears regularly in my dreams. However, despite these ties with water, I tend to resist it: I never drink enough water, and although I loved swimming as a child, I have not swum in six years. I resist gaining an even more intimate connection with water, possibly because of the various traumatic encounters with it throughout my life.

Cycles, Circles, Spirals

When observing storms, it is impossible to ignore their shape: cycles, circles, and spirals. These motifs appear and reappear in my life. One obvious example is the swirling imagery of Hurricane Katrina. One evening, while staring at a photograph I took of the interior of a rose, I saw a connection: the same spirals, and, staring out from the middle, an eye.

Both images capture the power and grace of the spiral and the strength of the eye that stands calmly amid the swirling exterior. Both images signify purity: the hurricane's white clouds and the rose's creamy petals. The rose even has half of a heart surrounding its eye, pointing to the love inherent in the act of purification.

Delving further into spirals, I found a connection with my name. *Katrina* derives from *Katherine*. One of the more famous, St. Catherine, ended life as a martyr tortured on a wheel that later bore her name. When I saw an image of the Catherine Wheel I sat stunned. It looked just like a hurricane. Spokes radiate out from the wooden wheel's center, a circle echoing a hurricane's eye. Curved spikes along the outside of the wheel evoke a storm's spiral motion.

The name Katherine also shares ties to the African storm goddess Oya, who dances in spirals representing tornadoes and winds of change. Like the Hindu goddess Kali, Oya brings destruction to create new beginnings and, ultimately, peace.

Although destructive, stormy Katrina brought change through her winds and rain. She laid bare the country's shadow of poverty and terrestrial desecration for us to face, and if we work to heal it we can renew and strengthen ourselves as a nation.

I am a big dreamer and I know that when a dream features a storm, I had better pay attention. One such dream connected directly to spirals, cycles, and Oya. In the dream, I am among relatives crowded in a basement to ride out a tornado. In waking life I am terrified of tornadoes, which occur frequently during Colorado summers. However, here I face the storm bravely, only hiding my eyes once. After the first tornado passes, I have a flash of clairvoyance and see, in my mind, two other tornadoes coming. These tornadoes, shaped like oak trees, hint at my ancestry. (My grandmother's maiden name is Ekblad, meaning "oak leaf" in Swedish.) In the dream I do not fear these storms; instead, I am calmly resigned about the inevitability of their presence.

I re-entered this dream through the technique of active imagination a few weeks after dreaming it. Almost immediately I became the tornado. I felt myself swirling in rapid circles that nearly brought on vertigo. Experiencing the raw power and force of the storm unsettled me. I heard a voice telling me I am a powerful center, I am bringing potent changes, and I am the sacred spiral. The journey and its message shook me and helped me realize how strong storm power is within me.

Circles do not manifest only in wind and water, but also in earth as spherical geodes and other rocky wonders. My grandparents were rockhounds, people who search for geodes and other rocks and then display them or sell them to other rockhounds. My grandfather practiced lapidary later in life, and I remember him constantly polishing rocks in the garage or creating jewelry in his downstairs studio. My grandparents' home was a rock haven: giant amethyst geodes decorated the living room, a beautiful collection of jade occupied a built-in case in the dining room, handmade intarsia rock mosaics hung on the walls, and stone specimens and fossils took up half of the basement. My grandmother wore cabochon rings crafted by my grandfather, and my grandfather sported his handmade belt buckles and bolo ties.

These rocks entranced me then and they still hold my imagination today. I own many pieces of stone jewelry, and I collect rocks from beaches and other locations. At a rock and gem show in Hayward I found myself transported as I instantly connected with a piece of ammonite, a spiral-shaped, 80-million-year-old fossil. The ancient water-born creature was shaped like a hurricane, with a central eye and wavy, radiating lines. The ammonite occupies a prominent place on my personal altar.

Spirals and circles signify cycles, and another area in which they play out for me is through my monthly menstrual cycle. Since it arrived at age twelve, my period has been painful, draining, and emotional, a somatic whirlwind one might say. Often, I suffer such intense pain I stay home from work or school. Making changes to my diet, doing psychotherapy, working with alternative therapies, and having two separate cysts removed from my left ovary has helped me heal, but something hidden remains that continues to cause pain. I am certain that ongoing embodiment of the storm's power will uncover the trauma stored within my womb.

Finally, the cycle motif has played out through my many rebirths. I reinvented myself from a newspaper reporter to a learning center director to an elementary school teacher to a children's author to a nanny to a photographer and freelance writer to a tutor to my current incarnation as a dreamworker, artist, intuitive, and writer. These reinventions all spiral together and represent new levels of my development.

Not in Kansas Anymore

With all this water and spiral/circular energy in my life, it is no surprise that the storm archetype has such impact on me. After examining my life events up to the present, it is clear to me that storms played major roles, perhaps in part to show me my own power. As a side note, my favorite book growing up was *Cloudy with a Chance of Meatballs*. It's about a town called Chewandswallow that gets its food from the weather: storm fronts made of pancakes, orange juice rain, and split pea fog. It makes sense to me now that a story about people getting nourishment from storms would call to me. But the stories of the storms in my life are not always fairy-tale in nature.

In 1976, eight months before my birth, the Big Thompson River flooded. Over the course of four hours on the evening of July 31st, more than ten inches of rain fell, causing the river to rise and sending a tidal large wave of water down the narrow Big Thompson Canyon. The flood killed 144 people; the next day the Army rescued 850 more trapped on mountainsides or on rocks in the river. This is remembered as the worst natural disaster in Colorado history. At the time, my mother was in the beginning of her first trimester of pregnancy, so this tragedy entered my consciousness through her reactions to it. We often drove up this canyon during my childhood as my parents told the stories of the devastation. I tried to imagine what it would look like for a giant wave to sweep down the canyon. This became my first introduction to storm power.

Thunderstorms, hail storms, and tornadoes danced through my first twenty-two summers while I lived in Colorado. These powerful, loud, and intense storms horrified me. In the past I attributed this fear to my mother's acute fear of storms, but I think there was more going on. I remember the afternoon that lightning struck in my backyard, splitting the air with a giant *crack*. I was nine or ten. A few years later, lightning struck in the street in front of my house. At eighteen, during my first road trip without my parents, I was caught in an intense rainstorm in Idaho. I could barely see well enough to pull off the road, and a semi nearly sideswiped the car. At twenty-four, days after moving back to Colorado, I witnessed a swirling cloud directly above my apartment, a funnel I thought would become a tornado. At twenty-six, weeks after moving back to California for the third time, a rare thunderstorm struck San Francisco as I drove home to Concord. As I crossed the Bay Bridge, lightning struck the bay, and I could hardly drive because waterfalls fell from the upper to the lower deck of the bridge. Newscasters reported tornadoes in Sacramento later that day. I had never seen anything like that in California, and it felt as though the storms of my Colorado childhood had followed me to my new home. These storms left me shaken and overwhelmed, and they recur whenever I face a big life transition.

Hurricane Katrina

Even with all of these storms in my life, it was a storm I did not meet first-hand that most impacted me: Hurricane Katrina.

The hurricane hit as I entered a very dark period of my life. I had just made a heart-wrenching decision to cancel fifteen children's book contracts months after going on a book tour to promote *Denise's Mold*, my first published book. During that tour I became aware of the unscrupulous actions of my publisher, and after weeks of crying and feeling unstable, I decided to end my relationship with them. Although the decision was the right one, I felt devastated. For three years I had walked on clouds, knowing I'd be a published author, but after I cancelled the contracts I was right back where I started. I began to believe I was not a writer anymore; that my career had ended. I did not know who I was, what I wanted to do, or where to go. Seven days before the hurricane hit, I wrote this in my blog: "I feel like I'm in a box. But I no longer wish to be in it. I'm breaking out." I felt lost and wanted out of my life.

At first, when Hurricane Katrina was still a tropical depression, I joked about how I would teach Florida a lesson for botching the 2000 presidential election. I felt heartsick (and guilty) later when the storm reached Category 5 and brought destruction and devastation to so many people. I resonated with their loss, for in my own way I felt lost, homeless, and overwhelmed too. I tried not to listen to National Public Radio (NPR) too often or log on to the *New York Times* website too many times because it hurt to see my name attached to such a horrible catastrophe. I tried selling some of my photography in order to raise money; I donated to three different relief organizations; I even tried starting a website called Katrina Heals to catalog stories of hope in the aftermath of the storm. It did not go anywhere, mainly because I lacked the willpower to move it forward. I did not know what to do.

A month after the storm, a newspaper reporter in Mississippi interviewed me; he had somehow found Katrina Heals. After lauding me for starting the hopeful website, he wanted to know if I planned to change my name. Other women had, he said. I told him I would never change my name.

In November that same year, my wrists hurt so much I had to cut back on writing for the second time. Two publishers rejected the manuscript for *Denise's Mold*, the book I had already published and sold. My cat Taffy died. But the most difficult event came in December when I went home, a trip that would be my last visit to Colorado. I spent a long night crying, mourning the parents I never had and feeling scared about a future in which the truth of my unsatisfactory relationship with my parents was no longer hidden. Narcissism, depression, anxiety, and low-self-esteem plagued my family, and I needed to do a great deal of work on myself before I could relate to them realistically. And so family life as I knew it ended that Christmas as the destructive storm archetype continued to work its salty medicine.

Meanwhile, by February it became glaringly apparent how completely the U.S. Government had failed the residents of New Orleans. People there as well as outside the city struggled to renew and give birth to a revitalized Big Easy.

By April a physical therapist helped me with my wrists; I also experimented with spiritual practices like mindfulness meditation. These powerful ways of healing were a glorious wind that cleared out all the old junk in my life. In May I quit my jobs and started my own tutoring business. This was a big success. In June I found an acupuncturist, radically changed my diet, began meditating, bought a new car, and made new friends. In August I bought my first house, and in October I moved into it and hung my first photography show at a local tea bar. 2006 had become the Year of Self-Care and Finding My Direction.

Even with all this movement I had not fully recovered. Neither had New Orleans. Many changes in city infrastructure were needed, and shadowy elements had to be illuminated. Racism, classism, government neglect, and the destruction done by the petroleum industries no longer lurked in the shadows.

In my case, the storm revealed that I ignored my inner guidance and my body, that I made wrong choices in friends, that I lacked boundaries, and that I treated myself terribly. But by October 2007, a little more than two years after Hurricane Katrina's arrival, I had entered graduate school and found my path. I am now grateful for that storm, because she caused me (and our country) to take a long look at the state of things and start to make some painful changes.

Storm power allows us to heal, purify, transform, experience death and rebirth, tap into the unconscious, go with the flow, trust in our power, listen to our intuition, and revere nature. I hope to combine all of these elements into a professional practice that will encourage deep healing in me, others, and the Earth. I now trust the storm to help me swirl all of these elements into a cohesive method, to aid me in gathering the people I can serve, and to remind me not to stay small, but to become large and powerful, blowing the winds of change through society.

Resources

Blum, R. *The Book of Runes: A Handbook for the Use of an Ancient Oracle*. New York: St. Martin's Press, 1993.

Campbell, Joseph. *Hero with a Thousand Faces*. New Jersey: Princeton University Press, 1972.

Hillman, James. *The Soul's Code: in Search of Character and Calling*. New York: Grand Central Publishing, 1997.

Sams, J., Carson, D. and Werneke, A. (1999) *Medicine cards: the discovery of power through the ways of animals*. New York: St. Martin's Press.

Katrina Martin Davenport, MA, is a dreamer. Her work involves reconnecting people with nature and illuminating nature's soul through her photographs and words. In 2009 she graduated from John F Kennedy University with a master's in Consciousness and Transformative Studies. She co-wrote and now oversees the online curriculum for the TerraPlaces Project. Find out more about her at www.katrinadreamer.com.

Sacred Scars:
Wildfire in the Southern California Psyche

Danielle Neuhauser

This essay explores the presence of wildfire in the chaparral forest of Southern California and how this natural phenomenon is reflected symbolically through the psyche of the region's inhabitants. Beginning with the author's personal narrative, the essay traverses the landscape of stories in the land and in the community and examines the role of alchemical fire to reveal an overriding myth of transformation through destruction and loss.

The night before I was evacuated I stayed at home in my yurt in the canyon. It was a warm, dry summer evening and the crickets sang loudly as I lay in bed and the curtain at my window softly blew in and out, tracing the contours of my hand. I had stayed up late listening to Forest Service radio updates on the wildfire two miles away, and had gone to sleep with some uncertainty about the fate of the place where I lived. I wondered about sudden changes in wind and being driven out by raging flames in the middle of the night. Although aware of a threatening blaze nearby, the perfect stillness in the air seemed to tell me to rest and appreciate this moment of peace.

The next morning I stepped out onto the deck to see the cloud of smoke above the next ridge now grown bigger and taller. As yet there was no chaos, no fire engines, and not much other traffic at all traversing the windy road. It was a picture-perfect day on the mountain; only the air carried an ubiquitous smell of smoke. The heat of the day had arrived. After a quick rinse with cool hose water, I immediately fell into a deep sleep.

I was awakened by a neighbor calling my name, then dressed quickly and made my way outside in a confused state. The moment of realization came when the firefighters who hiked down the sandstone trail to my door asked me to remove my propane tanks from the property. It struck me as ironic to have been in a dream state of naked vulnerability, nonchalantly napping at midday, while outside in the full sunlight, men in uniforms were rounding up residents to usher them to designated safety zones.

Within seconds I was disconnecting gas lines and packing a bag while surveying my possessions and trying to decide, what mattered? All the while the vibrations of helicopters sweeping overhead sounded a constant reminder of approaching danger. Someone asked me if I was okay with what was happening, and I replied, "Well, what can you do?" *It's bigger than us*, I thought.

By sunset my car was packed and I stood atop the boulders gazing down at the canyon in a silent goodbye. Birds still flew through the oaks, thickets still shivered in the breeze, and pink naked ladies of summer still bloomed with their otherworldly sweet scent. We departed without knowledge of outcome, likelihood, or forecast. *This place could be gone tomorrow.*

Community and Stories After the Fire

Stories told and retold during a wildfire activate the collective awareness of an area's inhabitants, creating an atmosphere of high-level drama that calls attention to how the community faces this natural calamity. Within panic and uncertainty, heroic bravery, highly organized recovery efforts, disheveled evacuees, and sympathetic bystanders, conversations are weighted with the latest news on where the wind is headed and whose homes are threatened, all below the darkening skies.

One way or another we all seem to be a part of this show. My story was only one of the hundreds of stories told during the fire, and their intensity and magnitude smoldered for weeks. One family with a newborn, it was told, had moved into their new home one day and been burned out the next. A husband and wife were able to save their house with good planning and a misting system. A woman narrowly escaped death by five minutes when she was awakened with a phone call. After a musician lost his home to the fire, he held a benefit concert to share both his losses and his new appreciation of life.

Normally content to be neatly placed in cozy dens, people find themselves stepping outside of prescribed social parameters and individual comfort zones. People are called to pay attention to their surroundings, to be clear and accurate in their communications, and to maintain an awareness of a rare, in-your-face kind of reality. I saw this in my own evacuation. While frantic and uncertain, I was also surprisingly grounded, energetic, and free. Listening to hourly radio reports and watching the skyline for smoke and flames as the fire burned through decades of dry brush and dense vegetation, I grew aware of a simultaneous internal incineration of my own emotional landscape. Unattached to material possessions and old emotional patterns, I felt empowered by my course of action. This was not bliss, but within moments of fear, disbelief, confusion, and outright denial arrived a concurrent state of awakening and sudden transformation. I was infused with life and joy, awakened as from sleep to the beauty and the danger in each moment.

Our ancestors lived in a way that industrial civilization has felt compelled to escape: in intimate relationship with the raw aspects of life in the physical world. In this state, eyes are open to see things in relationship, and your fate and place, whatever they may be, are acknowledged with lucid awareness. In contrast, modern humans are more likely to hold onto anxiety and the false idea of security to the point of clouding one's vision and inhibiting actions and decisions. Fire is a bell-ringing wakeup call to this error, a jangling of our individual response systems and our collective idea of safe reality.

This capacity for awareness may have been left behind in the age of information and technology. Perhaps spending hours on computers day after day, quickly filling our social hunger with a talking picture box, or flying across an entire continent in a matter of hours, all these grandiose, sweeping gestures of modern man remain abstracted from our basic needs as mammals. Depending on these highly sophisticated systems may leave us feeling powerless. Like the fearful narcissist who inflates his ego to mask deeper feelings of inadequacy, perhaps we use our superficial connections to the world to hang on to a false security. To make contact with the world in a more personal and intimate way might illuminate our emptiness and vulnerability.

And so we forget the raw taste of life, the cool spring water down a dry throat. Or the slow, natural cadences of a place still inhabited by other sentient beings. Or the sharp sense of moment-to-moment adaptation requiring instinctual action rather than calculated answers.

Alchemical Wildfire and Transformation

Fire is a story in the psyche, held in the memory of a place: black-charred limbs on the land, streaks of intensive change to the collective mind. In alchemy as understood psychologically, fire is a symbol of transformation, and we can look to this symbolism to discover an internal activity that mimics the outer activity of wildfire in the land. C.G. Jung said that the cyclical and mythical in nature— summer and winter, the phases of the moon, the dry and rainy seasons—"are symbolic expressions of the inner unconscious drama of the psyche."[1] In Southern California, fire often dominates the life cycles of our ecosystems, inviting us to look to its unconscious implications, its symbolic meaning.

Fire can offer a metaphor for systemic anxiety erupting from a need to remove what ails us psychologically. In an ecosystem, fire serves a similar function by regulating growth. Panic is fueled by hyperventilation, as fire is fueled by oxygen. A panic attack is brought on by breathing rapidly and shallowly, thereby retaining carbon dioxide gas in our circulatory system. Wildfire is like a hyperventilation of the land, its breath fed by oxygen and, in Southern California, by 70-mile-per-hour Santa Ana winds and sundowners.

In the alchemical vessel of old, destruction precedes renewal, just as wildfire aids the renewal of a landscape. For consciousness to grow, internal alchemical fire must erupt in order to burn and reshape the contents of the unconscious. Enduring the heat can be difficult and uncomfortable, but emotions like anxiety and anger emerge to give a voice to needs that have gone unanswered. When unspoken anxiety is fully felt and expressed, something shifts in our psychology; conversely, repression of these feelings creates more anxiety and paralysis. Depth psychologists as far back as Freud and Janet recognized that pathologies serve a natural purpose—so too with wildfire. Wildfire and alchemical fire bring transformation and renewal to their respective living systems.

If we look closely, transformation is revealed as a recurring motif in the land as well as in the self-help culture of Southern California, evident not only in rapidly changing landscapes, but in myriad offerings of yoga classes, therapy groups, spiritual gurus, candle-lit kirtans, and inspirational seminars; in a billion-dollar industry of cosmetic surgeries, cleansing therapies, weight loss programs, and fitness celebrities. People here crave acts of transformation and renewal: fuel for alchemical fire.

In alchemy, the phoenix is a symbol of the renewed personality.[2] This mythical bird, found in the mythologies of many different cultures, including the Arabic, the Egyptian, the Indian, and the ancient Greek, carries meanings associated with fire, the sun, death, rebirth, and transformation. Among other things, the phoenix myth illustrates how psyche possesses the will to burn, and how out of the ashes of destruction comes creation and renewal in the form of an entirely new bird. Losing one's home is a tremendous loss. Maybe your grandmother's love-letters to her husband were burned in the blaze, perhaps family heirlooms, books and music you loved, or your carefully planned vegetable garden. But when the burning comes to its end, you may realize that the world itself has not ended. A new world may emerge, where you have changed, and perhaps you no longer obsess over possessions or the remark that your brother made the other day, or the color that you want to paint the guest bedroom. You are faced with life moment by moment, and moment for moment.

Those who have experienced significant losses from fire can best tell of the hope that lies beyond the loss and the potent period of regrowth that occurs; of how life returns in the most beautiful and unexpected ways, just as a burned hillside suddenly springs up a sea of electric-blue lupine.

Looking further, we see that fire holds clues to the nature of this place, and therefore of its people.

Listening to Chaparral

Wildfire has always been a natural occurrence in Southern California. Fire scientists Robert Martin and David Sapsis estimate that between 5.6 million and 13 million acres of California burned annually from lightning and indigenous peoples' fire regimes.[3]

Southern California has one of the most fire-prone climates on earth. An estimated 800,000 acres burned in two simultaneous fires in Orange County and San Diego County in September 1889 alone.[4] They weren't catastrophic to humans because few people lived in the backcountry at that time.

Chaparral is a semi-arid, shrub-dominated association of plants shaped by summer drought, winter rain, and intense wildfire. It is uniquely adapted to outlive fire. The shrub seeds, for instance, resist fire and drought and can lie dormant for decades before they germinate.

Ecologist Richard Vogl has postulated that fire helped to shape three fourths of California's vegetation.[5] According to ecologist Joseph Connell, "Disturbances that occur at intermediate intensities and frequencies promote the greatest biological diversity."[6] Fire is vital to the health and biodiversity of the ecosystem. M. Kat Anderson reports that fire was the most significant, effective, and widely employed vegetation management tool of the California Indian tribes.[7] Deliberate burning increased abundance and density of wild edibles, controlled insects and diseases, enhanced feed for wildlife, increased the quantity of basket-making materials, removed dead plant material, promoted growth through nutrient cycling, and maintained specific plant community types, such as coastal prairies and montane meadows.

With so much of this wilderness now inhabited and developed, wildfire causes significant losses in property damage and poses a threat to human life. Additionally, fire frequency has increased with population growth, which in turn risks what experts in the field call "type conversion": as burn rates exceed the natural twenty-year recovery period, native shrub lands degenerate into desolate patches of non-native weedy grassland.[8]

Some believe that chaparral must be burned regularly to remain healthy and reduce risk to human communities. According to Richard Halsey, director of the California Chaparral Institute, these ideas are harmful because they promote actions that will eliminate the last remaining stands of old growth chaparral. Studies show that there is no evidence for species loss when fires are too infrequent, but there is evidence for species loss when fires are too frequent. "It is difficult for many to accept the uncontrollable. With support mechanisms in place, smoothing the bumps in life, the urban dweller may forget the intimate connection that still exists between civilization and nature."[9]

Halsey believes that awareness of the native chaparral ecosystem must increase if people are going to build a sense of personal responsibility toward the land and prevent wildfire disasters. "Chaparral is distinctly Californian. It is our own native wilderness and defines who we are. Both the landscape and our lifestyle have been shaped by the same natural forces, drought and fire."[10] He points to the need for education about the ecological conditions of Southern California. This can help us think more deeply about how we inhabit this place while grasping the ecopsychological truth that landscape is an inextricable part of our psychology. Without this ecological awareness, the Southern Californian may feel a symbolic drought within that yearns to be replenished, or an emotional wildfire that leaves a trail of devastation in its path.

We might take a paradoxical approach to these anxieties by turning *toward* the alchemical fire to consider what California is asking of us with her fires. We might also confront our own anxieties about nature, including our cultural notion of wilderness as something to dominate or avoid. Could the people of Southern California be in an emotional drought caused by psychic isolation from their home environment? As a result, are we unable to see beyond the smokescreen of chaos and loss from wildfire, blind to its more sober and life-affirming message?

In more ways than one, the symbiotic relationship of humans with nature has been overlooked. Psychologist James Hillman linked the loss of wild nature to the loss of internal wildness when he asked, "Is not a basic cause of contemporary environmental devastation 'out there' a continuation of Western history's determination to keep control 'in here'?"[11] As we continue to exclude nature from consciousness, natural aspects of ourselves are also excluded, ignored, and repressed. According to ecopsychologist Liz Evans, we now have little sense of ourselves as instinctive creatures, which leaves us "fundamentally alienated from the natural world as well as from our own inner nature."[12]

Can we mimic the landscape and its cyclical processes by integrating the outer eruption of wildfire with an inner dynamic of transformation? When we observe our own burning and re-growth, we begin to cultivate diversity in psychic life by allowing new parts of the self to emerge and old patterns to subside. As our internal landscape becomes weedy, desolate, homogenous, overgrown, or under-utilized, we may benefit from the disturbance of psychic fire. Anderson describes fire's "episodic perturbations" and how many plant species not only tolerate them, but also require them to complete their life cycle.[13] In a land of perpetual disturbance, some of us adapt to thrive on change, just as seeds in chaparral sprout only after a fire.

Communities too can find the means to transform their responses to wildfire. The voice of this particular Californian landscape may ask for a more "feminine" response to these disasters—one of community, of relatedness, and compassion and respect for the "other" that is our environment—beyond the heroic effort to save us all. Instead of reacting after each disaster, we might respond in a more adaptive and relational style, conforming to nature's limitations with more maternal prevention than perpetual battle and rescue. An adaptive response to fire could reflect an awareness of our fundamental connections to the land, and renewed maturity in our relationship to place.

Central to an informed response to wildfire is an understanding that culture and wildness are not in opposition. By examining wildfire and other natural phenomena as reflections of our inner nature and vice versa, we may uncover and deepen our own relationship to nature and to ourselves. The flames of these mountain blazes speak of the deep, enduring wildness characteristic of the Southern California landscape; looking inward, we connect with the land through awareness of and appreciation for our own enduring wildness.

Endnotes

1 Kidner, David. *Nature and Psyche: Radical Environmentalism and the Politics of Subjectivity.* Albany, NY: State University of New York Press, 2001, 267.

2 Von-Franz, Marie-Louise. *Alchemy: An Introduction to the Symbolism and the Psychology.* Toronto, Canada: Inner City Books, 1980.

3 Anderson, M. Kat. *Tending the Wild: Native American Knowledge and the Management of California's Natural Resources.* Berkeley and Los Angeles: University of California Press, 2005.

4 Halsey, Richard W. *Fire, Chaparral, and Survival in Southern California.* San Diego, CA: Sunbelt Publications, 2005.

5 Anderson, 2005.

6 Anderson, 2005, p. 18.

7 Anderson, 2005.

8 Halsey, 2005.

9 Halsey, 2005, p. 33.

10 The California Chaparral Institute. *Chaparral Mythology.* 2008. http://www.californiachaparral.com/factsmyths.html.

11 Hillman, James. *Pan and the Nightmare, (being the only translation from the German by A. V. O'Brien) of Ephialtes: A Pathological-Mythological Treatise on the Nightmare in Classical Antiquity, Together with an Essay on Pan, serving as a psychological introduction to Roscher's Ephialtes.* New York: Spring, 1972, 72.

12 Evans, Liz. "Developing a Jungian Ecopsychology" New Orleans: Spring Journal, Psyche and Nature edition, Fall, 2006, p. 131.

13 Anderson, 2005, p. 17.

Danielle Neuhauser, MA is a licensed Marriage and Family Therapist Intern who began studies in the field of ecopsychology at the age of nineteen.   Her formal education includes study at Northland College, Prescott College, UW-Madison, and Pacifica Graduate Institute. She currently lives in Santa Barbara, California, working as a trauma counselor, assisting in ecological restoration projects, and tending the human-nature connection.

Contrails

Craig Chalquist

For Fay Trowbridge Legg (1908-2001), nurse, hiker, wilderness defender, lifelong learner, grandmother. Her appreciation of the element Air extended to getting up on her roof at age eighty to rake off the leaves and clean the gutters. I always imagine her straightening after her labors to gaze up at the sky in wonder.

Something is up with my birth family's relationship to sky, and I wonder if I inherited it.

My birth father was a pilot who taught my birth mother how to parachute. Her sister, a firefighter and paramedic, flew helicopters. Her brother was an Army Ranger who jumped out of aircraft. Her father forecast the weather.

However, these straightforward and verifiable facts—you know, the kind that float research politics and public credulity—conceal a twist. My uncle sustained a permanent injury when he broke his leg on a jump ramp. My father liked to frighten pilot trainees by zooming his small plane under rocky arches in Hawaii. My mother survived a plane crash, only to crash in a cab on the way to the hospital. I have a photograph of her finishing a jump on her head. My aunt made a helicopter do a somersault; and although my grandfather was a Navy man who loved the sea, as a boy he saw lightning flash down through a chimney in the Midwest, a concussion from on high that left in him a lifelong fear of storms.

This essay takes its name from a poem written by my grandmother. One day she lost her wedding ring. Looking up, she saw streaks of condensation left by jets. As their contrails vanished, she reflected wistfully on the impermanence of things; eventually my grandfather divorced her. Evidently she had seen what the ancients called an *augury*, a word that derives from the ancient Roman practice of studying the flights of birds for hints of what might befall. (What does it mean that our birds have the flu?)

For me as well, sky has always carried a premonition of the uncanny. In my earliest dreams dragon-like beings chased me, flashing lightning as they came on. As a toddler I thought I saw lightning hit the lawn outside after my dad drove off to work, but when I went out after the storm to confirm my fears, I found no blast marks anywhere. In Nebraska a tornado spun a bolt of lightning near enough to knock me back inside the house.

From a friend's backyard I looked up one night as we wrestled, pretending to be knights at arms, and saw three greenish disks moving erratically against the stars. I glanced at my friend., a hulking childhood Lancelot rising from pinning a stocky but shorter Arthur. He saw the disks too. "They look," I remarked, "like cartoon searchlights running along a bank of clouds"; but there were no clouds, and in the morning our AM radios chattered about a UFO sighting over East County San Diego. (Jung wrote an interesting essay on UFOs as collective symbols of wholeness that counterbalance the chaotic breakdown of our time. Are UFOs psychic Round Tables looking for favorable earthly groundings?)

The sky writing that holds all this together takes shape for me when I remember that my parents woke me up very early on July 20, 1969, to watch Apollo 11 astronauts descend from their Lunar Module to leave human footprints on the Moon. (Watching this televised event, a birth mother I had never met threw her cigarette into the air in celebration and decided to quit smoking.) As one small step confirmed one giant leap, new futures of possibility opened over our heads. We could stand on other worlds—and look back in appreciation at our own blue-green marble floating in the blackness. Sky itself had become the only limit.

Sky = future then, as the Romans seers figured out. After being dazzled by a bolt from the blue, my grandfather turned to meteorology. My uncle's broken leg announced a new post-military career before he ever struck the earth. My mother planted herself twice, one foot in Hawaii and the other in San Diego, city of my birth. My father turned trainees into pilots and my mother into his wife. After a few aerial twists my aunt landed firmly in a Forest Service career. Having glimpsed strange green disks, I went on to read Jung and earn three psychology degrees as dragons and lightning led me into the study of myth. For all of us, the writing on the wall took form first in the sky. In the old Gothic language, the word for "sky" was "mirror."

People have always looked up for hints about what was on the way. As Columbus hove near a world new to him and his crew, a falling star struck the ocean not far from his three ships. His men were frightened at this omen, but not as frightened as the Aztecs who watched fire descending from above shortly before Cortés and his pathogen-ridden conquistadors arrived. "We are lost!" wailed the priests of weeping Cihuacoatl, goddess of childbirth and death, after lightning struck the rain god's temple.

Traditionally, stars that rise announce new beginnings: we have only to recall the story of Jesus born in a lowly Bethlehem manger, entering a world yet devoid of mega-churches to the humble lowing of cows. Comet Halley appeared just in time for the birth of inventive Samuel Clemens. In Arthurian legend a comet's tail suggested to Merlin the shape of a dragon's head just before King Uther Pendragon was born. It makes an odd kind of sense that futurist H. G. Wells was born at Atlas House, an abode named after the hero who bore up the sky on his shoulders. If Aer (lower air) and Aether (upper air) were the gods the Greeks supposed, these heavenly beings possessed a favorable vantage for seeing the shape of things to come.

IT'S HARD TO SAY WHERE the habit of breaking reality down into its supposed primordial components originated. The Greek classical elements written about by Empedocles before he hurled himself into a volcano had been influenced by earlier Orphic and Babylonian traditions. Babylon, of course, was once part of the Fertile Crescent from which monocrop agriculture spread horizontally across Europe, carrying writing, accounting, and urbanization with it. In a few thousand years those growing urban centers would replace the worship of earth goddesses with sky gods as all eyes (to paraphrase Lewis Mumford) turned upward.

Do the elements live? Do they possess some sort of proto-consciousness? Pre-industrial people thought so, as we can see from their myths and surviving oral traditions snidely dismissed as primitive superstitions, as though belief in Scientism or the Invisible Hand of the Market were exempt from irrationality. Even in the West, a long line of thoughtful writing about the possibility of mind inherent in matter weaves its arguments through Nature Philosophy, Romanticism, and panpsychism all the way back to the ancient Greeks ("All things are full of gods"—Thales) and beyond.

David Ray Griffin refers to "panexperientialism" rather than "panpsychism" to clarify what philosophers do NOT claim: that stones and breezes think like we do. Consciousness of the type that requires a neocortex is one animal, experience another; and if experience begins with the first photon to "decide" whether to bounce from a half-silvered mirror one particle at a time or to show up for an interferometer as a wave instead; if existence is woven of occasions actually experienced (Whitehead) or of brief, all-consuming pairings of quantum foam and flux; if a capacity for adaptation counts as cognition (Maturana and Varela); and if Teilhard de Chardin was right that everything, absolutely everything possesses a "within" as well as a "without," then by what right do we relegate experience only to ourselves? And if only we do it, where did we get it from?

In June of 2009, a team of Weather Channel storm chasers found themselves in southeastern Wyoming watching a tornado form. As they pointed their cameras at the oncoming funnel, they gaped in awe as it bent toward them, opened its eye, and stooped so they could see its rotating insides. By contrast, college football fans attending a game in spite of a late-season twister a week before were driven from the field by a team of tornados touching down to chase away the Iowa State Cyclones. "Coincidence," the hardcore materialist would claim, echoing without knowing it the ancient Roman habit of blaming events on "Fortuna" (chance). Yet if nature does bear some version of the subjectivity with which so many of her species are endowed, then perhaps, as a terrapsychological lens would record, Earth turns toward us the face that we turn toward it, addressing us daily in a tornadic language of symbol and image: "Look more deeply inside my aliveness! As you watch me, I watch you as well."

THE SPACE PROGRAM HAVING become a whipping boy for both conservatives trying to choke off "wasteful spending" not diverted into warfare and environmentalists in search of earth mother wisdom, its results come in for evaluation on both sides through the hard lens of fiscal practicality. *Besides weather-watching and vacuum industry, what does leaving the planet really do for us? Don't we have enough to worry about down here?* Imagine future representatives of an advanced civilization landing to congratulate us for pursuing our curiosity anyway: "Now and then we find the vestiges of species who stay on-planet, but because most live in solar systems filled with debris, these sad creatures are usually dead of an asteroid strike by the time we visit."

One often hears these days, including within this anthology, that humans are out of balance with nature. But developmentally speaking, is that not somehow the point? In permaculture we say that "the problem is the solution." *Homo sapiens* is of nature, and yet we also thwart, disrupt, and destabilize nature. We act like adolescents needing to feel independent in the service of a strong ego—and perhaps in service to the whole too, just as the manically experimental teen brings fresh insights and quirky learnings back into the family.

Parentified pragmatism, which in chronic cases ought to be diagnosed as a form of panic, easily forgets that sometimes big problems need the higher perspective of an aethereal view, as when humanity caught its collective breath to see photographs of Earth for the first time ever. That lovely blue-green ball floating in impenetrable darkness shifted perceptions in ways that mere money never could.

Knowing intellectually our local address—planet Earth, Solar System, Local Fluff, Local Bubble, Gould Belt, Orion Arm, Milky Way Galaxy, Local Group, Virgo Supercluster, all in a Universe perhaps daughter to vaster cosmic parents occupying other dimensions—is not the same (notwithstanding Dennett and the eliminativists) as *seeing* our home planet floating against an interstellar backdrop receding to reaches so vast that even imagination quails at their immensity. Home sweet home.

Astronauts returned to Earth have resorted to poetic utterances to describe the beauty they saw and the awe they felt. *A jewel hanging in the blackness of space. The scars of national boundaries gone.* Glimpsing the thin line of the atmosphere at dawn, all the protection we have against cosmic radiation, one returned traveler admitted: *I was terrified by its fragile appearance.*

What will our street corner look like to the rest of the cosmos a century from now? Can we finally get enough above our crazy ideologies to actively cherish our entire planet and its creatures? If not, the writing's in the sky: a tragic tale of a dead world divorced of life by unregulated greed, unchecked paranoia, and unacknowledged hatred of embodied being.

But if so, then blue depths below a bright bow of aer, its curve like a wedding band encircling Earth's round finger.

Craig Chalquist, PhD, depth psychologist and core faculty in the College of Professional Studies at John F. Kennedy University, is also a certified Master Gardener through the University of California Agricultural Extension. He holds certificates in permaculture and sustainable landscape design. His books include Terrapsychology: Reengaging the Soul of Place *(Spring Journal Books, 2007),* The Tears of Llorona: A Californian Odyssey of Myth, Place, and Homecoming *(World Soul Books, 2009),* Storied Lives *(2009), and, as co-editor with Linda Buzzell, the anthology* Ecotherapy: Healing with Nature in Mind *(Sierra Club Books, 2009). He lives and works in California's Bay Area. Visit his website at Chalquist.com.*

places

Among the Living

cartography
is really more of an idea
my teacher says
the map is not to be confused
with the world
it's just a metaphor
a mind wanting
to hear the whole of speech
in one story

pointing out the particulars
of mountains
and rivers does not quite
get at the sanctity of traveling
when you want to find your way again
having felt the land call you

egregious errors are made
by slipping past
the lightening strike spots
following red snakes
toward black dots

miss the stargates
and you'll never know
what you might have become
if you had been watching the clouds
that were watching you

as you moved through dust
throwing flakes of skin
to join the cosmos

—Catherine Baumgartner

Kings of the Crown:
Collision and Connection in the Crown of the Continent

Steph Paidas-Dukarm

Montana's Glacier National Park and the larger Crown of the Continent ecosystem are home to some of the most beautiful landscapes in North America. Prized for the abundant diversity of flora and fauna, this area is mostly known for one reason: bears. In this essay, Steph Paidas-Dukarm recounts her experiences with summer work supporting educational endeavors for older adults in the Glacier area. She draws from the natural environment and observations of its inhabitants to share how elements from the landscape permeated the psyches of those who came to seek the Crown.

That summer started with a bang—a loud series of bangs, in fact, that shook the small frame of my hundred-year-old house and woke me from a fitful slumber. While I'd punched my pillow, a female grizzly fresh from her den had crossed the railroad tracks to move from her subalpine habitat to the river valley below. As she crossed, she paused for a moment to investigate some smaller casualty of the railroad, and though the conductor did his best to sound the horn and scare her off the tracks, she lingered too long. The conductor hit the brakes, but the sheer force of the train and its inertia were too much. The grizzly was struck by the oncoming engine, her body propelled more than one hundred feet, so far that the conductor had to strain to see her landing. The cacophony of orchestral metal-on-metal was loud enough to wake my sleepy town—and me—several miles away. Echoes of her death became percussions that beat the rhythms of that season, for she was the first of nine bears to be killed by trains and autos that summer in northwest Montana.[1]

That summer I lived just outside Glacier National Park in a vast landscape known as the Crown of the Continent ecosystem. Extending into Canada to the north, the Blackfeet reservation to the east, ranchland to the west, and more than two hundred miles of pristine wilderness to the south, Glacier and the Crown of the Continent comprise ten million acres of the most intact ecosystem in the United States, and one of the better preserved ecosystems in the world.[2] This area, home to a greater species variety than found anywhere else in North America, houses the largest grizzly population in the contiguous United States.[3] This is one of the last vestiges of wilderness where grizzlies call home, but these bears have not always congregated in the Crown. Nor has the railroad always passed through. The Crown of the Continent serves as a central hub for both, where bears and boxcars have played major roles in the history of Glacier and—as the first railway roadkill of the year illustrated—in the histories of each other.

The grizzly death occurred during the first week of my summer job as tour director for an organization that operated educational vacations for older adults around Glacier National Park. Our first program had begun in May, and it was my responsibility to spend every day living, eating, and hiking among the groups of 30+ participants as I coordinated their adventures. Included in the curriculum were local and national experts in ecology, geology, wildlife biology, anthropology, and indigenous cultures who spent whole days teaching about the place that the groups had come to experience—my home. That morning, we were studying Merganser ducks on a ranch pond less than twenty miles from where the grizzly had been hit.

As we stood with binoculars and spoke in hushed tones, we had no idea that a van, pickup, and railway crane were executing a funeral procession for one of the Crown's most revered symbols—the grizzly sow, a fallen Queen. Standing at the base of the mountains in the blue light of morning, gazing out across a summer to be filled with grizzly encounters of every imaginable kind, I found myself offering prayers. I first prayed for protection of the ducks we observed, and then for their wetlands. The prayer extended to grizzlies and all the animals who shared the Crown with us. I prayed for their safety and well-being through what promised to be one of the biggest tourist seasons on record in Montana. And I asked for our safety as well. Looking back, that prayer may have been the only eulogy offered for the dead Queen.

Little did I know then that the Crown of the Continent would communicate through many collisions that summer, or that she would often send bears to deliver her messages.

Bears and Boxcars in the Crown of the Continent

Tourists and seekers come to the Crown of the Continent for many reasons: the call of the wilderness, the few remaining glaciers in the contiguous United States, abundant flora and fauna, hundreds of miles of hiking trails. An average of two million travelers visit the region every year;[4] my organization hosted some seven hundred tourists that summer. Although they arrived by car and air from their homes around the globe, a favorite mode of transportation was the method by which most travelers visited this area in its early days as a national park—the train.

Significant today as the single major railway crossing of the northern Rockies in the U.S., the railroad has played a prominent role in the history of the Crown since the 1800s. The Great Northern Railway was constructed by J. J. Hill when a large mineral deposit was discovered in Glacier territory in the late 1800s. Raw materials would need to be transported from the mountains to other parts of the country for refinement, and the idea was born to build a railroad through Marias Pass, the lowest throughway across the northern Rockies. Lands containing the mineral deposit and Marias Pass belonged to the Blackfeet Nation, so U.S. government officials and

Hill himself negotiated with Blackfeet leaders to cede their portion of what is now Glacier National Park in the Treaty of 1896.[5] However, mining quickly proved infeasible in the difficult terrain, and Hill struggled to profit from his substantial investment. Recognizing the stunning beauty of the area and its reliance on the rail for accessibility, Hill petitioned Congress and wrote personal letters to President Theodore Roosevelt advocating for the national significance of the land.[6] As a result of Hill's efforts, the area was officially designated as Glacier National Park in 1910. Hill initiated the advertising campaign "See America First," and Americans came in droves to see lands where bears were still free to roam.[7]

Today, the Great Northern Railway legacy still attracts tourism to the area, as visitors journey from around the world to visit grand park lodges built by the railway more than one hundred years ago. Some still seek to ride the rails through spectacular scenery. The tracks are busy; trains voyage through Marias Pass many times each day, though most now carry freight and cargo instead of the wealthy easterners of the early 1900s. There has been so much traffic on the rail line over the past decade that it has raised concerns about the safety of the area's animal life—most notably the bears. An average of one to two grizzly bears are killed every year on the stretch of railway that passes through this part of the world.[8]

Wherever travelers have journeyed from and whatever the particular draw, historically and today, visitors to the Crown of the Continent all seem to share an interest: bears. And while the ecosystem is home to hundreds of black bears, most visitors covet the King of the Crown, the grizzly, whose status as supreme species in this wilderness has been hard won. The North American grizzly bear (*Ursus arctos horribilis*) actually evolved in the American plains over thousands of years. It was there, digging for insects and small rodents, that it developed the muscular shoulder hump which has come to define it.[9] American Indians of the Great Plains held great respect for these massive creatures often weighing in excess of 550 pounds. The Blackfeet, who referred to themselves as the "Real People," venerated grizzlies to the status of "Real Bear" for the ability to stand on two legs, often more than six or seven feet tall. But reverence for these creatures was not shared by the waves of

European-descended human migrants who battled for the plains in the 1800s and sent the grizzlies running for the hills. Difficult-to-access mountain regions like Glacier were the few remote safe houses where grizzlies found protection from American settlers who decimated their habitat and killed any bears they encountered.[10]

Loss of more than 98% of its habitat and dwindling numbers landed the grizzly on the Endangered Species Act list of threatened species in 1975, which earned the bear federal protection.[11] No longer roaming the plains, American grizzly populations now center in Yellowstone and Glacier National Parks, where they have become the supreme species of those ecosystems and one of the primary tourism draws. Recent studies suggest that the *Ursus horribilis* population in Montana is faring better than expected given their isolated situation. An estimated 765 grizzlies call the Crown of the Continent home.[12] And every visitor I hosted that summer wanted to see one.

Grizzly Encounters in the Crown

In the week-long programs I helped coordinate that summer, we had many encounters with mountain goats, bighorn sheep, marmots, moose, elk, and deer, but none was so exciting as spotting the black bear or grizzly wandering a mountainside. When I look back now, it is the bears who stand out in memory. The hundreds of human faces I worked for have fallen away, and I'm left with images of the bears we regularly encountered. There was the giant male who patrolled the Swiftcurrent Trail near Bullhead Lake, intimidating hikers from making the seven-mile, 2,300-foot climb to the pass. There was the black bear family, a mama with three cubs who dug for bulbs in the meadow under Apikuni Falls. And there were the twins, a brother and sister duo of three-year-old grizzlies who had been kicked out of the den that spring by their mother, encouraging them to move out into the world on their own. The pair hunted together all summer on a ridge overlooking the remote Many Glacier Valley near the eastern edge of the park. Our groups spent many days in the valley below studying these familial bears through scopes, binoculars, and the naked eye. Week after week I memorized their features, the male with his silver-tipped fur and the female with a blonde mohawk up her back. I felt connected to them, coming to know them as I watched them dig and scratch their ways across a season. For my guests and for me, those bear encounters were the highlight of the summer.

But that summer was not filled just with romantic moments in sweeping mountain vistas in the presence of the Crown's Kings. It was also replete with strife, discord, and struggle. Like the bear struck by the train early in the season, the rest of the summer was impacted by collision. I had imagined small, intimate groups who would fall in love, as I had, and let anxieties fade with the blue-green sonnets of sunset in the mountains. That idealized image took a beating from my actual experiences as tour director. There were plenty of moments when camaraderie, humility, and reverence permeated the group; these I had fantasized about when I accepted the position. But there were many other moments when the illusions I'd come with were shattered. The groups could be quarrelsome, intolerant, and impatient. Many who came seemed perpetually dissatisfied and always clamored for more. It was my job to keep them happy, fed, satiated. Looking back across the four-month span of peaks and vales in my work, there was never a moment when I was fully successful. Many sightseers had wonderful experiences, but every time I turned around some guest was there to let me know how unhappy she was with the trip or how disgruntled he was about some detail of our travel.

Complaints usually arose from collisions of some kind. My guests bickered with each other, a lot, seeking me to mediate between sparring stances. The hotel that served as our home base near the park was understaffed and we often had only one strong woman to make breakfast for forty and clean all the guest rooms; demands for affordable accommodations clashed with the economic realities of a struggling resort. During the first month of tours, the Going to the Sun Road, the only road traversing Glacier, was closed as road crews worked around the clock to clear record winter snowfall from the passes; the willful fantasy of summer-long accessibility was smashed by the needs of nature. Instead of riding the road through the heart of Glacier, we had to bus our guests around the southern boundary of the park. There, we would pass the mountain striations of an ancient collision, where the Lewis Overthrust, a three-hundred mile long land mass from eastern Washington, broke off seventy million years ago and floated on the inland Belt Sea until it smacked into the Rocky Mountains in Montana and settled upon much younger sediment.[13] Past the Lewis Overthrust, we would venture into the Blackfeet reservation and come face-to-face with the devastating destruction of one of the most significant collisions in North American history, that of the European migrant and the American Indian. Those were long days in cramped vans when guests frequently complained about missing Glacier's definitive scenery, and pummeled the reservation with insults and ignorance.

Collision was present even in our itineraries. Less than two months before our groups arrived, we discovered that the park hotels had no room for us. Reservations for several programs had been irretrievably lost, the result of staff division in the corporation, and my supervisor and I found ourselves butting up against corporate management. The only place vacant enough at the peak of summer to accommodate our groups was a small hunting lodge on the Blackfeet reservation. Ironically situated outside the village of St. Mary, the lodge owners were happy to accommodate those who had been cast out of the inn, and they offered our groups all of the rooms in their barn-like building. We notified our guests of the change, that the idyllic lakefront rooms they had been promised in the grand lodge of the deepest valley in Glacier had been swapped for smaller, less majestic quarters on the reservation. Some cancelled, allowing us to better accommodate those who came. Of those who showed up, many ended up wishing they had gone elsewhere or stayed home.

The Great Divide: Human Beings, Bears, and Boundaries Collide

The Continental Divide passes through northwestern Montana, and this feature has partially contributed to the region's status as Crown of the Continent. The Blackfeet have long understood the importance of the rift demarcating watersheds, referring to its spiritual and ecological significance as "the Backbone of the World."[14] This line divides precipitation between two oceans and is responsible for the aqueous nourishment of the entire continent. The central spine that runs through Glacier National Park is one of its most prominent geological features, and the subject of thousands of photographs every year. As a group and I sat in its shadow one afternoon and learned about its formation, I began to recognize the great divide in my experiences that summer, which ranged from elation and reverence to deep despair and anger.

The weeks when we were able to stay in the Many Glacier valley were spectacular and enjoyable. The hotel itself sat on the edge of Swiftcurrent Lake, surrounded on three sides by craggy peaks and glacial cirques of incomparable beauty. We would awaken before dawn and hike from our hotel to stunning vistas. We wandered through meadows of wildflowers, waded in aquamarine lakes, and hiked up mountains to the remaining glaciers in the park. We learned about Blackfeet history, railway stories, and how the white man came to this place. We stayed in the grand lodge and feasted on its breakfast buffets and upscale dinners. We lived like wilderness royalty, served like kings, and we basked in the Crown.

Though we were treated as the royal family, our guests recognized only one King of the Crown—bears. While those of us who supported the tourist industry planned excursions for our visitors, our efforts to entertain paled in comparison to the real royalty who tread in that valley. Every evening on the back deck of the hotel, groups of strangers would gather with binoculars and excitement about what they might glimpse. One person would spot a grizzly, and the next hour would see hushed whispers, pointing in various directions, and a child-like eagerness on the faces of even the most curmudgeonly old coots. I stood on that deck day after day, week after week, watching the bears and marveling at the stories shared among strangers who found points of connection in the *Ursus* universe.

When we stayed in the park lodge, my coworkers and I shared a room. We'd wake and, still in our pajamas, throw open the window to start glassing the mountains for grizzlies. We'd often find them and call out their activities as we prepared ourselves for long, full days. We'd venture down to breakfast and eat scrumptious delicacies while still following those bears through the windows. Anytime a guest complained that breakfast wasn't hot enough, or that the hotel lacked Internet access, or that some physical ailment or conflict between visitors had acted up overnight, we'd draw attention back to those bears. Guests' worries would fade away as they fell into rapture, amazed that we could watch major predators hunting for food while we loaded our plates in a fine dining room—we at our buffet and the bears at theirs.

That rapture was harder to find once we moved to the reservation lodge. The rooms were small, with no air conditioning to cool the hot summer afternoons and few working heaters to warm the cold nights. With no private bathrooms, our guests had to share two showers down the hall, and I spent a month dealing with complaints about poor water pressure, broken faucets, dirty water full of iron, and fellow travelers who took too long to get ready in the morning. Breakfast beefs would replace bathroom battles—the food was too cold, the utensils were plastic, the coffee not gourmet. I'd mediate between disgruntled travelers and the overworked lodge owners, and I'd offer a prayer of thanks when we left the lodge each morning to head for the park. But it was the ride that I most dreaded.

Those twentymile drives of bumpy, windy roads through the reservation to enter the park valley were the worst of my summer, where I frequently found myself immersed in a seemingly insurmountable divide between cultures. No matter how the conversation started, it always seemed to settle on reservation life. My guests would criticize the dilapidated buildings, rusted vehicles abandoned in tall grasses, the way residents drove haphazardly, the garbage that seemed to cover the sides of the roads. A few expressed empathy for Native conditions, but most voiced harsh judgment against the predicament of the people. The staff and I tried our best to communicate about the historical roots of reservation poverty, but our storytelling did not impress those content to believe that this American Indian community must be thriving on casino profits and choosing to waste them on alcohol and junk food, the bottles and wrappers of which littered the highways like glass and paper wildflowers.

I attempted to explain history, colonization, and the lasting impacts of genocide against the people who had been here first. I tried to tell my exclusively white visitors that the Blackfeet had once been the most powerful of the Plains Indians, that their territory had spanned eastward to the Missouri River, north to modern Edmonton, and as far south as the Great Salt Lake.[15] I struggled to tell them that Glacier itself once belonged to the Blackfeet, but that their territory was tragically whittled away by conflict, famine, encroachment, and treaties which promised monies and services that were never delivered.[16] Blackfeet culture had been all but decimated by disease, violence, poverty, substance abuse, and unemployment when the 20th century rolled around; today's Blackfeet struggle to rebuild and find their way.[17] But many of my guests could not see the legacy of pain and suffering in the collapsing structures and highway litter, could not hear cries in the wind that scattered Blackfeet stories, like Marias Massacre and the Whoop-Up Trail, across the Crown of the Continent.

Those drives from the reservation to the Many Glacier Valley were difficult times for us all. I found myself praying for some larger force to breathe hope and understanding into the vans where prejudice and ignorance had sucked out the air. And then by some miracle we'd see bears: the twins, or the black mama with her cubs. Critical voices would hush and tones turn reverent. The melee of the day would fade away. We'd watch the bears pass as though royalty crossed before us. It was then that our discussions could turn to displacement, habitat destruction, and sheer will to survive and desire to thrive in places where encroachment is a dangerous, ever-present threat. Then, we could talk about the tragedy of great roaming creatures relegated to a small space on earth. Then, we could mention depleted resources and the perilous pursuits of humanity. Then, we could explore anguish at what is precariously perched on the edge of American expansion, and what might someday be lost. It was as if the bears seemed to know, seemed to appear when we most needed them, as if they sensed, as I did, that they could teach us what it really means to roam a territory, cooperate, and build a culture firmly grounded in a sense of place.

Not all animal encounters were enlightening. We watched from vans as tourists raced to bears grazing by the roadside, quickly snapped pictures, and then sped away. We saw private vehicles trying to nudge wildlife off the road after getting the snapshots their drivers desired. Hundreds of animals, mostly small rodents, were killed on nearby roads that summer, including several grizzlies. One of the park's shuttles collided with a ditch in an effort to avoid animals on the road.[18] And there was the ever-present threat of the railroad, as many animals, including grizzlies, died by train that summer.[19] The last to be killed, a grizzly sow relocated from this area to help repopulate another wilderness, died well after the tourists had gone as she tried to make her way back home.[20] I was gone from Montana by then too, having relocated myself to the deeper wilderness of Alaska for the sake of my husband's employment. I read about her death on the Internet and remembered my last trip over Going to the Sun Road the night before it had closed for the season.

By the end of the summer, my psyche had been pulled apart by tensions between what I saw of Blackfeet culture, what I experienced of mainstream American tourism, and what I knew of Nature. I felt confused, heartbroken, and struggling to find a vision of the Crown that could hold the extreme polarities of my experiences there. Park officials had announced the closure of Going to the Sun Road for the winter, and I decided to make one last trip through the park before it was left again to itself. I drove the road from west to east, lingered for sunset in the Many Glacier Valley, and began the long trek home in early twilight. Traffic was gone, the park deserted of human travelers, leaving me alone with my woes and the grandeur of Glacier.

I drove in silence as memory played a montage of the summer's events. I smiled at images of the animals and people I'd come to know, laughed at hilarious and embarrassing moments, cringed at attempts that resulted in failures, and cried in grief over what it meant to live and work in an industry that stripped more from the Crown than its majesty. At an emotional low point, I stopped and watched the last light fade on the shores of St. Mary's Lake. It was there that I said goodbye, not just to the park because I'd be moving away from it, but also to the image I had long held of its magical powers over people. Like that first spring prayer for the grizzly, this moment was a funeral, and I sat in the dusk with dwindling glaciers and felt the deep despair of loss.

I left Sun Point in a black abyss of grief. So lost was I in my mood that I barely inched along the road. As I rounded a bend, my still-quivering heart suddenly leapt back to life. In the road ahead of me stood a male coyote, startled by my headlights but confidently standing ground. I stopped. He looked at me, then in the direction of my headlights, then back at me. I crept forward to see what he might be looking for. He moved to the opposite lane, gaze darting between me and the path of my headlights. I inched forward, and he walked next to me, a few feet from my open window. He tentatively trotted, I accelerated to keep pace. We were traveling together, this coyote and me, and suddenly I felt a glimmer in that deep, dark abyss.

A few feet up the road we reached another bend. My headlights swept the shadows and revealed a dark figure hunched over on the shoulder. It was a grizzly. Coyote looked at me and we stopped, turning our gaze to await the bear's next move. She rotated toward the light, squinted against its brightness, and paused. I held my breath imagining a showdown, a collision of human, bear, and a coyote with whom I'd unknowingly become an ally. But instead of competitive clashing, Grizzly huffed, shrugged, and retreated into the forest. She did not go far. Coyote seemed to know this, too, and seized his opportune moment.

He ran to the place where the bear had been, quickly dug through the grass, and emerged with something small and furry in his mouth. He trotted toward me, prize dangling from his jaw, eyes shining with triumph. He passed within three feet of my open window and our eyes locked. Coyote nodded, bowed, blinked, then threw back his head to howl. The kill in his teeth made it more of a yelp, but it was unmistakably a celebration of gratitude. We had come together— Grizzly, Coyote, and me. A potentially catastrophic situation had morphed into heartfelt connection on the road that links west with east, White with Red, humanity with the natural world. And, like the land, the animals, the people, and the spirit of this place, the three of us had been transformed.

This was how I learned that the Crown of the Continent is not just about collision alone; it also holds the spirit of connection. Perhaps it was this spirit that inspired the formation of the world's first International Peace Park when Canada's adjacent Waterton Park joined Glacier in 1932, later earning Waterton-Glacier Peace Park designation as a World Heritage Site.[21] In a landscape that houses the entire continent's Triple Divide, where waters separate to nourish and replenish lands to the east, west, and north, there are also bridges, unions, and kinship to be found. This was the vision I had been seeking, one which could explain how a summer that began with a killing clang could end in one guttural, glorious yelp of unity.

Crowning Conclusions

I began that summer jarred and shaken with a grizzly death by train, and I ended the summer with much deeper discord, partially defeated by the collisions I'd become aware of and impartially inspired by the connections I'd witnessed and formed. Amidst it all were the bears. Feared and ferocious but beautiful and beloved, bears were the ways in which we—travelers and me—connected, for no matter what the circumstance, and no matter how great our divides, it was bears who would ultimately bring us together and teach us, making us remember and forget, even for a few moments, about all that the human world and its cultures contain.

What did I learn from the bears that summer? Once plains creatures, the grizzly has found a home in which to thrive in the mountains of western Montana. The bears we watched all summer seemed not to feel sorry for themselves, and they never complained. They didn't care if their food was hot, or their showers cold, or their companions too chatty. They were simply present to being alive, reproducing, finding food, and celebrating their existence in one of the most beautiful places in the world with a huckleberry branch and an afternoon nap cuddled against the warm body of a friend.

I learned that, as Chief Seattle is rumored to have suggested hundreds of years ago, what happens to the people, the animals, and the land is divisionless. Blackfeet and bears once roamed the plains; both were forced into habitats significantly smaller than, and lacking the resources of, the territories over which they had reigned. Both have suffered, sustaining tragic losses, casualties of an America that marches ever onward in pursuit of technology, progress, dominion. It is no longer just the animal and the American Indian who struggle, but all humans who come to this place torn between desires for Internet, television, human creature comforts and the deep and driving need for wilderness. Where contentious collisions over land ownership, water and mineral rights, genocide, and reparations divide east from west and White from Red—and Green—somehow, in the tingling reverie of bear-filled afternoons, we find ourselves on the same side, bridging our personal and cultural boundaries in unitary hope that Nature and all of her creatures can carry on somewhere, intact and whole, persevering in some of the grizzliest conditions imaginable—America.

Endnotes

1 "Area has seen 18 mortalities this year." *Daily Interlake.* 5 October, 2007. http://www.dailyinterlake.com/news/local_montana/article_15763bc8-8331-5969-96b2-8e35dedb31fa.html

2 Waldt, Ralph. *Crown of the Continent: The Last Great Wilderness of the Rocky Mountains.* Helena, MT: Riverbend, 2008.

3 Chadwick, Douglas. "Protecting the Crown," in Ralph Waldt, ed., *Crown of the Continent: The Last Great Wilderness of the Rocky Mountains.* Helena, MT: Riverbend, 2008, p. 155-164.

4 National Park Service. *Glacier National Park, Montana.* September 17, 2008. http://www.nps.gov/glac/index.htm

5 Manataka American Indian Council. November 22, 2008. *The Blackfeet Indians of Montana.* http://www.manataka.org/page255.html

6 Spotted Eagle, Edward, Juneau, Robert C., and Juneau, Robert J. *Blackfeet Sorrow: Crooked Agents, Whiskey traders, and Land Grafters.* Browning, MT: Juneau-Spotted Eagle Associates, 2005.

7 National Park Service. *History and Culture: Establishing the Park,* http://www.nps.gov/glac/historyculture/index.htm (October 25, 2008)

8 U.S. Fish and Wildlife Service, *NCDE Human-Caused Mortality Issues 2008.* http://www.fws.gov/endangered/

9 Schwartz, C. C., Miller, S. D., and Haroldson, M. A. "Grizzly Bear," in G. A. Feldhamer, B. C. Thompson, and J. A. Chapman, eds., *Wild Mammals of North America: Biology, Management, and Conservation,* 2nd ed. Baltimore, MD: Johns Hopkins University, 2003, p. 556-586.

10 Chadwick, Douglas. *True Grizz.* Berkeley, CA: Sierra Club, 2003.

11 Great Bear Foundation. *Brown Bear: Ursus arctos.* January 31, 2010. http://www.greatbear.org/brownbear.htm

12 Kendall, Katherine C. et al. "Demography and Genetic Structure of a Recovering Grizzly Bear Population." *Journal of Wildlife Management* 73, 2009, p. 3-17.

13 Tirrell, Norma. *Montana.* Oakland, CA: Compass, 1997.

14 Rockwell, David. *Glacier: A Natural History Guide,* 2nd ed. Guilford, CT: Falcon, 2007.

15 Rosier, Paul. *Rebirth of the Blackfeet Nation, 1912-1954.* Lincoln, NE: University of Nebraska, 2001.

16 Spotted Eagle, Juneau, and Juneau, 2005.

17 Belcourt-Dittloff,Annjeanette. *Resiliency and Risk in Native American Communities: A Culturally Informed Investigation.* Missoula, MT: University of Montana, 2006.

18 Wilson, Melissa. "Going to the Sun Road Shuttle Involved in Single Vehicle Accident." December 31, 2008. http://www.nps.gov/glac/parknews/news07-55.htm

19 "Area has seen 18 grizzly mortalities this year." *Daily Interlake.* 5 October, 2007. http://www.dailyinterlake.com/news/local_montana/article_15763b c8-8331-5969-96b2-8e35dedb31fa.html

20 "Second Cabinet Grizzly Killed." *Flathead Beacon.* November 4, 2008, http://www.flatheadbeacon.com/articles/article/second_cabinet_grizzly_killed/6442/

21 UNESCO, "Waterton Glacier International Peace Park." April 15, 2010. http://whc.unesco.org/en/list/354

Steph Paidas-Dukarm grew up in the deciduous forests of northeast Ohio as the eldest daughter of parents from Greek and European backgrounds. She studied creative writing and psychology as an undergraduate before moving west to Montana. There, she earned a master's degree in clinical psychology at the University of Montana in Missoula. Life in northwestern Montana brought Steph into close connection with the sense of place, and it was there in Glacier

National Park that her interest in ecopsychology was born. Though she remained in Montana for ten years, Steph has also lived in and explored the Black Hills of South Dakota and the San Francisco Bay area. She currently inhabits Eagle River, Alaska, where she lives with her husband and dogs. Steph is currently enrolled in the Depth Psychology doctoral program at Pacifica Graduate Institute, where she is in the early stages of ecopsychological dissertation work.

Coming Home: An Inquiry in Reverence of Flint

Chanda Möllers

It's one thing to dream about where you grew up: in this case the home town of filmmaker Michael Moore. But it's quite another for that place to show up in your dreams as a person....

Flint is a city in the state of Michigan and is located along the Flint River 66 miles northwest of Detroit. Known for being the birthplace of General Motors, and of the Sit-Down Strike of 1936-37 that played a vital role in the formation of the United Auto Workers, it has also become a symbol of the decline in the automobile industry. As my birthplace, the city has served me as both traumatized, grief-stricken mother and a vessel through which I seek to find healing, resolution, and hope. In this essay, I examine my relationship with Flint through the lens of terrapsychology, a systematic approach to encountering the presence, soul, or "voice" of places and things.

During those "get to know you" conversations I have with strangers, the question of where I'm from often lends itself to references to film director Michael Moore, violent crime statistics, looks of sympathetic dread, or blank stares that quickly turn into a wide-eyed expression of simultaneous sorrow and amazement. I have shared some of these reactions. But as I have been exposed to ecotherapy and terrapsychology, the distance I have felt towards Flint, both emotionally and mentally, has provided a broad terrain through which I can assess, and possibly heal, our relationship. By allowing my hardened prejudices regarding the city to melt, I've allowed hidden dimensions of both myself and the city to emerge.

I am now certain there is a direct connection between environmental degradation and other forms of oppression: the qualities of our culture that damage the Earth are also those destructive to the human soul. We need greener psychologists to develop better indicators of human well-being because of this synergistic interplay between planetary and personal well-being.

I am also interested in how we can apply Joanna Macy's Three Dimensions of the Great Turning—*actions to slow the damage to Earth and its beings; analysis of structural causes of damage and creation of structural alternatives; and deep shifts in consciousness*[1]—to slow the damage to Flint and, in turn, to the planet. How can we create alternatives to the defunct auto complex and the resulting blight and violence left behind? How can we create the conditions for shifts in consciousness—namely, cognitive revolution and spiritual awakening—to occur?

Beginning my inquiry with a brief biography—the life that Flint and I have shared—as an experience of place appeals to the idea that "home" is microcosmically significant, embodying some wider truth about the human experience. I will also note my emotional responses in the context of place, dreams, and self in relationship with the natural world as part of myself.

I was born on the winter solstice in 1976, a time in which the depth of the city's impending demise was only hinted at. Not only was Flint the home of General Motors, AC Delco (Delphi), and the Ojibwa tribes of long ago, it was also home to thousands of families that relocated from the South in search of prosperity, and at one time of a thriving middle class. But this is no longer true. As I compose this essay, memories that were buried are unearthed, seeking my attention: the fire that nearly destroyed our home when I was 12; the gunshots that were fired through our kitchen window; the numerous burglaries of our home during the height of the crack epidemic; the bullet that ended the life of six-year-old Kayla Rowland and highlighted the brutal plight of violence, poverty, and despair. Through a flash of images in my mind, I recognize and acknowledge that my personal story is inextricably tied to that of Flint.

Terrapsychological work began with a series of dreams about Flint, which, synchronistically, were followed immediately by a front-page feature and slide show published over a two-month period online by the *New York Times*. The dream sequence was frightening and I felt powerless to help.

Dream images of Flint, my childhood home, and its surroundings have continued to visit me over the last few weeks, creating a sense of both longing and confusion. I left Flint on the premise that I would never return. But like a mother calling out for her forlorn child, Flint has managed to seep into my dream life, causing me to think deeply of my time there and consider its meaning and mythology. And while I believe that dreams have provided me with insight into myself, from a terrapsychological perspective they have also become a means for place exploration.

Most of these recent dreams involved events that caused me to feel helpless, stressed, or afraid. In one dream

> *I flee my home in Flint in fear of my husband, Jürgen. I run to my elementary school, but he chases me there on his motorcycle. In the dream I'm child-sized, able to fit into small places and trying to hide. The husband figure is menacing, a larger-than-life character relentless in his hunt for me.*

That grammar school, Gundry Elementary, was closed two years ago due to budget cuts. After waking I feel anxious, wondering whether this anxiety, which does not belong to my marriage, is "felt" by Flint. The terrapsychological approach recognizes such a resonance of the indwelling spirit of place and its intimate connection to its inhabitants.

In the next dream

> *I'm at home in Flint with my mother. The home resembles a cinder block compound with large, heavy metal doors, and*

*she has just married a man whom I fear tremendously. When
I broach this subject with the mother figure, I'm baffled by
her uncharacteristic indecisiveness and ambiguity—not at all
like my mother. In the dream I have learned that this "man"
has somehow murdered hundreds of people and fear that my
mother and I may be next. When I tell her this, she insists with
a look of disbelief that there must be a misunderstanding*

*Later, this man locks us each in separate rooms. I'm
frightened because I know that if we don't leave now, we may
not get out alive. I manage to break the windows of the rooms
confining us. I plead with "my mother" to leave this place,
but once again she creates a number of reasons why she
should stay. I fight back tears as I try to get her to wake up
out of her apathy.*

Because of such dreams, I have come to see the fragile, frightened, and anxious mother figure as Flint. Perhaps her willingness to
avoid the problem is some kind of ecological coping mechanism.
Like a battered wife who cannot escape the danger and abuse of her
husband, Flint continues to cower in shadow of big industry's violent misuse and destruction of her. But where can a place go when
it's "afraid"? This is especially true if Flint also suffers from an infe-
riority complex.

While working with these images to create meaning and facilitate healing in my relationship with Flint, I shared these dreams with
my peers and my family. After detailing each dream, I gave my
interpretation of the location, characters, and their behavior. Often, I
felt overwhelmed by horrifying nature of the dream. My peers, however, were able to present a compassionate and unbiased container.
Many of the dream reflections were developed with their help.

The series of dreams concluded on a theme of hope, however. In
a final dream, I'm an adult rather than a child, and I've returned to
Flint to attend a home-buying seminar. The energy and mood of the
event feel good. Although everyone there is sad that I'm preparing
to return to San Francisco, they clearly realize that it is best for me
to leave. My first boyfriend arrives to say good-bye, and I notice in
his face the innocence and sweetness he possessed as a child.

Through his tears, he asks "Why do you have to leave?" I begin to explain, but awaken before I can finish.

The residue of this dream lingered with me throughout the day. What part of me is in Flint and what part of the city resides in me? What insights into woundedness— Flint's and my own—did I gain from work with these dreams? One important function of dreaming is integration: the combining of separate psychological structures into a more balanced and comprehensive personality. Portions of our personality which we knowingly or unknowingly judge become disowned, and are frequently projected outward in dreams, taking the form of aggressors, devils, monsters, intimidating animals or natural events. Jung referred to these symbolic figures many times as expressions of our disowned shadow side. Whether we become aware of such elements of our shadow through dreams or in other ways, I believe that re-accepting these judged and disowned portions of ourselves is the message and the awaiting gift.

Flint's impact on me will last indefinitely. After college, I visited less and less, initially because of work schedules, but after some time, I admitted to myself that I could not bear to see the place and its people in ruin. But now, with a new husband who had yet to meet most of my family, I sensed that Flint was calling me home. I felt prepared to do some of the work required of me to begin the healing and reconciliation; to ask, "What would a psychology of homecoming look like? How can I be present to the trauma embodied both in me and in this place? How can I continue to tend the sources of trauma in ways that transform them from scary to remorseful? What skills and resources do I have to enable this deep healing to begin?"

Over the course of two days, my German husband was introduced to Flint. Seeing the city through his eyes on that brisk winter day, I noticed the vast expanses of land with barren trees. He enjoyed walking through the downtown area which is experiencing a mini-revival—complete with new cafes, restaurants, and a karaoke bar. Backyard vegetable gardens have sprung up. I was beginning to see the city's return to wholeness.

Although I am no longer wedded to its pathology, this place birthed me, has dreamed itself into me and lives in me. Through my openness and active participation in this inquiry, the heart and soul of Flint have unfolded richly in me. As one of its chosen ambassadors, perhaps I can begin to summon the courage and the strength to act on her behalf.

Endnotes

1 Macy, Joanna. "The Great Turning." http://www.joannamacy.net/thegreatturning.html

Sources

Chalquist, C. *Theodore Roszak's Eight Principles of Ecopsychology.* Handout for Planetary Psychology course, 2009.

Gomes, M. "Ecopsychology and Social Transformation." *Re-Vision.* 20(4), 1998.

Orr, D. "The Psychology of Survival." *Conservation Biology.* 22 (4), 819-822, 2008.

Chanda Möllers is a yoga teacher and wellness professional in San Francisco. With a background in mechanical engineering, she is committed to creating holistic solutions to enhance the health of people and the planet. She completed her master's degree in Integrative Health Studies at the California Institute of Integral Studies in San Francisco.

Three Faces of San Francisco

Michael Steiner, Corey Hale, and Jane Tanner

The Displaced Waters of Dolores

Michael Steiner

What would happen if one walked through a neighborhood fully attuned to its images and metaphors? How would it respond?

In Clarion Alley, which connects Mission and Valencia streets between 17th and 18th, a mural can be found of a goddess-like tree figure who wears a tall, blue top hat and a skirt made of house façades. She rides atop a bicycle that, in place of normal wheels with spokes, has houses on wheels. As wind blows the curtains out of the open windows, the tree lady's roots find pedals instead of the ground. Pigeons flutter around her, and two help lift a scroll that has unfurled from the peak of her hat. The scroll reads, "The same wind that uproots the trees makes the grasses shine."

One of the first things I noticed after moving to the Mission District of San Francisco was how few people I met grew up here.

Most had migrated from other parts of the country and had only been here three or four years ago at most. In under a year, two friends I met had moved away and an old friend from my hometown arrived. Like the uprooted tree figure whose home is mobile, the motif of a neighborhood with a fickle taste for its residents soon formed in my mind.

I thought this trend could be attributed to the restlessness that comes in one's twenties, or perhaps to my inclination to meet other newcomers. Surely that was a factor. But as I researched the history of the "sunniest, hippest and most diverse"[1] neighborhood in the city, the connected themes of transience and displacement persisted. People came to live out a chapter here before being spit out. Some, like me, were drawn here by the sunshine, the arts, the grunge, and then pushed out by the rising rents of the dotcom boom. Some took refuge in Dolores Park after the 1906 earthquake and fires, then decided to stay.[2] The Italian and German restaurants, the fandangos and taverns, the shopping vein that pulsed down Mission and Valencia streets kept them here for a time, but after World War II, they fled to the suburbs. Whatever the specifics, the fun-loving, watery, fierce mother of the Mission didn't keep her children long before she became bored. She put on new makeup: a population of immigrants from Mexico and Central America that grew from eleven percent to over forty-five percent of the population from 1940 to 1970.[3] An influx of artists, punk rockers, and lesbians accounted for most of the remaining portion.

Spanish is still perhaps the first language of the Mission—issuing from the *Taquerias*, the *iglecias*, and the Verizon store. Yet this population too has faced displacement in the exponential housing price hikes of the mid-90s boom, when prices in some areas rose over 300 percent.[4] As one local reported,

South of Market, the Mission, and Hunters Point have been transformed into luxury consumption playgrounds for the region's nouveau bourgeois and professional/administrative cadre possessed of ample sums of disposable cash and the desire to live in close proximity to urban cultural amenities.[5]

That sounds a bit like me. I am young, have disposable income, and was drawn to the Mission because of its grit, its many cultures, its vibrant nightlife, its abundance of artists, and its resemblance to some streets I had walked in Latin America. I wanted to live somewhere tough, somewhere different, somewhere that would provoke the new level of self-understanding that comes from being out of my comfort zone. I did not initially count myself as part of the gentrification, and perhaps it's too far along in the game to be able to take that kind of credit. Had I moved here in the summer of 1999 and parked my luxury car on the streets, the Mission Yuppie Eradication Project might have keyed it.[6] Regardless, I was on the displacing end of the trend. Perhaps this is in part why She drew me here.

For many years I have grappled with questions of race and class privilege, often feeling a claustrophobic guilt for the abundance I have received. Did I come to the Mission hoping for some sort of redemption, some exoneration? To enter a world so different from my sheltered upbringing? To gain insight into the reality of low-income residents and the creative world of artists, only to become a force of displacement for these two groups?

These lingering questions were punctuated by a recent conversation at a teahouse on 14th Street. I told the girl serving tea that I had visited the old Mission Dolores. It took her a moment to realize which Mission I was talking about. When I specified that I had visited the Mission Chapel, she laughed and said, "When I think of 'the Mission' I think of being a little girl on a mission. I don't think of the Mission itself." Perhaps this mental disassociation and forgetting—for which I was responsible as well—parallels the general motif of displacement.

Not long ago, I took a walk down Mission Street while consciously asking the Mission what she might have to tell me. I stopped to look at an old vacant theater across the street. In an effort blend into the scene, I leaned my left shoulder up against another boarded-up and forgotten theater. I leaned there for a moment contemplating what sort of spectacles this theater might have staged during its heyday. Did the lines of people spill out the doors and wrap around the block? I reached for meaning there in this antiquated edifice, fumbling about, attempting to make connections to other things

I had seen in the neighborhood. When nothing came and I was not able to shake the feeling of being unwelcome, I moved on.

Later, I sat down in a café to write about what I had seen. When I removed my fleece jacket, I noticed a strip of white paint running down the left sleeve. My stomach sank and I became frustrated. This jacket had only recently resurfaced after a long hiatus in the back of my closet. I checked my backpack. White paint there too! I mentally retraced my steps, wondering where I could have acquired this unwanted garment paint job. It had to have come from that theater.

Not until much later did I consider the meaning of this event. Was it connected to the murals? Is the Mission so fond of her paint that she even paints her residents? The white color of the paint most closely resonated in its connection to ethnicity. The Mission painted the white man white.

The pattern of displacement and dislocation certainly did not begin in the Nineties. In fact it started even before the arrival of the Spanish. As Malcolm Margolin writes in his book about the Ohlone Indians,

> Sporadically, throughout the centuries, people recently settled were pushed out of their territories by more warlike (or desperate) invaders. The invaders settled down for a generation or two, grew content and peaceful, until they too were eventually edged out by still another wave of newcomers.[7]

Then, of course, the arrival of Captain Juan Bautista de Anza, and later Junipero Serra's Mission, instigated the horrors of native displacement and genocide. At the dedication ceremony of the first Mission on the shores of Laguna Dolores, "the Spanish soldiers shot off muskets, rifles and even rockets which caused the Costanoan tribelet to flee across the bay."[8]

In the founding years of the Mission Chapel, the building itself could not sit still. According to one source, in 1783, at the orders of Father Junipero Serra, the site of the Mission Chapel was moved about two hundred yards from its original location on the shores of Laguna Dolores (today, the corner of Camp and Albion Streets) to its present location at 16th and Dolores.[9]

In a recent dream a related image appeared:

I am in a pine forest in the mountains. I am next to a large, wooden cabin with a companion whose gender and identity I cannot recall later. A small brown bear cub runs through the area where we are standing and then quickly disappears into the forest. Shortly thereafter, a mother bear follows, frantically and angrily looking for her cub. She chases us, believing that we have harmed the cub. As I dart away from her, I notice that my companion is far less coordinated and quick than I. At first I try to assist but soon become frustrated, realizing that I will never escape from the bear if I continue assisting. I climb up a tall stump to safety and watch the mother bear continue her frantic chasing.

Here, the dream ends. Was this perhaps the extinct California Grizzly, or the angry mother of the Mission showing her feelings about how her child, the natural landscape, has been treated? Was she chasing anyone whom she thought might have covered her lakes or displaced her Indian (and much later her Latino) lifeblood? Or was my unconscious showing me something about my relationship to my own mother? Who was my companion? The homeless folks of the Mission? A less coordinated part of myself?

The apartment I moved into last February sits on top of a vanished lake once called Laguna Dolores (Lake of Sorrows). This lake used to occupy the area enclosed by 15th and 19th Streets and Dolores and South Van Ness. It was gradually encroached upon by houses, covered over by landfill, and became only a memory after the 1906 earthquake.[10] The street I live on is Linda: the name of the mother of my childhood best friend. At one end of the street lies the Mission Pool, and at the other, the Women's Building, with a three-story mural of a goddess-like mother holding water in her right hand. This house has been the place I have cried the most in my adult life, beginning quite abruptly with a long sobbing session on my birthday, March 7. Was I feeling the *dolores* (sorrows) of this place? I am also a Pieces—a fish in water. In addition, this flat has been the site of many hours of reflection and writing about my relationships with my mother and older sister.

The Mission knows recurring motifs of a mother and of water, indications of the emotional, the feminine, the unconscious, and the intuitive qualities still present here. The Virgin Mary appeared three times to me on one walk, as did Quan Yin, Buddhist Bodhisattva of Compassion. Las Muralistas, a group of pioneering woman muralists, painted many of the first and most famous murals in the neighborhood.

This feminine presence, it seems to me, has two faces: either nurturing or, at times, demonic. Her nurturing quality evokes tears and healing. But the same mother-water that washes and purges can also drown. While living in the Mission I had a persistent set of terrifying fantasies that an alien or a demon was poised to possess me. I lay awake many nights, afraid to drift off to sleep, for fear of letting down my guard long enough that this entity might to enter my consciousness. In the mornings I frequently walked to my favorite local bakery, Tartine, where the walls were covered with art of a strikingly similar theme. The central character of the work on display was a shamanic man who was always masked and naked and who possessed an obvious connection to the spirit world. In one piece he lay in the hull of a ship, absorbed by something unseen. In another he waded knee-deep in a pond, pointing into the distance in a gesture of rapturous trance.

In a dream from that same unsettling period, I found myself hiking up a hill through the mouth of a rock archway. The ground was sand, and I struggled to ascend. I realized I stood on a burial ground with the spirits of this place encircling me. I was terrified of them but felt I must battle them, determined to climb through this graveyard.

I see many "crazy," paranoid, and homeless people walking the streets here. The sirens of emergency vehicles frequently fill the air, as though the Mission were screaming out in pain—"emergency!" On three recent occasions I saw a drug user or alcoholic passed out in his or her own urine. One crowded weekend night on Valencia Street a man lay unconscious on a piece of cardboard with a trail of urine leading from him down the slanted sidewalk. Another afternoon, while walking home from the gym on 19th Street just before reaching Mission Street, I saw a woman sitting unconscious on the ledge of a low window frame, pants at her knees, genitals visible, and urine running down the sidewalk. These are perhaps displays of the Mission's demonic face.

Crack and heroin are sold quite openly on the block between 16th and 17th on Mission Street. The abundance of these drug sellers and users in the Mission can be attributed in part to another displacement. In 1989, "thousands of parolees, half-way house residents, and homeless, who had been put up by local government for years in South of Market and Tenderloin hotels"[11] were relocated to the Mission. A mural prominently visible on this block shows an enormous, distorted, frightening, black and white face. Like this mural, the Mission can distort vision into a hallucinatory fantasy reality with a paranoid quality about it.

Down Valencia, another alley is home to a mural that exhibits the more nurturing qualities of Madre Mission. The hair of a large female figure flows from the Mission over the city and blends into the Golden Gate Bridge. Her head is bowed to the earth, and in her hand rests an unconscious homeless man. Her other hand wraps around a man digging through a trash can; a common sight in the neighborhood. In the center two musicians play a stand-up bass and a guitar while another man sweeps the street. The archetypal mother presence of the Mission holds in her one embrace both the creative artists and the down-and-out.

This debauchery, pleasure and excess—which happen today among the not-so-down-and-out—have a long history in here. In the mid nineteenth century, with construction of a toll road connecting downtown to 16th and Mission, the neighborhood turned temporarily into a recreation destination.[12] "The Mission District, sunnier and warmer than many other parts of San Francisco, attracted many pleasure-seekers."[13] The Nightingale—a roadhouse inn on the corner of Mission and 16th Street from the early 1850s to the 1870s— "was known for wild parties, gambling and barbecues."[14] During this era, the Mission also hosted The Odeum Gardens, the Exotic Gardens, and The Willows, which were recreation establishments with outdoor cafes, gardens, small zoos, moonlight dances, and theater performances. The neighborhood was also home to two racetracks and, perhaps its most prominent destination, Woodward's

Gardens. These gardens hosted museum exhibits of live and dead animals, art, and other novelty items from Woodward's personal collection, including an Egyptian mummy. The gardens boasted a "sea-lion pond, an amphitheater, a lake with black swans, roller-skating rink, aquarium, playground, music hall and 'rotary Boat' or floating merry-go-round."[15]

The dirty and displaced waters left by these pleasure gardens have, perhaps, shown up in a dream:

I am traveling in a foreign country somewhere in the Global South. A close friend and I ride in the back of a truck. The roads are covered in brown, dirty water that extends out into the fields. This water and the surrounding country are filthy and, I suspect, full of disease. I am scared to touch anything or get out of the truck for fear of getting sick. We arrive at an upscale resort and begin to check in. I'm exhausted from a long trip and not excited to be there. A stray dog licks my hand.

It seems that the Mission is also a place where the gaze into the past and the gaze into the future remain at odds. The profusion of vintage clothing and furniture stores contrasts with the words of Junipero Serra, who said, "Always go forward and never turn back." Expensive new condos show up on the same block as an old television, a chipped desk, a pair of sneakers, all left on the curb for the taking. If you walk down 24th Street or past the murals in the famous Balmy Ally, you can see the faces of historical figures who fought for justice and led the indigenous, labor, and civil rights movements: Archbishop Romero, Cesar Chavez, Carlos Santana. Stories of Latin American oppression and immigration live there too. Through this remembering of cultural roots, perhaps a step is taken toward healing this displacement, pain, and suffering.

The Madre Mission is interested in that profusion of energy which gives rise to the creative act of remembering. Through murals, the subconscious of the Mission's psyche is uprooted, processed, and put on display. Perhaps they signal the Mission as a site of a trauma being worked through.

Endnotes

1 Nevius, C. W. "Worrisome Changes Roil the Mission District" *San Francisco Chronicle.* 25 Sept. 2008 http://www.sfgate.com/cgi-bin/article.cgi?f=/c/a/2008/09/24/BAPN134DC1.DTL

2 Stanford Research Institute. *Mission History: Walking Tour Guidebook.* 1973, p. 8-9.

3 Mission Housing Development Corp. *A Plan for the Inner Mission. Chapter 1: Inner Mission History, 1776-1974,* p. 13.

4 Negrete, Mabel. "My Home Is Your Playground". http://mabelnegrete.com/wb/wp-content/uploads/2008/11/mabelne-grete-ctb-sellis-sfai2006.pdf

5 Wetzel, Tom. "A Year in the Life of the Anti-Displacement Movement". 2000. http://www.uncanny.net/~wetzel/macchron.htm

6 Margolin, Malcom. *The Ohlone Way: Indian Life in the San Francisco-Monterey Bay Area.* Berkeley: Heyday Books. 2003, p. 58-59.

7 Mission Housing Development Corp. *A Plan for the Inner Mission. Chapter 1: Inner Mission History, 1776-1974,* p. 6.

8 Sandoval, Ricardo. *Viva La Mission!* San Francisco Focus. December, 1994, p. 58.

9 Stanford Research Institute. *Mission History: Walking Tour Guidebook.* 1973, p. 3.

10 Mission Housing Development Corp. *A Plan for the Inner Mission. Chapter 1: Inner Mission History, 1776-1974,* p. 9.

11 Mission Housing Development Corp. *A Plan for the Inner Mission. Chapter 1: Inner Mission History, 1776-1974,* p. 11.

Michael Steiner, who hales from the mountains of Colorado, is an artist, filmmaker and traveler. He has produced several short films, including a documentary about the traditional uses of the coca leaf in the Andes, as well as a dark comedy. Michael began his under-graduate studies at Brown University, continued in Cochabamba, Bolivia and finished at the California Institute of Integral Studies in San Francisco. These days he snowboards in the Sierras and dangles above the cityscape of San Francisco, cleaning windows.

Listening to the Soul of a Bridge

Corey Hale

This essay is about learning to listen imaginally to the soul of the place called the Golden Gate Bridge, and it is the narrative of a story of one possible way to develop a deep relationship with a non-human entity. By combining an ecopsychological perspective with the relationship between the researcher, a photographer, and a place, a methodology for further research creates a way of healing and reconnecting the human world with the non-human world via Place, Other, and Self.

Could a bridge have a soul? Could I learn to communicate with something other than a human? Was I crazy?

These are the questions I wrestled with as I contemplated my work at Pacifica Graduate Institute in January of 2006. I knew I was tired of writing about gender, feminism, and politics, which had been my focus in my undergrad work, but was surprised when this topic of place consciousness, and specifically that of the Golden Gate Bridge, popped into my head and wouldn't leave. I'd always been highly sensitive to my surroundings, but had not considered that it might have something to do with the life of the places I was in, and was not simply a flight of fantasy.

As I played with the idea and began to share it with others, I realized that although the Bridge is a tangible structure in the physical world, it also holds a magical place in the architecture of our imagination. What I wanted to do was find a way to hear the story of the Bridge, to hear if it had its own soul life.

I was agitated and excited by this prospect, worried that I might spend my summer in futile pursuit of a non-existent presence, and troubled that I might encounter something spectacular and not have the skills to interpret it. But my curiosity compelled me to pursue the possibility of breaching what might turn out to be a false void between the human and non-human world and discovering a foreign and unique perspective.

The synchronicity in this project began almost immediately with a chance encounter with an amateur photographer who, knowing nothing of my research, sent me a picture he had taken of his favorite subject, the Golden Gate Bridge. It was this picture that brought us together and changed the course of my research as the way "in" became the photographs he and I took together. As our relationship with each other evolved, there arose a dialogue between each of us and the bridge, a three-way conversation that would come to personify my work and which would eventually lead me into an triangular dialogue between Self, Place, and Matter, with Imagination holding the liminal space in between.

The possibilities for research were endless, so I chose those three which seemed most likely to facilitate an alternative way of communication: 1) Amplification through symbology and archetype; 2) Tracking how my experiences during the process illuminated and generated answers and ideas for further exploration; and 3) Noting how people responded to the photographs I shared with them.

I began by reading historical facts, then proceeded to visit the bridge, taking pictures and talking to people. The project culminated in sharing the pictures with participants.

The Bridge as Symbol and Archetype
The Bridge as a symbol of itself was distracting and challenging to move beyond. In psychological terms bridges can mean the con-

nection between the conscious and unconscious. When this image is taken a step further by the fact that the bridge spans water, we have a symbol not only of the unconscious but of transformation. I found myself struggling with a vast smokescreen of overused terms and theories that I found it difficult to get past.

Objectively, the Bridge is both a structure and a place, but subjectively, as symbol, it is consistently referred to in terms of feminine qualities and in words that suggest she has a lived presence. This helps to "place" her as an entity and to redefine literal place as an archetypal presence of Place. In this pursuit I found myself tangled in trying to suspend disbelief that a manmade object could have a lived history as a place in the natural world. "When places are actively sensed, the physical landscape becomes wedded to the landscape of the mind, to the roving imagination, and where the latter may lead is anybody's guess."[1] Although this idea loosely embodied mine as my work progressed, the land tended to feel full of its own life, whereas the Bridge exhibited a more ethereal, almost chameleon presence.

At what point does something come to have consciousness, and by what means could it be measured? Derrick Jensen referred to these questions in an interview with Neil Evernden in a discussion of Evernden's book *Social Creation in Nature*. In the book Evernden quoted Dennis Lee on neurobiology and the fact that "when we scientifically study the brain we find synapses but no trace of anything we could call consciousness." To Jensen's queries Evernden responded, "This is a dilemma: we cannot mistrust science, even when it proves we do not exist."[2]

Underworld Gateway

Although it is a documented fact that the majority of suicidal jumpers have chosen to leap from the center span of the Golden Gate Bridge rather than opting towards the west into the open ocean of the unknown, there has been relatively little research on the reasons for this choice.[3] It could be a simple issue of accessibility, but it could also be conjectured that leaping from her at this central point represents an unconscious release from inner torment into the wish to be held by the loving embrace of the womblike Bay.

Whatever the reason for the choice of such a gruesome release, the Golden Gate Bridge has been called the number one suicide magnet in the world, and because of this the mythic presence of Thanatos, the God of Death, was noted by us.

The influence of Thanatos became most apparent on one of my many walks across the 1.7-mile expanse in the company of my photographer. We had made the trip that day for a different set of pictures to be taken from Baker's Beach on the southwest side, but we encountered impenetrable fog. I had learned in the early days of my research to take whatever the Bridge offered, so after a few minutes' contemplation on the curb at Fort Point, vaguely listening to the foghorns plaintively mewl at each other, I suggested we walk across and get the bits and pieces of what was still missing from the conversation.

The three Fates—Klotho who spins the thread at the beginning of one's life, Lachesis who weaves the thread into the fabric of one's actions, and Atropos, who snips the thread at the conclusion—soon came to mind. The Bridge is comprised of eighty thousand miles of cable that would circle the world at her belly three times if stretched end to end. Each strand of cable was woven together by giant looms that swung from one end to the next for six months and nine days to create the suspension, and by supporting cables that strengthen a major portion of the entire structure. Most of the workers had never done this kind of work before but were willing to do so in Depression Era; and Lachesis the weaver kept them safe when the Bridge became the first to require the tie-off ropes that saved their lives. Old videos show the men blowing in the wind like spiders on a strand as they were swept by 40-mile-an-hour gusts from precarious perches on the partially built towers.

The Fates were possibly most prevalent in the silence with which I was woven into a relationship with the bridge, and, as the research progressed, with my photographer. There were times when both relationships threatened my stability as the stories wove strands between myself, the land, the structure, the people in my life, and even into the lives of the people I worked with. I felt myself being drawn into a conversation that was linguistically beyond my previous experiences. I could only trust that whatever was being spun would have some conclusion, however vast, to bring me back from the precipice, and that Klotho would not abandon me to eternally spinning stories without end.

When I walked across on the day of "bits and pieces," I did so slowly and with attention and intention, stopping at each supporting cable, which consisted of four bundles each, and touching each one, feeling the different level of vibrations and tension. I also paused to look over the railings at the track on which the workers perched, wheeled carts attached perpetually in the Sisyphusian struggle to maintain the iron structure in this salty environment. Interesting that Sisyphus and Thanatos both felt symbolically present considering that Sisyphus outwitted Thanatos twice. Was it the presence of Sisyphus that had preserved the two known suicide survivors? And what of the two who survived the scaffolding fall?

After months of spending time with this iconic Art Deco structure, I still found myself hesitating to embrace the dreamlike state that would overcome me when I was in her presence; but today, in this foggy blanket, I let the boundaries between what I considered "real" blur into a listening with senses beyond my ears. I allowed my vision to fluctuate between sharp attention to detail and that of the misty softness that often enshrouds the entire structure. She was like a cocoon, hidden from land, disconnected from a horizon, perceived only from inside the confines of her corridor.

On this day I felt my skin listening, as if to a low vibrating thrum. I watched people walking, driving, and biking, and I imagined I could hear the murmur of thousands of thoughts in this place at one time, voices of people commuting from work or exercising; the impressions of the shivering tourists. I wondered if the volunteers in pink boas walking to relieve Breast Cancer in the Avon-sponsored walkathon were thinking of the Bridge at all. My daydreaming wandered into the macabre and I wondered if anyone was contemplating suicide just then, and if they would pick up one of the prevention phones attached to the orange pillars instead. I wondered how it would feel to call for help, and who would answer.

In this dreamlike state I approached the center of the span, the place from which an overwhelming majority of the jumpers have chosen to leap. I shivered as I stood there in supposition, vigilantly monitoring myself to not wonder too deeply or too freely about how it might feel to plunge into the icy chill below. I was afraid that if I understood the level of pain that brought them here, that if I tapped into the intense feelings that had stood here before me, I might be forced to leap as well.

In this position I considered the possibility that a place so imbued with desperation and of promised salvation from inner torment might make itself felt so profoundly that even those not deeply lost could succumb to the mysterious tug to climb across the railing. I speculated what it might feel like to stand on the other side with no barrier to protect me from the seductive appeal of the womb of the Bay. These thoughts are mirrored in the words of M.F.K. Fisher, who describes a realization that "the whizzing cars on one side and the peaceful bay on the other were splitting me in two...and I was almost overcome with the terrible need to jump off and be more peaceful."[4]

As I stood in the alcove at this center, I felt the thrill of watching kite surfers crisscrossing the wake of the freighters passing below. The chill of the railing before me: the last thing thousands of people have touched before being crushed into the water below. As I considered this, my focus was shifted upward from the water back again to the railing. Instead of the usual litter of dropped lens covers, empty Starbucks cups, and wads of gum that had littered the railing leading to this spot, I saw a smattering of scattered and decaying coins. I was struck by their presence enough to catch the image on film. At the moment I could not remember what this meant; I knew only there was something significant about them that I needed to consider at another time.

As we continued to walk, I toyed with the idea of the Bridge as a Gate, not just the Golden Gate, but an archetypal Threshold into the Underworld. Both ends of the span felt imbued with the powers of Hecate's crossroads, places of power, opportunity, possibility, and decision, but what I had failed to consider until this moment was that the road to the Underworld might not be a linear one.

Later that day that I again considered the coins on the railing. They invoked the presence of the Ferryman at the River Styx. Whether they had been offerings from those who leapt, or were gifts from the living, or merely random coins tossed there as if at a wishing well, they were left in response to a deeper and undefined call. Consciously or not, they had paid the toll to Chiron and gained entrance to the Underworld.

Endnotes

1 Basso, Keith. *Wisdom Sits in Places*. University of New Mexico Press, 1996.

2 Jensen, Derrick. *Listening to the Land*. Chelsea Green Publishing Company, 2004.

3 Guthmann, Edward. "Lethal Beauty." *San Francisco Chronicle*, October 30, 2005. http//:SFGate.com/lethalbeauty

4 "Water Vapor." 6th ed., Vol. 4, 2006. (Original work published 1995.) http://cals.arizon.edu/AZWATER/awr/aug95/awtrvap.html

Corey Hale holds a Bachelor's degree in Gender Studies and Political Science from Sonoma State university and a Master's degree in Depth Psychology. She will complete her PhD in November 2010, in Depth Psychology at Pacifica Graduate Institute. Corey is professionally certified in Anger Management, Domestic Violence, and Sexual Assault Prevention, and has worked as a crisis counselor and family coach with the California juvenile probation system for almost ten years. She is the owner and founder of Blue Blazes Training, where she acts as coach and trainer for independent businesses and families in crisis. Corey is looking forward to teaching in a university setting once her doctorate is complete.

Spanning Dialectic across the Divide:
East Meets West in San Francisco

Jane Tanner

This essay intertwines two stories that occur twenty years apart. It looks at the terrapsychological implications of social and political polarization, from both a historical and geophysical perspective. If our collective psyche is embedded in the land, and the land is imbedded in our collective psyche, what is the interplay between these dynamics over time? Earthquakes crack open raw truths, and become the great equalizer affecting the entire social strata. Relief of dialectic stress at bedrock unleashes social distress, bringing out the best and worst of who we are, regardless of socio-economic and political differences.

October 15, 2009

Heading to San Francisco, I was struck by the thick stillness that lay in the air. Remembering past experiences of "earthquake weather" in the Bay Area, I pushed aside ominous feelings associated with the heaviness and instead, focused on the reason for this particular trip. I was looking forward to a fundraiser at the St. Francis Hotel, where I would listen to music by Tracy Chapman followed by a speech by President Obama. As I stepped onto the BART (Bay Area Rapid Transit) platform, I sensed a note of expectancy in the unusually muggy weather, and I wondered about the other attendees, supporters, and demonstrators that might be gathering at Union Square.

> What the cynics fail to understand is that the ground has shifted beneath them...We are shaped by every language and culture, drawn from every end of this Earth...[and]we cannot help but believe that the old hatreds shall someday pass, that the lines of tribe shall soon dissolve; that as the world grows smaller, our common humanity shall reveal itself.[1]
> –Barack Obama

October 16, 1989

Leaving my workplace in Emeryville, I turned onto the freeway and headed south for home. As I neared the 580/880 freeway split, I played the usual traffic guessing game: left fork or right fork? Congestion on the Cypress section of 880 or the potential bottleneck of 580? The left fork of 580 South rose to meet my tires. As I took a final glance at the double-tiered 880 viaduct, a sudden and violent image flashed like a piece of lost film in my mind: two slabs of concrete collapsing, creating a macabre sandwich of cars in their midst. Shaken, I quietly assured myself that such a tragedy could not occur. It was 5:04pm. In twenty-four hours I would have a different opinion.

The Cypress Street Viaduct was completed in 1957 to alleviate traffic on Oakland city streets leading to the Bay Bridge. It was the first double-tiered viaduct ever built: over a mile and a half long, with four lanes on each level. Constructed above Cypress Street, the new freeway split the declining neighborhood of West Oakland in half, isolating part of it from downtown Oakland.

After the overpass opened, thousands of its residents were displaced and many blocks of homes were razed. New projects such as a BART train station, the massive main Oakland Post Office, and a large housing project were completed. Unemployment, urban blight, and economic downturn followed in the wake of this development [2] built under the guise of "progress." As an emergent discontent grew out of this brand of "urban renewal," the once thriving port and railroad town saw a new trend of community activism. One of the most famous of the social activists, Huey Newton, was gunned down in West Oakland just two months before the 1989 Loma Prieta earthquake.[3]

October 15, 2009

The BART train was right on time and not too crowded. I emerged from the Powell Street station and breathed in all the familiar sights and smells of the city. San Francisco vibrates with its own unique quixotic energy. There is a buoyancy of purposefulness and color as panhandlers, tourists and business people converge. Stepping into the cadence of Powell Street foot traffic, I made my way to the St. Francis Hotel, the historic building that bears the name of San Francisco's patron saint:

> The converted psyche...of Francis of Assisi resembled a pendulum that had swung from one extreme to its opposite and stuck there...Centuries ahead of Muir or Thoreau,Francis loved the world and its creatures so much that he referred to sun and moon as his brother and sister.
>
> What he seems not to have recognized was naked, unblushing power. Too often the puer reformer remains a being of innocence in contrast to the old-man senex of entrenched authority.[4] –Craig Chalquist

The history of San Francisco is laden with exploits of wealthy power brokers operating against a backdrop of those who would seek to change the status quo. One of those historic power brokers was Charles Crocker, who managed to create part of his vast wealth via the Southern Pacific Railroad, which was financed "with fictitiously inflated capital stock" and built by badly paid Chinese laborers working 12-hour shifts.[5] The hotel was built by the Crocker family in 1904.

October 17, 1989

> *If you knew that you would die today,*

Saw the face of god and love,
Would you change?

–Tracy Chapman, "Change"

It was a clear and beautiful fall sky that capped the calm blue bay below as I drove west across the Bay Bridge towards San Francisco. It was 9:30 a.m. and the traffic was light. I would have plenty of time to make my appointment. Appreciating the stunning view as I traveled along the top deck of the cantilevered section east of Treasure Island, I felt a sudden jab and then a dropping sensation in my stomach as my body flooded with an adrenalin rush of fear. *"What is going on? I have never been nervous about crossing bridges"*—certainly not this one, which I had crossed hundreds of times before.

Jim Berkland, geologist for Santa Clara County, was not a stranger to controversy. Prior to his October 13, 1989 warning published in the *Gilroy Dispatch* that a major earthquake would strike the Bay Area during the World Series, he had used some highly unorthodox methods of analysis developed over years of study. In this particular case, he noted:

There were 27 ads for missing cats and 58 missing dog ads—these were unprecedented numbers. Baby beaked whales had beached themselves in San Francisco, a very rare pygmy sperm whale washed up in Santa Cruz and Homing pigeons were getting lost.[6]

He also looked at tidal flood tables and saw a relationship to the Earth's magnetic field, which shifts and changes with the movement of tectonic plates. In spite of a record for making accurate predictions, Berkland was given a two-month suspension from his geology position in late October. Government officials told him not to make any more predictions because they would "generate unwarranted fear."[7]

October 15, 2009

As I entered the ornate lobby of the St. Francis Hotel, I expected military-like efficiency complete with officials herding us towards a looping braided rope. Instead, I was greeted by a chaotic throng of equally mystified people. I struck up a conversation with the man in front of me. He assured me that we were in the right place, and we began to chat about the weird "earthquake weather" hanging in the air that day. As it turned out, the city of San Francisco had orchestrated an earthquake drill earlier that morning.

October 17, 1989

After a busy round of appointments in San Francisco, I offered my friend (and colleague) a ride home to the East Bay. Shortly after 5pm, we found ourselves on the approach to the lower deck of the Bay Bridge. Due to a World Series that had drawn people to Candlestick Park, traffic was unusually light. At that rate I would be able to cross the bridge quickly and be well on my way to 880 South.

At the first tug of the wheel in my hand, I immediately brought the car to a stop. We pitched and rolled form side to side. Grateful for secure seatbelts, I watched the road we were on sway and arch in a surreal dance, much too limber for my preference. As the 7.0 magnitude earthquake rolled on, I flashed back on the last large earthquake that I had experienced in 1971 in Los Angeles, when several overpasses had collapsed. I knew this earthquake was even bigger.

As the shaking subsided, I turned on the radio and was greeted by a dead silence. A few motorists got out of their cars; another driver made a U-turn and headed off the last on-ramp to the bridge. I was tempted to follow his lead. My friend broke through my indecision with, "Well, okay, the buildings are all still standing. No big deal, let's go!" I muttered something about bridges possibly being less stable than high rise buildings made to withstand earthquakes and reluctantly proceeded onto the lower deck of the Bay Bridge, gaining a little more confidence in the wake of my companion's unconcerned banter.

The San Francisco–Oakland Bay Bridge, one of the longest spans in the world, carries more than a quarter of a million cars over the Bay every day. The naming of the bridge had endured some dispute as each side of the Bay tried to claim it as their own. Many in Oakland and Alameda felt the bridge was their due. After all, San

Francisco already laid claim to the famous Golden Gate Bridge.[12]

Since the early days of the Gold Rush, San Francisco had become a major economic center, but by 1869, West Oakland presented itself as a rival, becoming a prosperous port and railroad city as the terminus of a transcontinental railroad. A large number of immigrants settled there, taking advantage of new jobs generated by the railroad, shipyard and trans-bay ferry system. Following the 1906 San Francisco earthquake, many survivors relocated to West Oakland as well.

The Bay Bridge was seen as a way to ease economic and political tension by extending the railway system to its sister city. Few could have predicted the dissipative effects of the Great Depression, or the blight created by the annexation of West Oakland.

October 15, 2009

We organized ourselves into a neat line that snaked through the lobby and down a side hallway of the beautiful hotel that houses the famed Magenta Grandfather Clock. This clock was installed in 1907, one year after the 1906 earthquake, and stands sentinel in the Powell Street lobby of the St. Francis Hotel.[9] St. Francis turned away from his powerful family's wealth and status, so it is significant perhaps that the clock marks the time (his and ours) in a place that connects his name to lavish opulence, just as his regular Offices of Prayer connected him to the wealthy Roman papacy.[10] The beautiful master clock controls all the other clocks in the hotel.

October 17, 1989

Six minutes later, the car was about to emerge from the tunnel running through Yerba Buena/Treasure Island when we heard a large bang like an explosion and felt the brief vibration as the whole bridge tremored. Slowly emerging from the tunnel, traffic came to a standstill. Suddenly throngs of people appeared, some running, threading their way through cars disgorging frightened passengers. As calm as ever, my friend laughed and turned to me. "I feel like I am in the middle of a disaster movie. How about you?" While she was lost in her cinematic speculation, I opened the car door, determined to get some credible explanation.

As people ran or walked briskly by, I received reports of "the bridge is falling apart" and "there are people dead up there" and "we all have to evacuate onto Treasure Island." Relaying these messages to my companion, her denial was still in full bloom, as though her belief in a system "too big to fail" created fail-safe protection. "Don't you think that we would know it if the bridge were falling apart?" To that I would now respond, "Do we ever recognize our fractured bridges as precursors to disaster?"

October 15, 2009

The wait seemed interminable, but finally the line began to inch forward, around and up two flights of stairs towards a windowless hallway. Clearing security, our line emptied out into a large, ornate ballroom where appetizers were passed and house wine served. The Secret Service was in full evidence as we were passed through to a smaller room with red-flocked wallpaper and large crystal chandeliers. Waiting patiently, facing two sets of double doors, I half expected them to conceal a surprise elevator reminiscent of the Haunted House ride at Disneyland. Instead, the massive doors opened, and the crowd surged forward into the enormous Grand Ballroom. I made my way towards the front of the room, relaxing into my seat five rows from the stage.

October 17, 1989

As we began to walk towards the guard rail that would lead us onto the grassy slope of Treasure Island, I remembered a conversation some years back with an engineer as we drove westbound on the upper deck. He pointed to the cantilevers and said, "If any part of this bridge were to fail during an earthquake, it would be in this section. The cantilevers are too long to provide much give in a large earthquake." Nervously, I asked, "Does anyone else know about this?" He laughed. "I presume so. It always comes down to money." Twenty years after the Loma Prieta earthquake, the new seismically safe span still awaits completion.

What is the pact we make when we turn over our power and trust to experts, hoping they will take care of us? How is it that we see our infrastructure as inviolable, that we trust manmade solutions over what we know to be true? Denial is endemic to modernity and its technological wonders. Wisdom we deem superfluous, yet our magic talismans of phone lines, water lines, electrical lines, gas lines, credit lines, brake lines, computer lines and bridge spans cannot tether us to guaranteed safety or civilized order. Lines fail; they can be cut; they can stretch and break, and we can become hopelessly entangled in them.

Sitting on a grassy knoll, looking out over the serenity of the Bay on a clear fall day in October, I noticed the quiet. The absence of what we all expected to be there but wasn't: no sirens, no police, no rescue vehicles, no helicopters and no reporters, just the silence of people milling about on a grassy hillside not quite knowing how the day would end.

Finally back on the bridge again, we all lined up, inching forward for an unceremonious return to the city. Unfortunately, one of the drivers misunderstood the directions to turn right instead of left on the top deck. Anxious to return to her East Bay home, she drove into the fallen gap before she had a chance to see it.

As I turned right onto the top deck, I looked in the rear view mirror at an empty roadway marred by a shadowed place where a roadbed once had been.

October 15, 2009

Tracy Chapman appeared on stage as a supportive audience cheered. Four songs served as an introduction to the spirit behind President Obama's campaign and as a prelude to his forthcoming speech. Enthusiasm and excitement emanated from the old and young of every hue and cultural origin. Here was something new: people who had never before contributed to a political candidate somehow justifying the extravagance of admittance. A palpable longing to hear their voices reflected in the song of a new paradigm.

October 17, 1989

> *How bad, how good does it need to get?*
> *How many losses? How much regret?*
> *...Makes you forgive and forget, Makes you change?*

–Tracy Chapman, "Change"

As the hours wore on, reports came in sporadically at first and then built to a shocking crescendo. The epicenter was not San Francisco, but somewhere near Santa Cruz. The Marina District sustained massive damage from predicted soil liquefaction and was in flames. As in 1906, access to water was cut off, with firefighters and volunteers passing buckets to put out the fires.

The fifty-foot section of the Bay Bridge that had collapsed onto the lower deck had injured several and resulted in at least one death. The double-tiered Cypress Section of the 880 freeway had fallen, possibly crushing hundreds of people.

October 15, 2009

I brought my full attention to the man on the stage. Who was this man that would be willing to take on the job of representing a country that for most of the world had come to symbolize all that was wrong and misguided?

He credited his election with a growing consensus that Americans were aware of a "huge gap between what America is and what America was. [The campaign] was about bridging that gap." There is a higher calling to close that gap and heal that fracture. "We are at a rare moment where we have the opportunity to remake our world for the better...We're going to leave something better for our children—not just here but for the rest of the world...You decide it's time to change."[11]

Critics dismissed his words as rhetoric, but to many others, he was simply stating the obvious. There is a profound need for humanity to change its course of action. Why has it taken so long to hear this basic message from those we empower to lead us? That life enfolds through change and that to resist change is to resist life? That continuous material growth cannot be sustained within the context of finite resources?

With Tracy Chapman's "Change" and "Revolution" still resonating through the room, a collective awareness of a barely seen, but radically felt wave crested. At that moment I knew this energy reflected a wider discontent that was too late to retract. No matter what events may unfold as a result of this cascade, it holds its course with a powerful and deep determination that goes beyond singular leadership.

October 17, 1989

I had never seen the city so dark, empty and silent. As I turned on my headlights, the night closed in around their tiny beams. Large chunks of concrete littered the streets. I couldn't imagine the extent of damage that had occurred throughout the Bay Area nor what it might take to clean things up and make them right again.

As I dropped everyone off and headed for home, the familiar background of my neighborhood somehow shifted into the foreground. Details never noticed jumped into view as I turned down the well-lit street. Pulling up to my dark house, I fumbled for my key, impatient to close the door on the never-ending day. The doorknob reflected dim light, reminding me that when things crack open, truth comes clamoring out from broken facades.

October 15, 2009

> The life of Francis compels those who would arrange rubrics, reshuffle administrative bodies, or form committees to ask whether that type of reform will move men to kiss the outcasts of today, or confront poverty in an open and loving way, to bless peace and tame the wolf of war and strife.[12]
> –Lawrence Cunningham

The people who poured out into the streets of Union Square were indifferent to the confines of the sidewalk. Cars inched around the human obstacle course. The parade branched off into various directions, limbs of the same tree. A lone police officer shouted for people to "Get off the street—you are jaywalking!" An ironic chuckle from the young man in front of me reflected a consensus: too late to contain the tide.

On the last darkened road before the turnoff to my well-lit home, my headlights shone upon a very large stag in the middle of the road, standing proud and still...as if waiting. I slowed the car and finally came to a stop, allowing for a respectful distance. Instead of a frightened gaze and quick sprint, he held my gaze and stood his ground. No denying the majesty in that look. With deliberation he slowly turned and made a dignified exit into the field beside the road.

A Celtic symbol of leadership and transition, the stag seemed almost to bring a challenge spoken by the world of nature. The challenge is clear if still unanswered: will we choose to span the artificial divide between ourselves and that world before our fortifications crumble of their own accord?

"What the cynics fail to understand is that the ground has shifted beneath them."

Endnotes

1 Obama, Barrack. "Inaugural Speech." CNN.com, January 2009. http://www.cnn.com/2009/POLITICS/01/20/obama.politics/

2 Douglas, Robert (Adapted from Olmstead & Olmstead, 1994). *Putting the There "There": Historical Archeologies of West Oakland.* http://www.sonoma.edu/asc/cypress...

3 Gale Group, Inc. "Huey 2001, Biography Resource Center," www.africawithin.com/bios/huey_

4 Chalquist, Craig. *Deep California: Images and Ironies of Cross and Sword along El Camino Real.* iUniverse, Inc. 2008. p. 529.

5 Chalquist, 2008, p. 549.

6 Upton, John. "Jim Berkland still predicting earthquakes." *The San Francisco Examiner*, Oct. 13, 2010. http://www.printthis.clickability.com/pt/cpt?action=cpt&title=Jim+

7 Walsh, Austin. *"Loma Prieta predictor Jim Berkland still picking quake dates." Santa Cruz Sentinel,* Oct. 16, 2009. http://www.santa/cruz/sentinel.com

8 McGloin, John B. "Symphonies in Steel: Bay Bridge and the Golden Gate." Virtual Museum of the City of San Francisco. http://www.sfmuseum.org

9 "Our History." http://www.westinstfrancis.com.ourhistory

10 Chalquist, p. 528-529.

11 Eamon Javers. "Obama speaks at DNC fundraiser." Politico, Oct. 16, 2009. p. 1-3.

12 Cunningham, Lawrence, ed. *Brother Francis: An Anthology of Writings by and about St. Francis of Assisi.* Harper and Row, 1972.

Jane Tanner is a master's candidate in Integral Psychology at John F Kennedy University, where she received her coaching certificate from the Graduate School of Professional Psychology in 2007. She has a BA in psychology from Mills College and has completed course work in Corporate Training from UC Berkeley. She has enjoyed over twenty years of success as a marketing professional in both large corporate settings as well as small entrepreneurial enterprises. Her work in the areas of management, product development, buying, merchandising, corporate training and sales have provided a range and depth of experience. The combination of academic, professional and personal experiences serves as the foundation for her current work as a professional coach. Jane lives and works in Walnut Creek, California with her husband and three daughters.

Dreaming Into Hawai'i

Jane E. Carleton

As we move through our lives we are typically unaware of our deep interrelationships with our surroundings. But when we take ourselves outside of this busyness, go into the natural world, and expose ourselves to the many opportunities for surprising encounters, we may find ourselves unexpectedly transformed through a dreamlike adventure not found in any guidebook except the one we write ourselves.

Events in our dreams and waking life are not separate; they live together, beautifully interconnected through us and through the land we walk. Enriched when we notice these relationships, we can enter profoundly into them and use the practical gifts and personal wisdom that are revealed, teaching ourselves to be active participants in the dialogue between worlds.

We begin by noticing dreams and coincidences, and by being alert for the wisdom coming to us from the land. Landscapes speak to us in feelings, sensations, emotions, images, sounds, scents, with all of our senses. Communication between us and the land where we live and work is alive with meaning. This dialogue may be deeply healing and nurturing, or it may alert us to disturbances in the land

and in our psyche. This way of perceiving the world is available to anyone who will take the time to be aware, to communicate with the land with openness and a sense of adventure. Dreamlike waking events are waking dreams and I am on the lookout for them.

Hawai'i initially became a strong presence in my life when I lived there as a young child. Pele, the goddess of the volcano, and other meaningful earth-based symbols have stayed with me ever since and have reappeared in remarkable ways. My time spent in the islands is rich and reviving; this sacred land affects me profoundly every time I visit.

I interpret waking dreams in the same way I read sleep dreams, but here I will not fully interpret the experiences I share; instead, I will simply recognize and honor the weaving I see between the worlds. My life is enriched in powerful ways by these meaningful inner and outer experiences, and I am convinced the internal alchemical processes that begin in Hawai'i continue to brew when I return home, further transforming my life.

Pele's Myth

Legends of Pele are many and varied. It is said she can manifest as the volcano in all its forms, or as a beautiful young woman or an old crone, usually dressed in white and often with red eyes. She may travel with her black dog, and she carries a *paoa*, a stick for digging, divining, and upturning the earth. She is a skilled *holua* racer, the ancient sport of riding a wooden sled down rocky lava mountainsides, and she may be seen balancing on hot lava. Pele holds sacred the delicious red 'ohelo berries, and if they are eaten without making an offering to her, unpleasant reminders of her power may follow.

Pele has many sisters; some are named Hi'iaka, "shadow bearers," after diverse moods of light and shadow glimpsed in clouds and steam. The youngest sister, Pele's favorite, called Hi'iaka-i-ka-poli-o-Pele (Hiiaka-in-the-bosom-of-Pele), was hatched from an egg that Pele kept warm under her arm as they journeyed by canoe to the Hawaiian Islands. This Hi'iaka is Pele's messenger and an important patroness of the sacred *hula*, a dance originally performed by men.

The chants were said to often be revealed to practitioners of the hula in dreams.

The ancient Hawaiians saw the goddess in the natural world, as described by historian Nathaniel Emerson:

One sees, as through a mist, darkly, a figure, standing, moving; in shape a plant, a tree or vine-clad stump, a bird, a taloned monster, a rock carved by the fire-queen, a human form, a puff of vapor...Or, again, a traveler meets a creature of divine beauty, all smiles and loveliness. The infatuated mortal, smitten with hopeless passion, offers blandishments; he finds himself by the roadside embracing a rock.

Pele has a frightening temper and waged a fierce battle with her former lover, Kamapua'a, the pig god who brings the wild boars that dig and turn the land so plants may grow. Kamapua'a called on rain to aid him in the battle. The elements of fire and water fought, but Pele summoned help from the underworld and won. Kamapua'a jumped into the sea and turned into a pig fish, Humuhumunukunukuapua'a, now honored as the state fish. Fire and water called a truce and now each finds its place.

I knew few details of Pele's legends when I first met her in my dreams. I knew she was powerful, and she was said to require great respect. She could be discerning and fair, and was known to reward kindness. I desired to manifest some of her power in my own life, the part of her that is sure and able, strong and determined, and makes no apology for her strength.

In a dream Pele shows herself to me. She visits me as a beautiful, young Hawaiian woman. I'm a little frightened of her. I've learned that appointments with wisdom and power can be frightening, when I am pushed beyond my small self.

In another dream I'm in Hawai'i flying with a beautiful Hawaiian woman who is my guide, bringing me to my life's path. She wraps a golden thread around her wrist and a piece of raffia, or twine, around mine. Together we dive down into a deep pool where I find and bring up a treasure box.

In another dream I'm with a black dog in a desert wilderness. The perspective shifts, and now I see a woman with long, straight, dark hair. She has a black dog. I'm her and not her, and she is on a little boat at a dock. Suddenly a plane flies overhead and I watch as she gets a rifle out. She stands on her jeep trying to shoot down the plane to protect the animals the hunters in the plane are trying to kill. I think of Pele, her dog, and the passion I developed later for protecting wolves from aerial hunting. In the dream she announced my future self.

Pele's Fire

It is February 25, 1995 and I'm visiting my friend Tom Paradise in the paradise that is the Big Island of Hawai'i. As a geomorphologist for the University of Hawaii, he has a permit that allows us to go out beyond the park ranger's barriers onto the active lava flow. We hike out at dusk on top of the shiny, uneven, crunchy warm black crust of the flow, scanning the massive horizon of the smoking field for the orange glows that indicate live pockets ready to ooze through. We came to explore, and we are risking danger to be under Pele's spell. We are thrilled with the beauty of this wasteland that is alive.

We carefully hike to an area with several windows of fresh lava the consistency of dense paste just beginning to break through the crust, radiating heat as they move in no hurry on the journey from the underworld to birth new land, as has been done since time began. The lava is over two thousand degrees Fahrenheit, and we are sweating. We brought offerings for Pele, and we place a green apple between oozing openings about a yard apart. The lava flows to the apple, embracing it, holding it between two arms, graciously accepting it. We also offer flowers, a cluster of fragrant white plumerias that slowly transform into a small flame. I huddle close to toss three copper coins as I ask for *I Ching* wisdom from Pele herself. After six tosses and the oracle drawn, I offer the coins, which melt instantly, unlike the slow flame of the flowers. The reading speaks of personal development, of slow gradual progress, step by step, like the land being formed here.

Tom takes a sample of lava, deftly pulling the molten earth like hot taffy, and we pause for photos, knowing this moment will never be repeated. The crust we stand on moves slightly with a barely perceivable crack; the heat begins to melt the glue on the soles of our boots. The spell is broken and we quickly and respectfully move gingerly away over black obstacles in the darkening night, charged with the power of place. The gratitude I feel will be with me forever from this unforgettable moment of play and respect. We have been initiated by the fire of Pele.

Dreamlike Oases of Shimmering Hearts

A four-day trip to Maui in November 2007. I've come to write by night and snorkel by day. I step into the following ecstatic waking dream:

I see magic today. I'm hiking across a treacherous brown field of sharp lava to go snorkeling in a remote and wild place. I lose the trail several times, and because I am alone, I feel afraid and vulnerable. I trip and lightly cut my toe on the lava, offering a drop of my blood to the land. I make up a little chant and sing to Pele, asking her to help me find my way. She has been an ally, a source of strength, and she is, after all, the volcano goddess who may allow passage over her lava. Soon I feel confident again and I find my way across the lava to the blue shore.

I find the bright and elusive little bowl-shaped bay; the wind is strong, and the water rough to snorkel in. But it is beautiful and deep and expansive and wild, and for a while I have it all to myself. And I have all day if I wish. After a couple of hours of snorkeling with wild fish and a lone sea turtle, I scramble across the lava, again challenged to find the trail. I sing another happy goddess song and eventually come to a favorite little lagoon I have been to several times before on previous trips to Maui.

Suddenly I realize I am standing in the midst of an ancient village I had not noticed before. It was as though I had been sleepwalking here before. On this day I am awake. I explore the jumble and find what appears to be a stone scraper tool near an old foundation of lava rocks. It feels to have been made to be held in a left hand. I look down from the platform I explore and see an inviting fresh water oasis hidden in a dip in the lava field below.

Climbing down, I find a gnarled ancient tree, one side dead, one side a vibrant green, near a shallow pond with a small lawn of tiny pink flowering ice plant at the base of the tree. Near the tree stands a large, perfectly smooth lava altar, with little shells placed like offerings. I add my stone and greet the land here. The oasis is alive with glittering trees of green heart-shaped leaves. All is ringed by dried branches of these trees placed radiating outward as a border. It is an inviting fairyland: an Oasis of Shimmering Hearts.

I lie down below the welcoming tree and look up through green branches at the sky and the clouds, thinking about how this could not be more perfect, and of how lucky I am. Then I begin to think of my worries back home, and tell myself to let them go. At that moment the only bird I have noticed, a seagull, flies by, releasing its droppings across the pond, with such perfect timing that I laugh. Message received.

Lingering here for hours, I fall asleep and dream of two translucent Hawaiian women in white robes blessing me. When I wake, I look at the shimmering hearts and know that I came here for healing. Sensing the nearby lagoon calling, I step in and swim, and soon I glide in the midst of an impressive school of lemon butterfly fish.

The next day I find the ruins of another ancestral Hawaiian village near the rough lava at the edge of a bay. I stop at a *heiau* (temple site) and offer respects to the ancestors. A pause at a large worn rock that feels like an altar to ask for some magic and wisdom; when a large fish jumps in front of me, it seems like a nod. I ask to be shown what I need most in my life at this time.

Continuing down the beach, I meet three merry men who are enjoying relaxing in a little lava cove. They've created a fantastic enclosure of hefty, impossibly balanced rocks. One of these resembles a heart with a soaring bird inside. A message? I can soar when I have balance; remember to create more balance in my life. I look beyond this white coral heart out into the bay and see a pod of dolphins swimming and spinning. Dance; don't forget to dance through life...

Hiking down the road and through the lava, I return to my oasis of shimmering hearts and say goodbye with tears of gratitude in my eyes. It begins to rain, and as I drive through Pele's lava field, I'm caught in a torrential downpour. The drops reflect my tears. The deluge requires me to pull over to watch and listen. I breathe in the moist air and revel in the power of this transformative place. I have been given another incredible day I will always remember.

Later that night I dined at a restaurant by the name of Humuhumunukunukuapua'a, the sacred fish, Pele's former lover, where a friendly waiter surprised me with the gift of a dozen coconut macaroons, my favorites, to take with me for my redeye flight home later that night. It was a kind gesture, an offering of sorts. As I left enchanted, I drove through a row of immense trees, a beautiful grove lit by tiny white lights, dwarfing my car in their magnificence, appearing to wave an island farewell.

Awake

I have traveled to Hawai'i again and again for healing and peace, for revival and recharge, for adventure, and for reminders of how it feels to be deeply alive. I listen with an expanded sense of possibility and see the ever-accessible outward manifestations of my interactions with this amazing land. Paraphrasing C.G. Jung, Craig Chalquist reminds us, "Nature turns toward us the face that we turn toward it." I turn a loving eye to these islands, and they to me, even when I'm not there.

Our dreams, too, turn toward us the face we turn toward them. We can ask for a dialogue with all kinds of dreams, those we have while awake and while sleeping. With intention we can share in the conversation that unites our dreams and the land, our lives and the land, our lives and our dreams. It is infinitely interesting, and great fun, to participate enthusiastically, inviting the earth herself to join in. She will answer. And we may find our lives become our best dreams.

Endnotes

1. Beckwith, Martha. *Hawaiian Mythology.* New Haven, CT: Yale University Press, 1940. http://www.sacredtexts.com/pac/hm/index.htm

2. Beckwith, 1940.

3. Emerson, N. *Unwritten Literature of Hawaii: The Sacred Songs of the Hula.* Washington, DC: Government Printing Office,

1909. http://www.sacredtexts.com/pac/ulh/index.htm

4. "Kamapua'a: The hog god." 2002. Retrieved from the Native Hawai'i website: http://www.nativeHawai'i .com/ legends/ hog_god.php

5. Wilhelm, Richard, and Baynes, Cary. *The I Ching or Book of Changes* (11th ed.). Princeton, NJ: Princeton University Press, 1974.

6. Chalquist, Craig. *Terrapsychology: Reengaging the Soul of Place*. New Orleans: Spring Journal Books, 2007.

Jane E. Carleton specializes in dreams as an educator of creative dreaming techniques. She holds a Graduate Certificate in Dream Studies and an MA in Consciousness and Transformative Studies from John F. Kennedy University. Since 2002 she has studied Active Dreaming with Robert Moss, and is a graduate of his extensive dream teacher training program. She is a professional gemologist, having earned her certification at the Gemological Institute of America in 1984. Jane's website is www.dreamsandgems.com.

Jerusalem: Know Hope

Aviva Joseph

*When a people's relationship to a place is frozen in defensive ide-
ologies, what happens in that place and to those who try to dwell
there? Do those who have keenly felt the pain of exile escape from
this pain by exiling others? Aviva Joseph's work of rebuilding homes
in Palestinian communities in Israel pushes her investigation beyond
exile and fragmentation into the very presence of the Holy City, riven
from below by ever-active fault lines, to witness what sacredness
awaits beyond ideology, conflict, and ruin.*

From the moment we are born, we seem compelled to travel
homeward. In places and people, we seek that elusive feeling
of being welcomed...Home is the goal of the epic journey of
the human spirit. Home is a container of Soul. The roof and
walls shelter and nurture the spark of life that animates our
modes of dwelling. They define the setting where Soul is
transformed from raw energy into the myriad experiences of
living.
—Anthony Lawlor

125

I thank you for helping us. By building Palestinian homes, you plant hope inside people, returning them to life. –Abu Musa, Head of Jahalin tribe, Anata

If you believe that it is possible to break, believe that it is possible to repair.—Rabbi Nachman of Bartzlav

For many years I repressed and oppressed my relationship with the people and the land of Israel, ignoring the rage and hopelessness, shame, guilt, fear, and love within me. I have been hesitant to re-vision and re-member this relationship, fearing the dammed power of grief and rage would break my heart...

My Jewish heritage emphasizes how for thousands of years we have been unprivileged and exploited by dominant powers. My parents, both holocaust survivors are a constant reminder of that reality.

Yet today, when I look at my Arab neighbors in Jerusalem, a very different image emerges. Who are the unprivileged now? Who is in power? Is it possible that we changed roles from victims to oppressors so quickly?

What has become of my land of milk and honey? Is it even mine—my land, our land? Why do the timeless words of our prophets fall on deaf ears? And I, how could I have become accustomed to the existing inequalities just outside my door? How can I continue to ignore or morally justify my privileges, my actions, the actions of my government, in face of so much human suffering? How can I support my people and at the same time be in integrity with my values? What is my part in supporting a different way of relating in and to that bloody-sacred place?

In the summer of 2007, I returned to Israel/Palestine, where I grew up, opened to knowing the other and myself; knowing through senses, knowing through reason, knowing through feelings and knowing through direct spiritual experience.

Fragments

How do I rebuild my Home? This question has preoccupied me for much of my life. I was born into a life deeply shaped by the long term effects of war. The house in which I lived in early childhood was built from bricks made out of the loud silence and fear my father carried from the concentration camp at Dachau and my mother from revolutionary Hungary.

Following my father's dream to live in our Homeland, we immigrated to Israel, but the heavy weight of my father's bipolar disorder and my brother's schizophrenia combined with my mother's lack of Hebrew, profession, and money to shatter what was left of our sense of "Home."

Fragments. The only Home I was left with was made from memories and legacies of loss and displacement, and the land of Israel itself. I did everything I could to feel at home there. I studied the history and archeology of Israel and became a tour guide and a teacher traveling throughout the country. Through these experiences I realized that creating peace at home requires people getting to know each other in genuine relationships in community.

So I led seminars aiming to bridge people from different backgrounds (i.e. religious and secular Jews, Israeli and American teens) in a setting where a safe space for dialogue could happen. But in all these efforts to build and find home, something was still missing. Although I was in my "Homeland," I felt like a stranger in a foreign land.

For a period of over two weeks, then, I joined 25 men and women from around the world for a summer camp with the Israeli Committee Against House Demolitions (ICAHD) to see and feel firsthand the daily reality of Palestinian displacement.[1] ICAHD aims to resist the Occupation by rebuilding Palestinian houses—mainly in East Jerusalem—previously demolished by government agencies. On the third day we witnessed a house demolition in close proximity to our working site. Together with ICAHD we decided to build two houses at the same time.

Anata

On a roof in the Old City laundry hanging in the late afternoon sunlight: the white sheet of a woman who is my enemy, the towel of a man who is my enemy, to wipe of the sweat of his brow. In the sky of the Old City a kite. At the other end of the string, a child I can't see because of the wall.

> We have put up many flags, they have put up many flags. To make us think that they're happy. To make them think that we're happy. —Yehuda Amichai[2]

I enter east Jerusalem, the "Arab zone." I leave behind my home in the modern Jewish west side, notably different than its eastern neighbor, just on the other side of Highway 1.

Looking without seeing, I drove in East Jerusalem many times before. Passing through this place from the distance of fear and control has kept me safe from change. This visit, I recognize by my fast-beating heart longing to experience, is significantly different. This time I am ready to break through the walls of fear that confine my head like a knight's helmet; ready to question clouding normative ideologies; ready to see and listen in for myself to different realities, namely Palestinian ones, on the other side of my home. Resistance is spreading all over my body like warm sticky tar. How would my father, who doesn't know about my fieldwork site, respond to this? What would my friends, many of them Orthodox settlers in the West Bank, say about my unorthodox behavior? Will my brother, a soldier in the Israeli Defense Force, be willing to listen to my journey? Will they say "you are a traitor, you don't belong here any more," or will they be curious and open?

Organized by the Israeli Committee Against House Demolitions, the two-week-long summer camp at the Anata village in East Jerusalem was about to begin. As we enter the village, I recall the only thing I heard about this place in the past: Anata is an unfriendly and unsafe place where children throw stones. It is curious to me now that I never questioned this statement, as if this condition was to be expected from an Arab village. What and who determined that it was unfriendly? Were the children provoked before throwing stones? Are the residents really unfriendly and do they genuinely hate Israelis? I notice how my questions refer to "them"—children and adults—as monolithic groups that seemingly have no room for shades of complexity; as if everyone has one opinion or behaves the same way.

We stop at the checkpoint at the entrance to the village. Israeli soldiers look into our vehicle. I look outside. I see a long line of cars waiting to leave the village. Residents in East Jerusalem must have a blue ID card or a special, rarely granted permit to enter Jerusalem, and these are checked often by soldiers or policemen. Though the village is considered one organic place, some parts of Anata reside within the municipality boundaries, others don't. These borders keep changing, leaving residents in confusion and fear because losing residency in Jerusalem means losing travel permits into the big city, the economic heart of the area. Many of the residents in the Palestinian villages in the outskirts of Jerusalem were born in the old city but now either don't have permission to enter or are concerned that they might lose it. Inside the village I notice the hard conditions of the roads. Some are paved but others are just dirt and rocks.

We travel to edge of the village where we are staying and find ourselves within the boundaries of Jerusalem yet also in the middle of the desert. Not a sight you would find in the west side of the city. Residents of East Jerusalem pay the same taxes, but the differences are astonishing. In Anata there is no trash pick-up; garbage piles up on the sides of the streets and on the slopes of the hills until burned. Toxic smoke hovers over the village. Residents don't have mail service, are not connected to the main sewage system, don't have parks or gardens, malls or entertainment facilities.

I keep asking others and myself how it is possible there is such a different world so close to us Israeli Jews. What creates and perpetuates this blindness? What stands in the way of my seeing more clearly? How is it possible that so many Israelis rarely find out about the daily reality of Palestinians: about systematic policies to provoke violence instead of promoting peace; about the daily humiliation Palestinians undergo by Israeli soldiers at checkpoints; about the thousands of houses that are demolished over the years for lack of permits almost impossible to obtain. "Occupation policies thrive in the dark," says Neta Golan, one of the leaders of the International Solidarity Movement (ISM). There have been incidents in which oppressive rules and laws have been changed due to public pressure, but generally, she says, the public doesn't know and doesn't care enough to create such pressure. For those in power who create the oppressive regime, the less people see, know and care, the less resistance to one-sided plans which benefit some while ignoring those who are "othered."

This feedback cycle supports the status quo. Lack of perception and understanding leads to lack of caring and lack of action. A key principle behind the transformation and healing of oppression is found in simply turning the lights on.

> To see and to be seen are not just the results of mechanical and photic energies, but also of social energies. What we see is influenced by what we believe about the world. So, too, what we see is influenced by how we feel about the world and other people. What people around us believe and feel about the world and others also influences what we see.
> –Kelly Oliver[3]

Limits and boundaries, physical or psychic, that differentiate organisms, whether individuals, societies, psychic entities, or biological cells, form naturally and are necessary. But what are the consequences of a boundary becoming an impenetrable wall that prevents any kind of communication between sides? By taking away the possibility of communication, by forbidding the free movement of energy, we take away life itself. If cells in our body were separated by a nonporous membrane, would anyone be surprised when our bodies were not able to function? How can we expect the iron wall between Israel and Palestine to bring anything but symptomatic dysfunction and death?

Another way to hide the presence of Palestinians from Israelis, whether intentionally or not, takes place through the well maintained road system in Judea and Samaria, which allows Israelis to travel in heavy populated Palestinian areas, bypassing most Palestinian villages, without needing to witness the conditions in which Palestinians are living. According to Israel, this bypass road system was created for security reasons. Palestinians are allowed to drive only on a much smaller and poorer road system divided by six hundred roadblocks.

Many Israelis are unaware of the road conditions and checkpoint system Palestinians are forced to face. I heard someone comment that he noticed fewer Palestinians on the road these days.

> When whole populations are forced to not-know what is going on around them, when the media choose to not-name injustice, watching-without-seeing becomes the most dehumanizing of acts. This kind of renunciation establishes a split within the self, where certain knowings are exiled and unavailable for the negotiation of one's life.[4]

About 27,000 Bedouins face displacement at this time, and many more thousands have already been moved from their land because of war, building of Jewish neighborhoods and settlements, building a wall, and other state-sponsored moves. Abu Musa, head of the Jahalin tribe in Anata, told us how they remember being thrown out of their tents in Tel Arad in 1948 by Israeli soldiers. They were moved to Hebron, which at the time was Jordan; later on, when Hebron became part of Israel, they were moved again to Anata, where 2,000 members of the tribe reside in houses in contradiction to the traditions of Bedouin life.

The displacement also caused economic devastation because the Bedouin rely heavily on an intimate relationship with the land. In Anata, for example, their goats have no place to graze, and they must buy grain to feed them.

"We and our ancestors lived here for many generations," stated the head of Anata's Council, "and now we are foreigners in our own land."

Demolition

At 6:30am on the 21st of November 2005, a very cold and rainy morning, ICAHD staff, volunteers, and activists witnessed and documented the demolition of the Hamdan family home, as well as its next-door neighbor's.

By the time we arrived, the area had already been blocked off by the Israeli Border Police, making it difficult to approach the houses. As we watched from afar, a Daewoo bulldozer systematically demolished the first house, leaving a pile of rubble where a family once lived. The bulldozer then moved on to the next house and began drilling into it as well. After a few minutes, the roof began to collapse, and the nine members of the family were left homeless in the pouring rain, wondering how they would rebuild their lives.

The demolition of their home left the Hamdan family in serious debt and without a house of their own. Shadi can no longer perform his job because he has no money to buy a car (he used to be a super-market distributor and now works as a builder in West Jerusalem). Mohammed's wife was three months pregnant the day of the demo-lition and had a miscarriage as a result of the shock. Mohammed is an engineer, but cannot find a job, and Ashraf is jobless as well.

Salim Shawarmeh, ICAHD's West Bank field coordinator, believes all this is a process of quiet transfer: "They demolish your houses and then make it impossible for you to have a job. What is the message? Get out! This is our land! You have no business here!" and "Where shall I go now?" I've heard Palestinians ask me again, and again.

At the end of our first day on site, the demolished home we were trying to rebuild was caught in the crossfire between children throw-ing stones and soldiers firing back with rubber bullets and teargas. It is of course a huge game (not to minimize the element of resistance in the act) for an eight year old to throw a stone at a soldier. And the soldiers, often going out of their way to drive past the Palestinian kids, know that their presence presents an irresistible provocation.

We had just started laying out the blocks for the roof when the Israeli soldiers arrived, accompanied by a Jerusalem municipal building inspector. They informed Jeff Halper, the ICAHD repre-sentative at the site, that the building was illegal. Jeff replied that on the contrary, the demolition of the home was illegal. According to international law, the Fourth Geneva Convention forbids home dem-olitions in occupied territories. "We go by Israeli law," the inspector replied, then proceeded to take photographs of the site.

Since a stop-work order would imperil both the Palestinian workers and the building equipment (which could be confiscated), the ICAHD staff and camp participants decided to postpone the work on the Hamdan family's home until a later time.

Women and children in particular physically suffer after the demolitions. Most women I met told me that they needed to go to the hospital to recover. Arabyah, in whose house we stayed, was sent to Jordan for a month after she was unable to speak after an unexpected demolition of her house. Her son was blind for a few days after the event, and his sight came back as suddenly as it was gone.

> Domicide is defined as the deliberate destruction of home by human agency in pursuit of specified goals, which causes suffering to the victims. In addition, we specify that the human agency is usually external to the home area, that some form of planning is often involved, and that the rhetoric of public interest or common good is frequently used by the perpetrators...The notion of suffering is crucial.[5]

I was holding my digital camera, a video recorder, and a digital tape recorder. Together with others, I was standing on the third floor of an unfinished building, looking out where, less than a couple hundred meters away, soldiers, jeeps, dogs, and a Scorpio looking tractor were starting to demolish a house. I felt the growing sense of responsibility to witness what was happening there, and to take as much footage as I could. Only two days after the camp started and here I was, doing my first research fieldwork. I knew I had the technology needed to bring home sensational material to communicate the insanity that we were witnessing.

Because our rebuilding project with ICHAD was illegal, we were asked not to raise much attention from the soldiers. After all, we did not want to put in danger the home we were rebuilding at the time. We witnessed the events from a distance, looking out a window in a nearby building. I grew impatient and started making my way closer to the actual demolition. Meir, the ICAHD field coordinator, knew that I was on a research "mission," so he allowed me to get closer.

On my way I encountered three woman, two of whom I did not know at the time. They were talking in Arabic. With my video camera in my hand, I was ready to shoot whenever the opportunity presented itself. I stood by them trying to get what they were saying. I recognized Um Mohamed, wearing a white head cover, from her presentation the previous night at the camp site. She was the owner of the house that we were building. She was very stressed; she thought that the soldiers were coming to destroy her house for the third time. A woman in a black dress started crying. I didn't know if it was her home that was being demolished.

Like in a scene from a dream, while the drama of the demolition was taking place, Um Mohamed came to me with a perfect red rose in her hands. She said, "Here, Habiba"—a name of endearment that sounds like my first name—"this is for you." I was surprised and speechless. Where did she get the rose? She is the one who needs to be comforted, I thought, but here she is comforting me. Now when someone tells me that Anata is a dangerous and unfriendly place, I know what I will tell them.

Exile

Galut, "exile" in Hebrew, shares its root with the word *Legalot*, "to discover." In leaving home, we discover things that we can't perceive from the vintage point of a familiar setting. Certain things can be only known when seen from outside, and a journey to exile must be endured to find the treasure.

Abraham, father of both the Jewish and the Arab nations, began his journey in a movement that lead him out of his physical and psychic familiar space: "The Lord said, 'Abram, go forth from your native land and from your father's house to the land that I will show you.'"[6] This journey out of home led Abram toward a new place, a new home born out of a personal connection with God.

In Genesis we read that the reason for creating human beings was that "there was no human [Adam] to till the soil [Adama]."[7] God placed man in the Garden of Eden in order to tend it. Yet he did not tend the soil until *after* being taken out from the garden. Why? Perhaps working the soil from which he was made was not possible until taken outside it, outside himself. "So the Lord God banished him from the garden of Eden, to till the soil from which he was taken."[8] We tend to view leaving the garden as a punishment, but we might understand it instead as an organic evolution for Adam. This exile was needed so he could discover himself anew, work the soil, and tend himself and his own psychic ground.

If we look at the stories of the Hebrew patriarchs leaving Canaan to go to Egypt, the big kingdom in the area at the time, with a symbolic eye through the language of myth, we must note that "Egypt" in Hebrew, *Mitzraim*, comes from the root "T.Z.R.": the essence of a narrow place. *Mitzraim*, a biblical version of the archetypal place outside of home, away from the homeland. This narrow place became the womb in which the nation of Israel was born. This birth did not take place at home, but outside of it.

Why did the people of Israel have to walk through the dessert for 40 years after being freed from their enslavement in Egypt? Couldn't they just go straight to the land of milk and honey? Some interpretations hold that although the people were freed from physical slavery, they were still slaves in their mind.

How is the experience of leaving home by choice different from being obligated to leave home? How is the experience of Abraham choosing to go to Egypt different from the experience of Hagar and Ishmael, who were forced into the desert? What is the relationship between the invisible voices exiled by a heroic, dominant consciousness, and the heroic ego out on a journey, away from home?

In archetypal psychology we direct our attention to the voices and images of pathology, to that which suffers, often in exile from heroic consciousness. But it is not only to the margins we turn. Indeed, much listening is done to the heroic ego itself, attempting to discern which ideas it has identified with, literalized, and taken for granted. These identifications have exiled other points of view, laying claim on reality and truth...Seeing through or deconstructing ideas is an on-going process of liberation which allows us to create with ideas, rather than remain enslaved by them.[9]

Somebody asked me, why did I come to live here [from the U.S. to Israel]. This is home. I couldn't think of living anywhere else. And for me, home, here, in a very real sense, is everything from the Mediterranean to the Jordan. That's home for me. After I said it, I realized, I sound like a settler, don't I? But that's from the heart. That's the way I feel. And that's the way a great many Israelis feel also. That it's home. And it's also the way Palestinians feel. It's beyond rationality. It's beyond any ideology. It's a sense of place. A sense of belonging. A sense of where one is supposed to be in this world. Is here. And the issues around being here are so ideological because between the Zionist narrative and its exclusionary aspect that being here for Jews means preferably that nobody else is here, and for Palestinians for many, today even, it means being here is better off without Jews—and yet our sense of place, our sense of belonging here, is very parallel, it's very similar. It's the same...

> On a personal level I don't see any contradiction between the Palestinian narrative and the Jewish narrative. There is room in the land for everyone to have that sense of place and to honor that heritage. The reality is that ideologies of nationalism and religious nationalism in particular have taken those feelings and twisted them into something ugly.[10]

The Rock

> Natives and non-natives alike are embroiled in a shared predicament of placelessness and its aftermath, and the only way out of this predicament is to regain living contact with place itself, to remember that place is a remarkable thing...An important part of getting back into place is having a place to get back into.[11]

A verse coined by mystics from the Talmudic period says that God is the dwelling-place (*makom*) of the universe; but the universe is not the dwelling-place (*makom*) of God. Philo the Alexandrian (1st Century) says a similar thing when commenting on Genesis 28:11: "God is called *ha-makom* ("the place") because God encloses the universe, but is Himself not enclosed by anything."[12] A Lurianic Kabalistic explanation for the source of the use of *makom* has to do with the *tzimtzum*, the contraction of God so a space is created for free will and for the physical world.

Does Place dwell in God? Does God dwell in place? What is the quality of this dwelling? Is it a literal dwelling? Is place a literal space, a location, soil and matter? Many people believe that Israel, and Jerusalem in particular, were literally the dwelling-place of God until the Jews were exiled from the land 2,000 years ago. They hold a strong belief that God will dwell in the land once again, and that, with the return of the Jews and the establishment of the State of Israel, the return is already happening.

But there is one place that is different than all others. A traditional belief holds that the *Schinah* (sometimes written "Shekinah"), the dwelling feminine essence of God, never left the area of the Temple Mount and the Wailing Wall in Jerusalem even after the exile took place. A new sign stands by the Wailing Wall today that explain this to the visitors. What might be the ramifications of such a belief? How is it be used for political purposes? Beyond that, can this traditional "myth" when de-literalized become a source beauty and inspiration for a deeper love of place?

One morning, while working at the building site, Um Mohamed came to me and quietly said, "I want to take you to see the Rock." I was confused. Um Mohamed and I had developed a close relationship by then, but I did not expect her, a devout Muslim, to suggest such an invitation. "The Rock next to Al Aqsa mosque," she confirmed. "I want you to come with me to pray."

Because camp was coming to an end, the only available time for us to go was on a Friday. Friday, of course, is a holy day for Muslims, and they gather by the hundreds to pray at the Noble Sanctuary (the Temple Mount for Jews), the third most sacred site for Muslims after Mecca and Medina. I would probably not have accepted the invitation had the Rock not appeared to me in a dream weeks before, as if preparing me for this.

Naturally, I was somewhat concerned because on Fridays only Muslims are allowed on the mountain. But through much prayer and meditation, I felt guided and safe to go with my new friend to visit the Rock. I felt that somehow the invitation was extended directly from the Rock and its many hidden layers.

That Friday morning I woke up sick. I had fever and my chest hurt. I understood those symptoms as energetic expressions of release and preparation and decided to continue with the plan. Since I needed to look Muslim in order to enter the holy site, I put on a head cover and a black dress which Um Mohamed loaned me before entering the restricted Muslim area. Passing through the Israeli guards at the entrance, we encountered no problems entering the Temple Mount/Noble Sanctuary. Slowly, I realized that I was somehow relating to the Rock, which according to Jewish ancient traditions goes back to the creation of the world. From that point, the world was weaved through.

> A transcendent function involves the creation of practices of dialogue with whatever new images and events emerge spontaneously in our inner and outer worlds. In developing such a function, we work at critical reflection and imaginative interpretation, a hermeneutics that brings the already known into contact with the new...[It] would lead to "a considerable widening of the horizon" and "a deepened self-knowledge" which might also "humanize" us and "make us more modest"...Finally, there would be, Jung wrote, "no distance, but immediate presence."[13]

During the first few weeks of my visit, one of the challenges I had faced was movement between the two different worlds. From East Jerusalem to West Jerusalem and back. From left to right and back. From Arabic to Hebrew to English to Spanish, each language holding its own memories, myths, and feeling tones. Moving from a crowded city with green in it to the open space of the dessert around the village. Traversing the space between one ideology and the next.

But the more I moved between the worlds, feeling as if I am embodying the transcendent function, I felt less a judgmental attitude toward sides and a growing appreciation of the opportunities and the wounds that each side carries. Moreover, with time, I came to feel the underlying e-motion in each "side." There was no difference here. They no longer seemed like "sides," but more like cells of a magnificent organ in confusion.

Heartland

How do we interpret Jerusalem? Zion? A literal place contained in time and space? A symbolic metaphor for a psychic experience? An energetic field of essence?

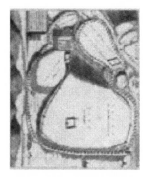 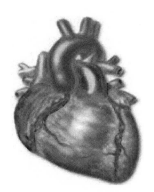

Map of Jerusalem, 1712

Oh, the walls of my heart! My heart moans within me, I cannot be silent...Hear this, O foolish people, devoid of intelligence, that have eyes but cannot see, that have ears but cannot hear...[Who] sense no pain...feel no shame...[non of you] acts justly, seeks integrity. Mend your ways and your actions...execute justice between one man and another...do not oppress the stranger [and the indigenous], the orphan and the widow...do not shed the blood of the innocent in this place.[14]

On the eve of 9th of Av, when Jews around the world remember the demolition of the Temple in Jerusalem, the destruction of the city and the exile of its people, I sit here in Anata, the city of Jeremiah, where only a few days ago we witnessed another temple, the sacred space of a family, crumble down. I cry, feeling shame and anger both for the wounding that my people suffered for so many generations and now for the needless suffering perpetuated by that wounded and traumatized consciousness. "Demolitions for security reasons," I always thought; but now I know after being here that demolitions are not enacted to secure Israeli lives or to protect Israeli law. The destruction of the heart of the Palestinian families comes as a symptom of our own broken heart that has not been listened to.

For years I was afraid to literally hear someone's heart. I hated hearing my mom's heart in her chest when I hugged her. I needed to pull away immediately. I imagined that by my listening to it would stop its rhythmic life, as if my consciousness creates death.

Years later an image appeared to me: I was lying beside another being. I stretched my arm and penetrated his chest and touched his heart. Held it in its rawness, alive, bloody, tender yet solid. My own heart was touched, it was held. We lay there side by side with each others' hearts in our hands, becoming one with the circulating rhythm of life.

Endnotes

1 Israel Committee Against House Demolitions (ICAHD) is a non-violent, direct-action group originally established to oppose and resist Israeli demolition of Palestinian houses in the Occupied Territories. As our activists gained direct knowledge of the brutalities of the Occupation, we expanded our resistance activities to land expropriation, settlement expansion, bypass road construction, policies of "closure" and "separation," the wholesale uprooting of fruit and olive trees, and more. www.ICAHD.org

2 Amichai, Y. *Poems of Jerusalem.* Jerusalem. Schocken Publishing, 1987.

3 Oliver, Kelly. *Witnessing: Beyond Recognition.* University of Minnesota Press, 2001, p. 24.

4 Shulman, Helene, and Watkins, Mary. "Depth Psychology and Colonialism: Individuation, Seeing Through, and Liberation." 2002. http://www.mythinglinks.org/LorenzWatkins.html

5 Porteous, J. D., and Smith, S. E. *Domicide: The Global Destruction of Home.* McGill-Queen's University Press, 2001, p. 12.

6 Genesis 12:1.

7 Genesis 2:5.

8 Genesis 3:23.

9 Shulman and Watkins, p. 9.

10 Interview with Fred Schlomka, ICAHD board member, July 2007.

11 Casey, Ed. *Getting Back into Place: Toward a Renewed Understanding of the Place-World.* Indiana University, 1993, p. 39, 111.

12 Philo of Alexandria, *De Somniis*, i. 11.

13 Shulman and Watkins, p. 8.
14 Jeremiah 4:19.

Resources

Breaking the Silence. A group of Israeli soldiers that served in Hebron decided to br the silence and speak out about their experiences. www.breakingthesilence.org.il

Combatants for Peace was established in part as a result of a public letter written by high ranking Israeli soldiers who refused to serve in the occupied territories. Palestinian ex-combatants also joined to end the occupation using non-violent methods. "Only by joining forces we will be able to end the cycle of violence." www.combatantsforpeace.org

International Solidarity Movement (ISM) "is a Palestinian-led movement committed to resisting the Israeli occupation of Palestinian land using nonviolent, direct-action methods and principles." www.palsolidarity.org

B'Tselem, the Israeli information center for human rights in the occupied territories. www.btselem.org

Bustan L'Shalom. "BUSTAN is a partnership of Jewish and Arab eco-builders, architects, academics, and farmers promoting social and environmental justice in Israel/Palestine." www.bustan.org

Machsom Watch was established to bring awareness to the checkpoints system operating primarily within the Palestinian areas. "Women against the occupation and for human rights." www.machsomwatch.org/en

Badil for Palestinian Residency and Refugee Rights.
www.badil.org

Sulha Peace Project (SULHA), a grassroots organization inspired by the indigenous approach to mediation, aims to rebuild trust, restore dignity and move beyond the political agenda.
www.appricom.com/sulhaReferences

Born in Chile, Aviva moved to Israel when she was eight. In Israel she worked as a tour guide and taught seminars that brought disparate groups together. She has also worked as a middle school teacher and director of Safe Routes to School in California and is currently a doctoral student at Pacifica Graduate Institute.

bodies

Half-Made

what if this is it?
no opulent palace halls await
just a simple singer's existence
my hands learning to be instruments
my voice finding its range

cloth garments, hand-made shoes
a basketful of morning berries
light shining on a wind-swept lake
and the mountain, always the mountain

I have walked along the edges of myself
for too long, searching for arabesques
that would lift me up out of the bracken
and turn me into a swan for good

but they always broke, just paper wings
hollow sounds that popped like bubbles
leaving my ears aching
my heart cored out like an apple

what if this is it?
plain white sheets, a cheese sandwich
letters as my kitchen friends
and teachers, stories by the fire
words growing in my chest, a new garden

what if this, just this
is the cobblestone trail
I have seen in my dreams

—Catherine Baumgartner

Walking the Skyline

Laura Mitchell

For Laura Mitchell, direct, nonpossessive, "nomadic" encounter with the terrain opens its "eco-imaginal" features to closer, more intimate exploration in ways that homesteading or settling cannot accommodate. This methodless method of listening, watching, and embodiment serves "the unbinding of the imagination as ways of mending the interrelational fabric of our communities."

The sharp incline of the mountain slope leads from the valley floor up to my skyline, the one I see daily from my front porch in the valley floor. As I stop to catch my breath at the top of the ridgeline, I find myself sitting on "my" skyline, gazing down at the valley, reversing my usual perspective.

From here I look down at the sharp, almost ninety degree, bend in the river as it loops around to enter the gorge where the valley floor narrows and the steeply rising mountainsides turn the river westward toward the ocean. As a bird flies, I am lined up directly with the "songline" connecting this part of the skyline to the built part of the community where I live—to a small clutch of houses bordering the riparian edges of the more densely wooded creek bed of willow, oak, sycamore, and eucalypti. I like touching this familiar skyline, a prominence we residents of the valley call Petroglyph Ridge, and sitting on her shoulder touching near at hand what only my eyes normally see from afar—yet also bemused at this comical sense of ownership.

For of course "my" skyline no longer exists and a new horizon, another skyline, has taken its place, shifted to the opposite side of the valley where a softer mountain ridge scribes the valley edge: the far side I can't see from my house. My body, reorienting to this new skyline across from me, contemplates the total depth and curvature of this hollowed out basin formed by the ancient persistence of water carving and sculpting the coastal foothills into a distinct bowl. The valley floor nestled into the steep mountain slopes where I sit is not broad and open like the pancake valley of the larger neighboring "hidden valley" of Escondido city. As part of the coastal watershed, a richly diverse ecosystem of coastal chaparral scrub, Harmony Grove is home to a small, soon to be erased, agricultural community of dairy and chicken ranches spread out along the flat lands, flanked by residential clusters and orchards here and there rising up along some of the more gentle slopes of the basin.

Sitting on top on the ridge contemplating the entire reach of the valley, it is hard not to fast-forward this scene of mixed-land-use and replace it with images of its future housing development: it is hard not to brace for a loss not yet executed. And even more disturbing, like a nervous tic that is unavoidable, is the contemplation of the irrevocable disruption to the richly entangled relationships of the natural and human community that have lived together here continuously for over one hundred years and, when counting in the seasonal nomadic settlements of the Kumeyaay Indians (whose inscriptions mark the petroglyphs at the north end of this ridge), for 1,500 years.

As a community, we are all settled in together. The animals and plants know us, have woven trails through the human layer. The native chaparral—itself a complexly rhizomed root system, a whole living organism consisting of diverse numbers of companionable plant species—has held on tenaciously to corridors even in the developed areas: built and natural still move together. Only the relentless slow degradation of creek life, the disappearance and diminution of frog, sunny, bluegill and even crayfish, and the clogging of creek with river moss and pollutants in the summer, tell the true tale of the persistent threat to habitat, to the rights of the land, and the inevitable erosion of the historic and present day character of the human community.

I think about the way we are spiraling out of ecological control and the concomitant disturbance in the way we are entwined in the imaginal fabric of our home communities, an invisible renting of human-nature bindings. I feel this rent reverberate in my own body like the sound of a deadening rush of footsteps going nowhere or an oncoming army, a speeded sense of urgency in a void. I began wondering how the landscape and habitat of a home community inform the collective identity, and how this tear in ecological viability affects us, and what new frameworks of thinking can bring such events into our ken.

Nomadic Awareness

As I move across the ridge toward the place where the petroglyphs lie exposed to the elements, I notice this rising and falling away of successive moments of contact along the path coupled rhythmically with a continual relinquishment of the places I pass through. Immediate perception, in the first flash of awareness, itself is a nomadic awareness: an openness upon the world of direct experience, an embodied alternative to our modern legacy of ownership and appropriation. This rhythm is one of opening and closing the spiral of localized encounters with the terrain and its inhabitants.

As I move along the pathway, the storied existence of this ridge comes into relief: the sensorial surround of smell, sound, texture, sight, and rhythm open up the immediacy of the living landscape. Yet it is my sense of intimacy and "attachment" that makes me part of, that weaves me into the landscape, particularizing and intensifying these moments—an attachment that is continually relinquished and returned back to the other, that cannot be possessed; a temporary ownership in the sense of being part of the terrain as I experience it at each point of contact: the sharp stones on the path, the mountain laurel now dried in summer brittleness. This innocent kind of ownership implies a familiarity and noticing, a connection that is implicitly also a letting things be free.

Nomadic awareness does not imply nonchalance or rootlessness, rather an ardent presence to each place and situation whether that be a walk in the hillsides, one's home place, work, art or relationships. To not corral or colonize events into one-sided automatized responses keeps us on our feet—attentive, fluid, nomadic.

We can no longer settle even staying in the same location. We are always adjusting to a loss that we don't even realize we have had and, on regaining ground, find we have lost it again. That is certainly my experience in becoming an advocate of place and authentic community in my home valley. I hear Rosi Braidotti's message in my head: the nomadic is a modern response to placelessness. As a metaphor and an approach to place-relations, the Nomadic is both an orientation and a critical mode of thinking based in deterritorialization. It is a response to the need to redefine person-place relations, to think differently, to unbind the imagination, and release the originality implicit in direct experience.

Nomadism requires a different kind of thinking, one not based in linearality and the intellectual modes we have been educated into, but in new forms of collective interrelatedness—modes that are more recursive and cyclical, a spirality that returns but is never the same at each new turn. The spiral is the signature of nature, the archetypal schema written in all natural forms: in a fingerprint, in plant growth, in weather patterns, in the sound print of a violin. As a species, humans were naturally nomadic, says Bruce Chatwin, and developed a prodigious sense of orientation.

For the nomad, deterritorialization is a relationship to the earth characterized by orientation, directional variability, and polyvocality. The nomad relies on sets of relationships where each particular place becomes a nonlimited locality (a universal and a particular at the same time, or global locality). For the nomad, locality is not delimited. The absolute, then, does not appear at a particular place but becomes a nonlimited locality; the coupling of the place and the absolute is achieved, as Ed Casey points out, not in a centered, oriented, globalization or universalization but in an infinite succession of local operations.

I am here and also there throughout within a nonlimited locality. My being is at home at any moment and also moving and distended everywhere into the region. The nomad is the path itself, fully present to the particularity of each place and simultaneously to the absolute—a condition where everything is everywhere at the same time. Nomadic awareness brings one into direct contact with place while at the same time being diffused throughout the environing region.

With the nomadic, we rely more on navigational aptitudes, our reading of the "songlines" (the interlocking network of ways through the land), our wayfinding, and the way we sense our journey by moving deeper into the sensory system, into orientation, directionality, our auditory and haptic senses. Movement, rhythm, bodily responsiveness reads its environment: micro-movements hold conversations with the immediate surround. Our first language is movement. Intrauterine imaging shows that the fetus develops an elaborated sound-specific set of micro-movements in precise response to its mother's voice tones—literally a bodily analogue to spoken language: not just inducing movement, but as a movement language.

Nomadism is both an acute sense of emplacement without appropriation or territorialization and also a polycentric orientation that cuts across categories and responds to contemporary conditions with fluid boundaries, and the recognition of difference and inclusivity. It is this deterritorialization, both of locality and social artifacts, that constitutes nomadic relations and that allows for, as Braidotti expresses it, a poetic re-involvement with the earth.

Here and Everywhere

For the nomad, the journey itself is the ritual and the way rather than the contemporary focus on economic viability and use value. The nomad is simultaneously placed throughout all locations of his journey (physical, cultural, imaginal) and also accountable and intensely present at each locality. For the nomad, experience is particularized and at the same time a globalized universal: global locality amounting to an intensive interconnectedness. Nomadic awareness brings one into direct contact with place while at the same time being diffused throughout the surrounding region and also centered in the absolute context of the planet and even the cosmos. To be here and everywhere at the same time is the ultimate freedom of nomadic awareness. To re-enter our home-places is a gesture toward this freedom in its call for an open society and the unbinding of the imagination as ways of mending the interrelational fabric of our communities.

It is with this nomadic attitude that I wish to enter my community, listening for polyvocality in the interviews and the appearance of fresh resources. The writing itself is an unpredetermined journey, a wayfinding through the accumulated material and interviews, an open-ended responsiveness to what turns up and what voices want to be heard. Wandering re-establishes the original harmony which once existed between the human and the universe—one that does not necessarily require physical travel. Intentional wandering, nomadic presence, is a practice I have tried to follow in this writing and wish to hone in my relations in my home community.

Laura Mitchell, PhD, is an art therapist who works and lives in northern San Diego County. She is the director of the Expressive Arts Program at Sky Mountain Institute.

Exiled from the Land, Exiled from the Body: Investigating Connections

Rebecca Wyse

Sometimes it's as though a place selects its storyteller. This role sometimes conforms to a family lineage. But in cultures that lack storytelling tools, the tales resist total silencing by resurfacing in the body, bearing witness in what ails us. Rebecca Wyse responds by crafting her own tools for reconnecting body, lineage, mind, and place.

Dedicated to the land in Marion Township, Iowa, and to the story-tellers who kept its spirit alive.

> For it is the body, the feeling, the instincts, which connect us with the soil. If you give up the past you naturally detach from the past; you lose your roots in the soil, your connection with the totem ancestors that dwell in your soil. You turn outward and drift away, and try to conquer other lands because you are exiled from your own soil. That is inevitable.[1]

The land in Marion Township, Washington County, Iowa I call home has felt alive as far back as I can remember. When I say, "I miss the land" and consider returning, friends tend to say to me, "I don't know if it would be a good idea for you to go back there." It is not the people who live there I miss, but rather the land itself.

Ever since leaving Iowa for college at the age of seventeen, I have followed my curiosity, always wanting to know more about the ordinary lives of "my people," those who had gone before. I'd write to my aunts, including long lists of questions about their younger years, which they answered with patience and good humor. Over years of brief visits home, I developed what I came to call "My Pilgrimage," an internally directed route I would take, no matter how short my visit, to points that held meaning for me: the cemeteries with the remains of my great-great-grandparents, who had come from Switzerland and the Alsace region of France; the remaining homesteads of my great-grandparents, my grandparents, and my parents. All of these places fell within a few square miles in Marion Township. Although my parents had moved to a farm several miles into Henry County by the time I was born, the rest of my extended family on my mother's and father's sides of the family remained in this first-settled area.

I was fortunate to grow up in a family of gifted storytellers: my father Mahlon, his mother (my Grandma Wyse), his brother (my Uncle Vernon), and his sister (my Aunt Esther). My dad came from a line of people who loved the land. Grandpa and Grandma consulted *The Farmer's Almanac* to determine the best time to plant their garden and crops. When my Aunt Esther developed a growth on her spine, my grandma took her to the local natural healer. This was confessed in a whisper, for "those people" were considered strange and dangerous by the majority of Mennonites in our community.

My family's stories, especially those of my father, planted deep in my psyche a connection with the spirits of the people who had lived on the land long before the arrival of my relatives. Grandma, born in 1889, told of Indians coming to her house when she was a little girl to beg for food. Grandpa uncovered signs of these early inhabitants as he plowed in the fields along Crooked Creek. Two of the best preserved—a heavy stone axe head and a flint arrowhead— he wrapped with care and passed on to my father, who honored the spirits they held. My father kept the axe and arrowhead in his shop.

I would pull open the drawer that held them and stare, awed by an awareness of the ancient people who had walked before me in this land we called home.

My father told stories of the Black Hawk Wars, and of the Plains Indians who had been displaced from their lands and their homes. My little girl ears heard the indignation in my father's voice as he told the stories. He would take me on the Black Hawk Trail that ran next to the Mississippi River in Burlington, whispering the story of how Black Hawk's warriors took this dirt path on their way to their camps on Crooked Creek. My senses were alive, and my heart pounded. In the silence, broken only by the lapping of the muddy water against the riverbank and my father's soft voice, I expected Black Hawk to appear on the trail, for his spirit was there.

A reverence for the land on which we lived grew naturally in me. For the first eleven years of my life, I came to regard the land on our farm, and the land on which my parents, grandparents, great-grandparents, and great-great-grandparents had grown up as my home. I was the last of five children, nine years behind my siblings. I came to enjoy many hours of solitude, which I spent with my dogs taking walks in the pastures and climbing up into the haymow or the corncrib for hours of imaginative play. I discovered hidden bluebells and lilies of the valley sticking up from the rich, black Iowa dirt under thick fern fronds. Each afternoon, I gathered the cows for milking. Every so often I watched my mother cut chickens' heads off, and their headless bodies would flop around the back yard, spattering the grass with blood.

When I was eleven we moved to Mt. Pleasant, a small town fourteen miles south of our farm. My father's health no longer allowed him to farm or butcher, and our family doctor found him a job as a maintenance worker at the county hospital. A few years before, my mother and father had joined three other couples to form a mission church in Mt. Pleasant. So instead of traveling three times a week for services, we were in the same town. My life was forever changed during this transition from living on the land to living in town. An essential part of me felt cut off, repressed, silenced.

In recent years, as I mused on my early connection with the land, a question took root and began to grow: might there be a parallel between the control, repression, and silencing of the land and the control, repression, and silencing of my individual nature? Might there be a parallel between my exile from the land and my exile from my body? I decided to dedicate time to listen to the land, and my body, and record what they might have to say.

Land and Body Speak

Wednesday, June 25, 2008: I'm thinking of my papa's map, shared at a family reunion in the early 1980s as a memorial for Elmer and Mary, his parents. My father's map mirrored my inner map of the land with which I felt most connected. I knew stories about the people who lived in each house marked by an X on my father's map, but it was the land itself that had hooked my belly and my heart and sprouted the roots that grew from the bottom of my feet deep into its rich soil. I have a suspicion, a curiosity: I wonder if my aching loneliness and broken heart speak through my weight gain, creating padding against the pain of rootlessness.

Monday, June 30, 2008: I can hardly move. My back on both sides, in the area of my kidneys, is aching, as is my midriff, where my liver lives. I keep thinking of the photos of fatty liver on the liver doctor's website. I'm so disconnected from my body. It's as if I'm a walking head severed from everything below my neck. I'm into what I want and the fact that I want it NOW—everything from candy, to cake, pie, ice cream, and doughnuts. I want it, I want it, I want it, and I don't care that I'm overworking my liver and other organs to the point of numbed-out exhaustion. They are fine, beautiful, perfect organs. What I am doing to my body, I realize, is no different from what we human beings are doing to the Earth. I take care of my car and my cats much better than I take care of my body. I find this dichotomy puzzling.

Exile: the price I pay for not fulfilling my mother's wishes, and for breaking the community's moral code. My body is sick. It needs a long, long rest and plenty of gentle sun, rain, quiet, soft music, nutritious food. My heart cries for love, for belonging, for a feeling of being at home, of being rooted.

Wednesday, July 16, 2008: I set my timer for twenty minutes and ask the land as a whole to tell me which parcels want my attention.

I sketch out the boundary led by my heart and ask the land what it wants me to know. The boundary, I'm surprised to discover, isn't confined to the square mile, but meanders, following the path of my father's stories.

The land and I have this imaginal dialogue:

The Land: I miss you. I miss your love of me. I miss your company. I feel abandoned and lonely. The people who live here have forgotten me, are unaware of me. I ache. My sadness runs in my soil, my trees, my streams. I miss your grandma, and your father, and your Uncle Vernon. They loved me, too. I was part of their lives, part of the stories they told, the stories you loved.

Your grandma and grandpa lived close to me. They shared their love with me. Your grandma planted her garden and her flowers, and your grandpa his crops, with care, by the moon and the seasons. Your grandma and I grew beautiful flowers. They were beautiful because she planted them in me with love. I used to listen to her telling you the stories of when she was a little girl, of her playing with Danny in the fields, and of Indians coming to their back door for food. Your grandpa gave your father the Indian axe head and arrowhead he found when plowing in the field as a young man, and now they have been passed on to your sons.

The stories tied me to you and your family. The storytellers have passed on. Now there's a disconnection. I am not seen. I am not heard. I am not given attention, care, or love. I am not honored or respected. I miss you. I want you to come back and tell the stories crying to be told. I want you to tell my story—our story—to keep the connection between people and other natural beings alive. I miss hearing the laughter of children and the feel of their feet padding over me. This is a sacred place, but the people who lived here and felt it are gone. I'm calling you because you feel it. You know I'm here, that I'm alive. You hear the voices of the ancestors calling you.

Rebecca: I'm sorry I live so far away! I love you so much. What can I do?

The Land: Reconnecting with you makes me very happy. For now, it's enough to know you're still here. I want you to tell the stories. Will you do that?

Rebecca: Yes, I'd be honored to tell the stories. Will you tell me what you'd like me to say? Can we tell the stories together?

The Land: Yes, we'll tell them together, with the help of the other beings that live in our world and long to be heard.

Twenty minutes are up, and the timer rings. I continue to sit, wondering how this communication from the land reflects my life. The direct parallel jolts me. I too feel disconnected from, betrayed by, my people, my tribe. I also feel sad; the loneliness is a pain. My intuition pulls at me to tell my story. Like the land, I feel silenced and unheard.

Is it significant that over the past few days my liver has been extra sensitive, my stomach extra bloated, and that I feel heartburn and flatulence just as I'm focusing on the land and asking what it has to say?

I hold my belly and begin a gentle rocking. I caress it and ask if it has anything it would like to tell me. I hear it say that the umbilical cord that connects me to the land has been ripped away. To fill the void and numb the sorrow of separation, I devour the foods that represented love to my family: ice cream, pie, cake, and candy. These were the foods of love, all made from scratch. Emotions weren't allowed, and sex was never discussed; the way to my mother's heart was to be silent, not be a problem, and show my love by eating everything she set before me. Eating these foods now is my attempt to reconnect, to fill the gaping hole that longs to be filled with love and connection and a feeling of home. The pain in my belly is at crisis point for a reason. The timing is indeed significant. It's time to reconnect with the land I love.

July 17, 2008: I'm stroking the grass in Sommers Cemetery, the place where my ancestors are buried. Pain pushes up from my throat, opens my mouth, and emits a silent but powerful cry. The intensity, the pain, the longing for that plot of land I call home are too much to bear.

"I'm so sorry," I cry out to my body, asking its forgiveness for feeding it yet again: twelve doughnut holes, an apple fritter, a decaf latte, and a scone, all in one sitting.

The land feels lonely and cries for attention, companionship, love. My body feels lonely and cries for attention, companionship, love. In a Derrick Jensen interview with Dolores LaChapelle and Julien Puzey, Puzey states, "Dolores is really helpful with this, because all these addictions are substitutes for real community."[2] I know that I eat because I'm excruciatingly lonely. I eat to numb the pain, to block out the reality that I am in exile from my community. It seems a conundrum: I'm pulled to the land of my people as though by a strong magnetic force, and yet I'm exiled from my people. It's clear I long for community. Perhaps in listening to the land, and the stories she holds, I will be led to the community I seek. The reconnection with the land, and with the voices of those in her past, is certainly a beginning.

July 18, 2008: I ask the land how it feels to be covered by a concrete road.

The Land: I'm smothering. I can't breathe. The tires roll over me, going faster each year, the humans steering the car focused on where they're going, minds far removed from me. I don't exist for them. I'm what they walk on. I'm what they stand on. I perform a function for them, nothing more.

Rebecca: How does this feel in my body? I'm smothering. I can't breathe. I must run away, away from my family's attempt to control my spirit. Making me like them is all that is on their minds. They don't see me. I don't exist for them, except as a challenge, a problem, needing to be fixed.

I ask the land how it feels to have a turkey farm covering its body:

The Land: Smothering. I can't breathe. It's forever night without air. I sense the turkeys above me, seemingly oblivious to their fate. They haven't seen the sun or walked on my soil or soft grass or snow-covered ground. They don't know I exist. Their world is crowded.

Rebecca: How does this feel in my body? I feel nauseous. I can't breathe. Just five minutes in the presence of my family, and I feel myself slipping into their world, where everyone must live according to plan, or be judged a problem, a sinner. They don't allow themselves curiosity or doubt. Different, to them, spells danger. For comfort, they surround themselves with others who believe as they do.

I'm thinking about myself in relationship to the earth, and how I'm a living thing, just like the birds and squirrels, the trees, the grass, the air, the earth herself. I'm thinking about the idea of having a love affair with the earth, of being in a mutually satisfying relationship where we share quality time, feel joy in each other's company, feel a sense of being protected and nurtured by each other, feel heard and fed deep in our souls.

Surely, feeling cut off from my body and from my present physical environment reflects feeling cut off from the land in Iowa. Just as the cement was poured on the road past Sommers School in the name of progress, smothering the land's spirit and its ability to live and breathe, so my spirit was smothered, cut off from the sunlight of community and love and attention and belonging.

When my exile began in the early 1980s, just after my divorce, the farmers in Iowa were struggling. There was a growing demand to either give up the family farm or go into industrial farming. They felt despair, depression, and a preoccupation with survival. Farmers suffered a forced reorientation from the lives they and their fathers and mothers before them had known. They were compelled to find other ways to make it in the world. Those who had farmed now took jobs forty miles away at the University of Iowa to work as hospital orderlies, or as factory workers in small surrounding towns.

I'm thinking about Craig Chalquist's comment that exile happens when something is turned against its own nature.[3] What is my body's nature? What does it naturally want? It wants attention, love, connection, and warmth. It wants to ingest foods that nourish its growth and to be in the company of people with whom it feels at home, with whom it has a sense of belonging and esteem. My body longs to follow its natural course. What is its natural course? I'm not sure I know. I can ask it to let me know. I can ask it what it wants.

I love to think about the land being allowed to grow back to its original wildness. I love it because I want to allow myself to grow back to my original wildness. Just as there are conservationists and environmentalists who help nurture land that is scarred and ill from misuse and disuse, so there are healers who can help me grow back to health. My body is at the front of the line; it wants to be healthy and will be able to speak to me itself if I stop pouring cement on top of its sensors.

Friday, July 25, 2008: I began reading Abram's *The Spell of the Sensuous*[4] last night. I'm moved by Abram's discussion of death, and by the idea in indigenous cultures that the body is "a magical entity, the mind's own sensuous aspect, and at death the body's decomposition into soil, worms, and dust can only signify the gradual reintegration of one's ancestors and elders into the living landscape from which all, too, are born."[5] No wonder indigenous people view nature as sacred if they believe they become part of the cosmos after death!

After my father's funeral, I stayed at his grave after everyone else had left, "to tuck my father in," as I explained to my family. My sons and I watched as the coffin was lowered into the ground. At the bottom of the grave an open concrete vault had been placed, awaiting the coffin. My father's body had been embalmed and, after the funeral, sealed in a heavy coffin. We watched as the coffin was lowered into the waiting concrete, and as the concrete lid was secured in place. Finally, the gravediggers began filling the hole with dirt.

How different from the indigenous practices Abram describes. In the United States we seem to do all we can to deny the naturalness of death. Death is often feared and not discussed. We embalm our dead with chemicals and barricade their bodies from the earth in coffins and vaults. I wonder if there are parallels between our fear and denial of death and our fear and denial of nature?

July 30, 2008, 4:45am: I woke up with a start, thinking of the trauma surrounding my birth: my mother's hemorrhage and near death, my delivery by cesarean section, my separation from mother and breast, my days spent in isolation in the airlock. My mother was my land, and I was literally ripped from her belly, just as I later felt ripped from the belly of the land I love. The coincidence seems too pointed to be accidental.

My mind jumps to the rage I felt as I read Susan Griffin's *Woman and Nature: The Roaring Inside Her.*[6] As I was reading the chapter "Timber,"[7] anger so possessed me that I had to stop, shut the book, and leave the house. The containment of the airlock at birth seems to have set up a theme of containment and control in my life. I think about containment and control initiated in the name of governments, religions and greed and the consequences for the land and the people. I intuit that my rage is a clue to key issues held, unspoken, in my belly.

August 1, 2008, Solar Eclipse/New Moon in Leo, 5:30pm: Lafayette Reservoir. I felt stiff and awkward as I left the car and walked toward the ranger station in search of a picnic table near the water. I felt conspicuous and kept talking to myself as I felt the urge to hide, not be seen. Thinking about my intense desire for solitude and the realization of my differentness. Testing being at home with who I am inside. Can I accept that I'm different? Can I accept how often I feel I don't fit in? Can I accept that sometimes I antagonize people in authority and am scapegoated by their insecurities? Can I be okay with seeing what I see? Knowing what I know? And sitting with it? Being with it? Not flicking away out of fear of my truth? Accept the thoughts, feelings, and perceptions as mine? Not abandon myself? Look myself full in the eye?

I walked, searching for an empty table where I could sit down and meditate. No luck. I sat by the side of the trail on some straw grass above the water. I had trouble letting go, relaxing. I kept breathing. I asked the earth what it wanted to say. I sat for many minutes, waiting, listening. Trees rustled. A plane engine droned. I kept getting "fear." I fought the word, thinking, "But this is a protected area. I don't think I'm doing this right." But "fear" kept coming up. When I went into it, I widened into awareness of the vulnerability of the land to the whim of humanity. I was aware of a feeling of anxiety in my body and an inability to relax and feel safe. I picked up a handful of dirt: dry, tiny clods. I didn't feel a connection. I felt a surge of longing for the land in Iowa.

I sat a bit longer and then went to look for a tree to hold. I didn't find one close to the trail, so I kept walking back to the car, stopping once to visit with a talkative blue jay and once to allow the gentle lapping of the water draw me in and soothe me. The water seemed safer, less vulnerable, than the spot I'd sat in. That place had felt

stiff, awkward, and unfamiliar, vulnerable. I felt faint points of connection, but not a feeling of being at home.

August 3, 2008: On my oldest son's thirtieth birthday I'm filled
with an acute awareness of the stories that want to be told, of the
pain that wants to be heard and honored. I'm thinking of the pain of
the exiled, the ignored, and the marginalized—the pain of the land
itself, and of the Ioway people, of the Sac and Fox, of Harriet, Rosie,
and Rebecca. These people have lived on the land, and the land
holds their pain as well as its own. I'm thinking of the power of
story, of its potential for reclaiming a connection with place.

Tuesday, August 5, 2008: I'm reflecting on the concept of biore-
gionalism, the practice of humans living along with a region's natural environment, and how cutting the Iowa land up into counties,
draining the marshlands, and plowing up the prairies did away with
this idea. By the time my older brother Gene purchased the farm,
monocropping was dominant among farmers in southeast Iowa. I'm
intrigued by Chalquist's comment that monocropping "starts working its way into relationships."[8] It seems to have worked its way into
the religious aspect of the community I grew up in. Only one set of
religious beliefs fit into the box labeled "Acceptable." It was around
the time farming practices changed that I became acutely and
painfully aware I did not fit into the box.

Chalquist also mentioned that in Jung's view, everything casts a
shadow, and that when a "flashlight of consciousness is turned on"
specific areas, the rest lies in the darkness.[9] In my family and community, the flashlight shone on being a "good" Christian and on the
"Acceptable" box. All things outside that box were in shadow and,
thus, repressed, just as only crops in the "Acceptable" box were
planted, year after year after year. Any plants native to the land were
dug out and killed. In both cases, diversity and wildness were suspect and stamped out.

Investigating Connections

I have become obsessed with the land, and with questions of how
what has happened to the land relates to my personal history. I'm

also intrigued by a pattern that has emerged: of people exiled from the land, and of the land's exile from itself. The land and its exiles share a silencing of voice and spirit. I'm determined to continue my exploration, for the land and the silenced voices call to me. They deserve to be heard. As Chief Seattle is thought to have said, "You must teach your children that the ground beneath their feet is the ashes of our grandfathers. So that they will respect the land, tell your children that the earth is rich with the lives of our kin."[10]

I invite you to join with me in this process of listening to the land and telling its stories, and perhaps, along the way, discovering your own. Is there an area of land that calls to you? Have you considered your connection with this land? Does its historical story hold parallels with your own? Deep listening is an act of respect and love. When we quiet ourselves enough to listen to the earth around us, we not only hear its pain and wisdom, but also the pain and wisdom we hold in our bodies. When we listen deeply to the land, we both begin to heal.

Questions for Further Investigation

Does alienation from the land parallel alienation from the body?
Might healing our alienation from the land heal our alienation from our bodies?
If we listened to the call of the land that pulls us, what would it say? What does it want from us?
If we listened to the call of our bodies that whisper through our intuition, what would it say? What does it want from us?

Endnotes

1. Meredith Sabini, *The Earth Has a Soul: C. G. Jung on Nature, Technology and Modern Life* (Berkeley, CA: North Atlantic Books. C. G. Jung (in Sabini, 2008, p. 73–74).

2. Derrick Jensen, *Listening to the Land: Conversations about Nature, Culture, and Eros* (White River Junction, VT: Chelsea Green Publishing, 2004), p. 243.

3. Craig Chalquist, personal communication, 2008.

4. David Abram, *The Spell of the Sensuous* (New York: Vintage Books, 1997).

5. *Ibid.,p.* 15.

6. Susan Griffin, *Woman and Nature: The Roaring inside Her* (San Francisco: Sierra Club Books, 1978).

7. *Ibid., p.* 58–66.

8. Craig Chalquist, personal communication, 2008.

9. *Ibid.*

10. John Seed, Joanna Macy, Pat Fleming & Arne Naess, *Thinking like a Mountain: Towards a Council of All Beings.* Gabriola Island, BC, Canada: New Catalyst Books. Chief Seattle (in Seed, Macy, Fleming & Naess, 2007, p. 71).

Rebecca Wyse, MA is a master's degree student in Consciousness Studies at John F Kennedy University. She lives and works in the San Francisco Bay Area.

The Shape of our Habitat

Pam Greenslate

The shape of our habitat reflects the shape and state of our physical being. When we are unable to live connected to our environment, we become separated from our true nature, and often live disenfranchised and pain-filled lives as a result. If we can learn to see our physical world and learn to live in and create the natural beauty and harmony we find there, we insure a richer, more alive environment both in the outer world and within ourselves.

Lines and Curves

I find living in squares difficult. Roads that run in straight lines that intersect at right angles making boxes take us out of our circular thinking and into a straight, goal-oriented routine. When we lose the softness of curves, the beauty of roundness, and live only in squares and straight intersecting lines, we loose our connection to our instinctual creativity. We no longer listen to the whispered soft voice that pulls us down a winding and rambling country lane.

I love a curving road. I love a path that I cannot see to the end and must adventure through curves and turns to find what lies beyond. When our ancestors were forced to move from living in round places—living in circles—and made to live in squares and boxes, they began to loose their connection to nature, and to the aliveness, sentience and intelligence of the Earth.

As this living separate from nature continues, humans began to relate to the Earth as an object to fulfill our desires, not as a sentient being to co-exist upon. The human race began sliding down that straight slippery slope and soon lost footing, continuing to plummet down that angular hill.

No longer an ally, the mantra for the human race has become "I conquer," forgetting that to conquer Her is to destroy ourselves in the process.

Nature became the symbol for an adversary that must be conquered, controlled, and bent to human will. The perfect balance between humans and the environment was upset.

Our bodies like nature are cylindrical—more rounded than straight. Life is a cycle. Our breath is a circle; our exhalation a release our inhalation a connecting. The moon cycles ever twenty-eight days—growing from the dark new moon to the full rounded moon back to the tiny slip of the dying moon—and is reborn. The sun also cycles every year: from the rebirth of the sun at winter solstice, to equal dark and light at spring equinox, to the longest light at summer solstice, and the gradually fading of light moving toward fall equinox, until it reaches winter solstice again and is reborn.

We see cycles/circles repeated throughout nature, and when humans began to live disconnected from living in these circles/cycles, humanity lost its understanding of the natural world.

When flying I like to look down on the landscape below and see how that world is laid out. Roads laid out in perfect symmetrical shapes are often reflected in the lines of houses and buildings that populate that place. By contrast, areas that follow riverbanks and streams where the roads begin to curve often have houses and buildings that reflect this creative bend.

When driving I like to follow the "blue highways" (state and county roads) and stop in places that are not on the main thoroughfares. I am looking for how the hills, valleys, winding creeks and riverbeds impact the consciousness of those living there.

Talking with people I have traveled down a winding country road to visit is a different conversation than ones I have after driving along straight highways. Curved lines and roundness invite the visitor to slow down and come into their embrace. A straight line cannot embrace us; it can only move us forward. Perhaps straight lines and right angles shorten our stay. They are not inviting or receptive, but always moving us ahead with little time to stop and reflect.

When our ancestors moved from living in a circular society into one with straight lines and boxes, they not only lost connection to nature, but connection to each other. A world of right angles is an impersonal world. A world of curves is an embodied world, filled with invitation and acceptance.

The psychology of place is overlaid by the structures we place upon it. Land holds power and carries memories. We are drawn to places because we sense the power and we recall the memories. Many times the land's memory is a shared memory with us. Unfortunately, human energy feels the raw power of a place, and a desire to tame the energy, contain it, or own it becomes the foremost thought. We often build boxes to become these containers.

These boxes can be found from the myth of Merlin, who kept the simple chapel in the forest, clearing it of any association with a belief and opening to all who passed by, to the grand churches and cathedrals built on ancient places of power. From humble structures to imposing ones, all have long attempted to contain the power and energy of place.

When humans lived in circles with their gently curving lines that described more of a true blueprint of nature, perhaps we could communicate more easily with the natural world. Today we walk on straight, paved paths. Our feet rarely touch the natural landscape of the ground. We plant gardens in neat rows and boxes, and tend to these gardens so that no weeds or pests will disturb the perfect picture we have created.

We hide in this perfection, believing that we can control the natural order of things. But can we? Watching a raging river at flood time reveals how little control we have over nature. Two decades ago, I watched with fascination as the Mississippi river swept over its banks to destroy straight-line dams and levees, flooding and reclaiming its natural habitat. The dams and levees had forced the river into an unnatural course; flooding took the river back to its natural course.

Earth Bodies

Dreamtime carried me to the fouled waters of the Gulf, where drilling and piercing of the earth's outer layer to tap the oil lying deep beneath has begun a tragedy unseen before. My tears flow as the image and reminder of this disaster enters my mind, and in the full light of morning I wonder if my tears, and the tears of others, can clean and replace those waters. Like the water of the oceans, tears are salt water. Perhaps enough of our tears can begin the healing.

We humans are made of the same stuff as our environment: there is a connection of recognition between the human body and the body of the earth. As we harm the environment, so we harm ourselves. I recall the teachings of an elder a few years ago. He asked, what is a leading ailment of humans? Asthma, he answered, is a chronic inflammatory disease of the airways, one that makes breathing difficult. The defoliating of rainforests is systemically destroying the earth's airways and lungs. Our body illnesses reflect the illness of the earth. As we pollute our planet we also pollute ourselves.

Different Shapes

I imagine Earth and ask her to speak of her pain. I close my eyes and listen. I hear the mechanical sounds of modern day life drowning out her words of reply. I must listen more closely to hear her natural sounds. I step off the paved paths and wander barefoot on her body. I find trees and woods to sit still and listen. I feel her energy vibrate up through my feet, rising up my legs, abdomen, and chest, into my heart and traveling through my throat, to my face and then into my crown and pulsate outward. She is alive and her heartbeat is strong. My own heart beats in rhythm with her.

When we think in circles or spirals we open to unlimited possibilities. It is limitless thinking that allows access to our intuitive creativity, and this is how we can solve problems and make new creations.

This means we must to learn a new vocabulary from which we

speak and think. Our descriptive words outline our internal beliefs. So we change the paradigm of our thinking and our speaking to change the reality of our world.

The shape of our habitat is formed by the shape of our thoughts. Thinking in straight-line goal-oriented patterns creates that structure in our daily world. Thinking in curves and multi-solution goal patterns creates a different shape in our world. The more we think in circles and curves, the more they will express themselves into our physical realm of existence. With our eyes drawn to the curves and circles of nature, we begin to seek solace in these shapes. As we do this we begin to create these gentle shapes in our homes and buildings. Like the highways that curve and ramble along the riverbeds, the buildings and structures along these roads reflect these easy curves. The shape of our habitat is changed by our involvement with the natural world.

The body of the place of our world is intricately connected to our human bodies and we back to that world. As one is affected, so is the other—they go hand-in-hand. Our tears reflect the waters of the ocean, our breath is the wind moving over the landscape, and our heartbeat is a perfect echo of the earth's vibrations. The rain that quenches thirsty grasslands is the same rain that creates the waters in the streams and rivers that we will drink to relieve our own thirst. The healthier our physical landscape remains, the more healthy grow our mindful bodies. They are forever connected.

Pam Greenslate is the founder and director of CASA, Center for Therapeutic Services. Her therapeutic emphasis is on dream work and the use of archetypes and metaphors in daily life. Pam is a Reiki Master/Teacher who combines her therapeutic background with Reiki work to bring a unique approach to her work. She believes that all life is inter-connected, so for humans to heal, we must be willing to heal the world around them.

Touch, Awareness, and a Deepening Relationship with the World

Kevin Filocamo

We normally think of sexuality as a capability to be confined within our own species. But what would it mean to cultivate an erotic relationship with the natural world?

Introduction

From November 2007 to April 2008, as part of my master's thesis, I embarked upon an experiment in which I explored the possibility of cultivating a relationship with the world that was meaningful, healing, *and interpersonal.* The word *interpersonal* is important here, as I wanted to explore the possibility that the Earth (or, in this case, non-human "individuals" that emerge as part of the Earth) could engage me in such a way that I might become familiar with different aspects of their experience, developing a sense of their *interior* experience in such a way that some form of knowing or intimacy might be established between us.

To take this experiment one step further, I entertained the possibility of engaging the world *erotically.* What I mean by erotic engagement is that I explored the possibility that I and a non-human being could "energetically interpenetrate" each other—meaning that

I could "feel into," interact with, and perhaps impact the inner world of a non-human being.[1] And that this non-human entity could also energetically penetrate into my own body and awareness, impacting my experience in fundamental, energetic ways. (For the purposes of this paper, when I write about "energy," I am generally referring to the sensations or vibrations that we feel within our bodies. It is my experience that this "felt-sense" that we have of ourselves changes when we are in physical contact with another being, whether human or non-human.)

I will briefly explain why I embarked upon this exploration, how I prepared myself for this experiment, what tools that I used to engage the being that I worked with during the process (a Monterey Cypress tree, whom I will refer to as "Tree" from now on), and what I learned as a result of this experiment. I am hoping that this writing may inspire readers to explore the potential of relating to the world intimately, and to hold the possibility that a non-human form or being, or even the Earth itself, can reciprocate this intimacy with humans.

The idea that non-human entities living with us on the Earth, or the Earth itself, can share in relational or erotic intimacy (as I've defined it here) challenges the dominant perspective that the world of form lacks awareness or consciousness, and that non-humans have no intelligence (or no intelligence that can offer humans anything of value). Though generally accepted as true, these beliefs have limited our perspective of the physical world (including our own bodies) and our relationship with non-humans, thereby restraining the ways in which we receive communication and relate with these entities. On some levels, this "humancentric-materialistic" worldview has offered us much in terms of a material understanding of how the world and our bodies work. On another level however, this limited perspective has created a sense of alienation from the Earth and our bodies that is creating harm to ourselves, to other creatures, and to this world.

I hold the perspective that some form of consciousness or awareness infuses all of creation. While this consciousness may not be self-reflective, I do believe that humans can experience this consciousness or awareness if we can open ourselves to the possibility that we live in a world that communicates with us and seeks relationship with us.[2] The responsibility for opening to this more intimate relationship with the Earth seems to lie with humans, since we are the ones who closed the door to this intimacy, and in closing ourselves to these relationships, have risked the lives of not only these other beings, but ourselves as well. It is my hope that by opening to intimacy with the Earth, and to beings with whom we share the Earth, we can begin to experience a deeper communion with the world as well as with ourselves, and through this intimacy, invite deeper healing and wholeness for all that exists.

Drawn to this Work

There have been a number of experiences that have opened me to the possibility of a relationship with a living world. One of the most vivid events in my life which suggested that there might be more to the Earth than what appears materially happened in the spring of 2001.

While staying at a retreat center in northern California, I decided one morning to hike along one of the trails that surrounded the valley in which the retreat center is located. At one point during the hike, I stopped to look across the valley toward a small but prominent mountain. As I did so, I suddenly felt an energy that seemed to come from the mountain enter my body through my perineum, and I experienced wave after wave of orgasm. Standing there, not stimulating myself in any way, *I felt the mountain engage me erotically.* Feeling astonished awareness, I laughed as I felt wave after wave of the mountain's energy enter me.

After a while, I asked the mountain to stop. I felt the energy withdraw from me as easily and willingly as it had entered me. I was left with feelings of amazement and wonder, as well as many questions regarding our own embodied experience, and the nature of the world and the beings with which we live.

When I revisit the memory of this experience, I intuit that this encounter was not some random energetic event. Rather, I sense in this experience a connection which seems to have been intended and initiated by the mountain, or some energy contained or "personified" by the mountain. It feels, for me, that it was a very personal encounter. Since then, I have had other experiences with other places that suggest to me some form of consciousness or sentience that infuses all that exists and that may seek to communicate with us. I wanted to explore how I might be more ready and receptive to receive these communications if or when they occurred again.

Another contribution to the exploration began in 2006, when I began to explore the mysteries and wisdom of the body in a process called Holistic Sexuality.[3] Originated by Ramon Albareda and Marina Romero, Holistic Sexuality utilizes a number of embodied meditative exercises designed to awaken us to the unique wisdom our bodies can offer us using touch. The intention in Holistic Sexuality of meditative touch was not to move or change energy, but to allow participants an opportunity to experience what might be stirred in their bodies as a result of the touch, and to bring into conscious awareness information or experiences that may have previously been out of consciousness. In short, the capacity for deeper embodied presence can be facilitated by this *presence-in-touch* (or *presencing* touch). While the touch can be as simple as laying one's hands on another's body, the effects can be deeply felt and illuminating for all participants, whether they are giving or receiving touch. My work with Holistic Sexuality deeply inspired me and became the basis for the techniques and frame of mind with which I employed the touch with Tree. These tools will be described in greater detail below.

Finally, I am motivated by a deeply-felt reverence for Life, and for the Earth which offers and sustains life. This reverence informs the variety of feelings, ideas, and desires that inspired this exploration. As part of this reverence, I feel deep concern about the current environmental crises we are facing. Climate change, mass extinctions of species, shortages in drinking water, food sources, and energy, are all concerns that I share with other people. Some, such as the extinction of species, bring me to tears. I worry about the loss of quality of life that we are creating for ourselves and future generations, and I worry that we are losing something whose value is not fully known. Without developing a relational engagement with the Earth, it is my belief that we cannot know how to slow down the destruction or how to participate in the healing that needs to happen among humans and in the world. In an attempt to contribute to this healing work, I will now briefly describe the relational experiment I embarked upon with Tree.

Exploration

I worked with Tree for five and a half months, from November 2007 through mid-April of 2008. My experiment required that I still my mind and awaken a fuller felt-sense awareness in my body so that I could invite communion with a non-human entity. My companion in this exploration was a Monterey Cypress tree (whom I called "Tree") located in an area of San Francisco's Golden Gate Park called the Panhandle. I felt drawn to this particular tree even before I began the process for reasons that are not fully clear to me, though it may have been the size or strength of the tree and its expansive crown of branches.[4] After attempting to connect with other trees in the area, felt that this particular Monterey Cypress was the "right" tree for me.

The process that I am about to share may be simple to describe but was sometimes difficult to practice. Initially there were fears that nothing would happen, but as I began experiencing changing sensations in my own body that seemed directly related to the contact with Tree, other doubts emerged that I may be "imagining" what I was experiencing, or attributing the experiences to something that had no relationship to what I felt. On other occasions, I resisted being present to myself or to Tree, feeling vulnerable and exposed to the environment around me. Finally, there were times when I felt restless and uncomfortable, waiting for the visit to end. In each of these cases, I brought myself back to the present by re-focusing on my breath and on my awareness of sensations within my body, and bringing awareness to the part of my body that was in contact with Tree.

My intention with each visit was to spend an hour with Tree every week to ten days over a six-month period and journal about my experiences. In that time, I attempted to open my awareness and my body to whatever energies or sensations arose through physical contact with Tree. Generally speaking, the tools that I utilized included mindfulness and touch, accompanied by an attitude of curiosity and an open acceptance of whatever arose (or didn't arise) during the time spent with Tree. I felt that I was attempting to *listen* to Tree with my body's awareness:

I found myself focusing on "listening" to Tree—my straining to wake up and tune in to Tree. Though my head was leaning in towards Tree—as if I were leaning into Tree to hear better with my ears—it felt as if my whole body were leaning closer *into* Tree in an effort to "hear" Tree better (Thesis Journal entry, January 1, 2008). It was as if I used my body as a kind of "tuning fork," attempting to come into some energetic harmony with Tree's energy or experience.

The metaphor of listening became a central one for me during this experiment, one that suggested not only an awareness of the being or environment with which I was interacting, but also an increasingly acute awareness of my own body, especially internally. This metaphor of listening signified my attempts to not only deepen my connection with Tree, but also to deepen awareness of my own body.

To me, listening implied a deeper, more subtle focus than the more habitually-used visual sense. To listen fully, I felt that I needed to move my awareness more deeply within my own being, and from this depth, to invite an experience of the "within" of Tree to enter me. It felt to me that the only way I could sense into Tree's "interior knowing" was to open my body more completely to the felt sense of Tree, and to the physical and energetic sensations of my body as it contacted Tree: to be energetically open and available to receive whatever might be exchanged in this contact with Tree. As I opened my body more completely to the experience, my awareness of myself and Tree seemed to deepen.

This is how I prepared my body for "listening." I started by placing my hands on Tree and, closing my eyes, invited my awareness to "sink into" my body by moving my attention toward what I felt was the core of my being.[5] In this way, my body became an anchor for me and an open vessel for what I might experience. At the same time, I established another anchor, which was the point of physical contact that I shared with Tree and the sensations and awareness that arose when I brought my attention to this experience of contact. At some point, contact might include other parts of my body: my head, my spine, my chest, my abdomen, my pelvis, my feet. Whenever my mind wandered from the connection with Tree or I lost awareness of my body, I used my breath to invite my attention back down into my body and to the area of my body that was in contact with Tree.

This dual or expanded awareness was very important to the process. One of the things stressed in Holistic Sexuality is that each participant stays primarily present to his or her own experience, even if they are offering touch to another participant. This was important to my explorations with Tree because my own felt experience while touching Tree was the only experience I could know. I could not ask Tree about *her* experience. (I am not sure why, but for the most part, I referred to Tree as "she" or "her," and only occasionally as "he" or "him.") My awareness of Tree, and of myself in relation to Tree, could only be experienced by me through sensations and images that arose in my body and in my mind as I made physical contact with Tree.

During my visits with Tree, I was attentive to the sensations, thoughts, and images that arose within my own body, as well as *where* in my body these experiences arose. I noted within my body any fluctuations in energy, any changes in physical sensation, any shifts in my embodied sense of self. In effect, I was expanding my awareness in two ways. By focusing my awareness on the sensations that emerged in the physical contact with Tree, my attention was drawn outside myself and into the environment. At the same time, my awareness became strongly focused on the sensations, emotions, thoughts and images that arose within me as a result of that physical contact with Tree. This effort both expanded and deepened awareness of myself and of Tree (and, to some degree, the environment in which we both were situated).[6]

These encounters produced changes in the ways I experienced Tree, myself and the environment we inhabited. Many of these experiences were subtle shifts in energy felt in my body, an experience I also had whenever I used similar techniques with other humans. A few times, the sensations or energy shifts were so strong that I felt as if particular experiences of Tree (or perhaps, archetypally, *Tree-*

ness) were penetrating my body. During one particularly vivid instance, I felt as if different qualities of Tree's being were penetrating my body as I touched Tree:

> I felt as if Tree's energy were "pushing into" my spine. While remaining aware of my own being—my own subjective experience—I felt myself filling with Tree's experience. The experience was energetic, and it was physically experienced: a sense of the woody experience of Tree entering my body. It felt as if I were becoming a part of Tree's trunk—a bumpy extension of Tree's being (Thesis Journal entry, January 13, 2008).

This was a powerful moment for me. While a fundamental sense of myself remained intact, I simultaneously felt that I was having a direct experience of one aspect of Tree's experience—its "woody character"—in my body. This subtly altered my sense of self, at least for the moments during and immediately following this experience. In ways that are difficult for me to explain, I felt as if I were experiencing the world as a "woody extension" of Tree.

Here is another account that is particularly descriptive of this shift in energy within my body as I connected with Tree. It occurred after some moments of distraction, and I felt as if I was called back to Tree by an energetic "bump" that seemed to come from Tree:

> The connection came after my attention and intention began moving more deeply into my body. I felt a concentration of energy moving into and down my body...I *felt* the contact of my body to the tree, with its relative softness in relation to the relative hardness of the tree...And what was amazing about this experience was that I felt that the tree had somehow reached out its sense of hardness—had in some way "bumped" me to get my attention. It felt as if the tree reached out to me energetically to bring my attention to the contact my body had with the tree—*and the tree with me* (Thesis Journal entry, November 13, 2007, emphasis in original).

With this energetic bump, I felt as if Tree was inviting me back into presence with *her*.

Other qualities of Tree were communicated to me as I became focused on particular aspects of Tree's physicality. For example, during one visit with Tree, I was initially bothered by the hardness of Tree's trunk. I could not find a comfortable place against Tree to rest my body. The experience initially made me feel restless. Then, I somehow quieted the resistance and recognized the possibility that the prominence of the sensation of *hard* during this visit could be an opportunity for me to get to know this quality of Tree's existence: its hardness.

So I surrendered to the somatic experience, holding the possibility that being attentive to and curious about this quality of hardness could be one more step toward knowing Tree more intimately. I later wrote:

> As part of me getting to know Tree, I needed to get to know Tree's hardness, just as I had been fascinated by the contours of Tree's bark in a previous session. I began to try to deeply *listen* to Tree. It felt as if my attention shifted somehow—deeper into my body. I pressed my head and body more closely into Tree. I literally bent my head, striving to get closer, to listen more closely (Thesis Journal entry, December 23, 2007, emphasis in original).

There were other occasions where my attention was drawn to particular aspects of Tree's physical manifestations: the contours of Tree's bark, Tree's height, and the breadth of Tree's root system as it spread beyond the length of my body. In each of these cases, I allowed myself to sink into the experience as one more way to "get to know" Tree more intimately by knowing more completely the details of Tree's experience as they emerged in my awareness.

One particularly *erotic* experience happened as I was sitting with my back against Tree's trunk. Here is how I described it later:

> It started with a quivering in my spine and abdomen...It intensified...The quivering emerged from deeper within me, and

moved powerfully through my abdomen and spine. As I watched and experienced it, it felt similar to times when I've been [penetrated sexually]. Not so much as a full orgasm; more like being filled physically and energetically, and that energy being released in quivering waves that continue...The quivering continued to "wave" through me from deep within me (Thesis Journal entry, March 18, 2008).

As the quivering began to subside, I placed my hands on the earth to help ground me. While I cannot say for certain what the source of this experience might have been, I do believe that the experience arose as a result of the time and energy spent *in open, attentive, embodied contact* with Tree.

During these times of contact, my relationship to the environment around me seemed to at times become more vivid. In one particularly vivid example, I sensed the "aliveness and presence" of the world. After one visit, I described an increased sense of communion with different elements that seemed to come together into this one experience: "the light of the sun shining through the trees...I wondered at all that surrounded me—the trees, the grass, the sunlight, the air, and all that holds or contains it/or all that it holds or contains" (Thesis journal entry, November 22, 2007). This increased felt-sense awareness of each of these elements contributed to the vividness with which I experienced the moment, and the clarity with which I remembered that experience.

My experiences with Tree impacted my sense of self and of the world outside of these encounters. For instance, I was left with a lingering "felt-sense" of Tree even when I wasn't with Tree. After a number of these visits with Tree, I could recall in my body and in my imagination what Tree was like—not only what *she* looked like, but also how *she* felt in my body, and that feeling was unique in my experience. This experience of Tree in my own body and awareness is similar to the experience I have felt when relating intimately with another human. This felt-sense of Tree became so vivid that at least one person commented that I communicated the *feel* of Tree as I described Tree.

I also became more attuned to the "aliveness" of the environment and to those beings with whom I came in contact. My curiosity about these beings' experiences increased, and I felt a stronger sense of compassion for these creatures. For instance, during one visit, I became fascinated by a spider that had made Tree its home; I examined its color and form, and marveled at its stillness. Another experience I had soon after my visits with Tree ended was to try to capture a moth that had become trapped in my room, in order to free it outside. In the past, I would have avoided contact with the moth, or perhaps killed it. During this encounter, I calmly captured it and set it free outside. I had become more aware of the preciousness of each "individual" form or being that exists in the world, and more willing to engage these forms or entities with more curiosity and openness.

Finally, my sense of the wonder and blessing of all that surrounds us and inhabits us increased. I took from this experiment a stronger awareness of the interconnectedness of all beings, and of the impact that the Earth, and the forms and creatures with whom we share this Earth, influence our sense and understanding of who we are. Perhaps more accurately, I sensed that the quality of our awareness of and relationship to these concurrently-emerging forms or "selves" determines, in a fundamental way, our experience of ourselves and our world. These understandings remain with me today.

Conclusion

At my core, I believe that we exist as an interwoven part of the Earth and that the Earth, and the beings with whom we share this world, provide an essential foundation of our own awareness. It is my belief that the healing relational path of humans with other humans, with other creatures, and with the Earth *herself*, must come from a perspective that affords the possibility that we can experience a direct relationship with these other forms of existence.

My desire in this experiment was to offer a possibility, through direct experience, of inviting a meaningful and interpersonal relationship with particular manifestations of matter and life on Earth. It is my hope that we will learn to be in relationship to our own embodied selves, to other beings, and to the Earth in a way that allows us to actively participate in the healing and wholeness of this world *in partnership with* these other beings, and with the Earth. I believe that it is the world, and our dynamic and intimate relationships with the world, that can teach us how to live in harmony with each other and with the Earth, growing as individual beings within *One Being*, toward fulfillment and wholeness.

Endnotes

1 For my thesis, I defined erotic energy as the primary creative and evolutionary energy in the universe. It is the creative life force that moves through all that exists, encouraging interaction and *inter-penetration* among beings...Erotic energy is therefore relational in that it seeks to join, to bring together. Through this joining, new entities or forms may be created. (*The Alluring Universe: Exploring an Erotic Relationship with the World*, December 1, 2008, p. 25, unpublished manuscript)

While I acknowledge that there can be a destructive side to erotic energy, or the ways that erotic energy can be used, I was focusing on the creative and relational qualities of erotic energy, as I continued to do for this writing. Brian Swimme's and Freya Mathews' writings contributed to my evolving understanding of the qualities of the erotic as it is experienced relationally, and the possibilities of engaging the world erotically (see below).

2 I want to mention a few books that support the perspective that the world has some form of sentience or consciousness with which we can engage: Craig Chalquist, *Terrapsychology: Reengaging the Soul of Place* (2007); Christian de Quincey, *Radical Nature: Rediscovering the Soul of Matter* (2002); Freya Mathews, *For Love of Matter: A Contemporary Panpsychism* (2003); Brian Swimme, *The Universe is a Green Dragon: A Cosmic Creation Story* (2001). Each of these books has, in their own way, strengthened for me the possibility of a world that is alive and relational. I'm sure there are others.

3 For more information about Holistic Sexuality, go to http://www.holistic-sexuality.com.

4 One question that arose for me during this process was whether

I "chose" Tree, or Tree "chose" me. Or perhaps we "chose" each other in a mutual attraction that could mirror our attractions to other humans who become our friends or lovers. This question remains alive for me as long as I *imagine* the possibility that the world, and all that emerges from or with the world, is *subject*, meaning that these non-human entities have a capacity for some form of awareness of interior experience—which of course may be different than humans' capacity for awareness of interior experience. And through that awareness, non-human entities can connect with other beings, including humans, in their own distinct and "personal" ways.

5 I don't believe that there is a specific location in the body for one's center or core. It is rather an *experience* of center or ground, and where you experience the center or "core" of your being may differ. The felt-sense of my core is one of dynamic stillness or ground, and relaxed alertness. I believe that the core of one's being is felt with one's intuition and ability to "sense into" or be aware of one's own interior space.

6 I believe that this dual or expanded awareness helps deepen the "knowing" or intimacy between relating beings, whether that encounter is between humans, or between human and non-human beings. By knowing what is happening within yourself as you relate to another, you become more grounded in the experience, and can be more present and responsive to what might arise in the relational encounter.

Kevin Filocamo is the author of the unpublished master's thesis entitled The Alluring Universe: Exploring an Erotic Relationship with the World, *on which this chapter is based. He earned his master's degree in Integral Psychology from John F. Kennedy University in 2008. Kevin currently lives in Seattle Washington, and is hoping to begin offering introductory workshops in Holistic Sexuality in the near future. For more information, please visit www.kevinfilocamo.com.*

Earth Dreaming: An Overview

Karen Jaenke

Dreams carry the wisdom of the natural mind, capable of restoring humanity's psychic kinship with the earth. Considering the human-earth relationship through the lens of dreams provides an approach to the global ecological crisis grounded in human subjectivity and evolutionary psychology. A small sampling of the author's earth dreams point to three themes: earth communing, earth destruction, and earth healing. Earth communing dreams reveal the necessity of recovering psychic and somatic kinship with the earth. Earth destruction dreams ask the dreamer to bear witness to elemental destruction through the earth-body connection. Earth healing dreams show the human-earth relationship is healed through balancing opposites found in the psyche and in nature. Altogether these earth dreams illustrate the process of restoring humans to a participatory relationship with the earth.

Dreaming: The Leading Edge of Creation

In the soft womb of the psyche lay the seeds of all creation. We enter that fertile darkness each night as we dream. Before anything enters into being, it must first enter imagination, and dreaming is the pure font of imagination. This truth is echoed in the Australian Aboriginal creation story, where everything in the universe comes

187

into existence after first emerging in the dreamtime. If humans are to bring forth a new relationship to the Earth, its seeds will be in dreaming. Our dreams express the leading edge of creation.

Dreaming is an ancient biological function present in mammals for 220 million years. Dreams are an information processing system that "evaluate current experience against a store of encoded information...assembled over millions of years of evolution, and...[provide] a reliable template for guiding our actions."[1]

Throughout our human presence on the planet, dreams have served an adaptive survival function, transmitting vital guidance for individuals and communities in times of crisis. We should expect no less, and indeed, far more, amidst the current global ecological crisis, which threatens survival for untold species.

Our current environmental dilemma presents an initiatory threshold for the human species. It announces an evolutionary call to unfold the next phase of species development. Our present-day ecological revolution is akin to three other major human revolutions—the agricultural revolution, the industrial revolution, and the technological revolution. Joanna Macy names our current initiatory threshold the Great Turning.[2]

Global warming presents a crucible for humanity, a heating up in which not only the planet but the human psyche is being cooked for alchemical transformation. Amidst this heating up, dreams offer sacred inklings and divine hints of the collective transformation that is both possible and necessary. Although dreams are only one pathway, they are our greatest source of inspiration and imagination, a perennial friend to the human soul in its trials, travails and triumphs upon earth. As the global crisis heats to boiling point, earth dreams offer the first bubbles of awakening in the planetary imagination.

Each night the universe addresses us personally in our dreams, and we are offered the opportunity to reconnect to our essential relatedness. Dispelling the illusion of separateness, our dreams pull back the veil, revealing the hidden fields of energies into which our lives are cast. We are intimately part of the living splendor that spreads out continuously in every direction; dreams transport us into this seamless fabric of being. Dreams reveal afresh each night the interior depths and hidden threads that bind together the web of life.

Not only do dreams help individuals work through personal psychological issues, the dreaming soul carries and expresses a much larger agenda—as wide as the cosmos itself.[3] Dreams labor to heal the fragmented breaks in our relationships with our deep nature, our nuclear family, our ancestors, the immediate community, and the entire web of earthly life. Dreams restore connection to what is essential. Our immersion in this world—our dreams will help us remember that as well.

The relationship between the individual and the collective, between microcosm and macrocosm, is an intimately interwoven one. Unresolved conflicts in the collective become deposited within the psyche of individuals, where they are carried and suffered by the individual—often escalating towards an unbearable acuteness that demands attention. Through personal angst, individuals are prodded to wrestle with conflicts that are simultaneously personal and collective, so that their own lives can flourish. When tensions in an individual's life closely mirror unresolved tensions held in the collective, the individual soul becomes a cauldron and laboratory for resolving such conflicts. By engaging the deep work of inner wrestling, an individual participates in attending to troubling patterns in the collective. While consciously bearing such conflicts, our dreams may surge with archetypal images that point toward healing resolution for conflicts that cut simultaneously through the individual soul and collective culture. Tending to one's deepest fractures and wounds paradoxically carries medicine for the collective.

A growing chorus of voices today recognizes that collectively as a species, we have reached critical impasse. Here I contend that we must plummet the depths of our own psyches in order to heal the human-earth split, outwardly manifested in our ecological crisis. The most direct bridge from Nature to the human being is through dreams. Indeed, Jung viewed dreams as the language of Nature herself. "Nature speaks to us directly in dreams and myths."[4] Our dreams are the pure voice of the natural mind, offering our best clues, drawn from humanity's ancient database of images, about how to restore the human-earth relationship. Even the chronicle of a single person's dreams can illustrate the process of a dissociated, postmodern person being woven back into the web of life.[5]

This ancient, evolutionary wisdom is available to us because within each of us is a two million year old human.[6] Dreaming sleep is an evolutionary function that allows an animal to update its strategies for survival by integrating the recent experience of the individual with the total behavioral repertoire of the species encoded into the brain.[7] "Our dreams nightly put us in touch with the wisdom of the two million year old human being who exists as a living potential within the collective unconscious of us all."[8]

Earth Communing Dreams

I have been blessed to receive many dreams of the earth. These extraordinarily beautiful and poignant dreams, among my most treasured ones, came over a period of approximately fifteen years at midlife. Each time I come back into contact with them, I re-experience some of their power. Here I recount three of my most significant earth dreams, along with the meanings I made from them.

The first set of earth dreams to appear on the shores of my psyche seemed intent on restoring my psychic connection to the earth, and on mothering me. They provided essential mirroring for a psyche sealed in a void, badly cut off from humanity and the world, through a series of recurring traumas that occurred at birth and in early childhood. Counteracting my extreme psychological isolation, these earth-communing dreams conveyed most dramatically that I was seen in the depths of my being by a larger-than-life presence, and that I belonged intimately to the earth.

One such dream transported me to the deepest place in the ocean, staging an encounter between solitary human and vast ocean:

I float on the surface of the ocean, at the place of its greatest depth. Alone in the expanse of the ocean, I am aware of an unfathomable abyss beneath me. Fear of being swallowed by the force of field of this abyss arises in me. At the mercy of forces unfathomably greater, I experience trepidation and awe. Aware surrender is my sole source of protection in this moment.

Never having traveled remotely near this spot in waking life, the dream inspired geographic curiosity. I imagined the depths of ocean floor to be located somewhere in the vast expanse of the far Pacific. Consultation with a world map confirms the location of the Mariana Trench, near the Mariana Islands, east of the Philippines. The lowest point on earth is Challenger Deep, at the bottom of the Mariana Trench, at a depth of 35,797 feet, nearly seven miles below sea level.[9]

For Carl Jung, the ocean conveyed the fluidity, depths, mystery, and inexhaustibility of the unconscious psyche. For me, the ocean is saturated with personal memories and meanings. As a child, my family made frequent weekend pilgrimages to the Atlantic Ocean, a three-hour drive away. Never was I happier than during this family ritual to visit the ocean goddess. The ocean held a wonder that magically soothed my fractured psyche, although I did not yet have that story. As a child, the ocean simply was a great power and presence, to be revered and enjoyed. Failure to respect her majestic powers brought swift correction—in the form of crashing blows—with sand, surf and self tumbling in a murky mixture of threat and thrill.

The ocean was also a generous giver of pleasure, offering full-bodied caresses in the waves. And she granted endless wonder, along with visual delight—the endless play of shimmering sunlight dancing in motion across the surface of dark, unfathomable depths. Many years later, as a young adult, at a major crossroads in my life, when the psychic waters had all but dried up, I again sought refuge in proximity to the ocean, moving across the continent, far from family and friends, merging my life and destiny with the coastline of that other great ocean, the Pacific.

However, lacking any personal connection to the deepest place in the Pacific Ocean present in the dream, I plunge into searching the subjective meanings of the dream, eventually concluding that the place of greatest oceanic depth offers a mirror for my essential life's work. It speaks of a central psychological necessity of mine—to cultivate a relationship with the depths. The dream, acting as travel agent of the soul, arranges a visit to a place of soul significance that echoes my life calling as one who must learn to swim in the depths of the unconscious and share the fruits of this gift with others.

Individual destiny refers to the purpose and path that fulfills one's potential while bringing alignment with the depths of the soul. Knowledge of one's personal destiny may be accessed through initiatory ordeals that open the gates of visionary perception and through destiny dreams. When a dream reveals an individual's core life purpose, that is a destiny dream.

Such destiny dreams weave us not only into connection with our higher purpose, but also into connection to the earth, tying the threads of biography to the threads of geography. The sacred place that marks one's destiny carries profound personal meaning, recasting a life in a wider web of signification. By aligning with our destiny, the haunting sense of alienation and meaninglessness that stalks modern persons at the edges of awareness is quelled. We find the single thread that connects us to the entire web of life.

Earth-communing dreams may touch places in the soul that have slipped through the safety nets of family and society, reclaiming us as children seen by Mother Earth. Mirroring, mothering, and mending the isolated and wounded soul, earth communing dreams generate in the dreamer deep feelings of kinship between person and place.

Earth communing dreams also inspire and enliven, bestowing infusions of numinous psychic energy. Through the portal of a sacred site, we may be granted entrance into the secret interiority of special places upon the earth. Dreams journeys to sacred places can impart a sense of specialness at being chosen to receive a life-affirming or healing transmission. Such transmissions are simultaneously personal and transpersonal. Something transcendent and objective permeates these revelations, as the scale of forces encountered is so beyond the ordinary as to be transpersonal. The connection to macrocosmic forces can both expand and humble, activating awe and vulnerability before the grandeur of creation.

Dreams of the Earth's Destruction

Once the process of mirroring and mending had rooted in the soil of my psyche, the focus of earth dreams seemed to shift, inviting me to enter into scenes of the earth's destruction. Being met by Mother

Earth in the fractured places of my psyche, next I am asked to witness our earth in her afflictions.

In memorable dream of this kind, a few days after arriving in New Zealand for the first time,

> *I dream of the virgin land of New Zealand being bombed during World War II. As the bomb falls nearby, a small group of us scatter into the woods, hoping to lessen its impact. I feel the bomb's assault enter the earth-body, which is simultaneously my body. My chest cavity, now synonymous with the land, heaves with unspeakable grief and anguish.*

I awaken to the sensation of receiving the bomb's impact into the tissues of my flesh, with tightening across chest cavity and heart. Waves of profound grief roll through me in slow motion. The grief permeates my body, resetting my bio-rhythms to the heavy heaving of heartache. Blanketed by grief, I lay still, breathing and absorbing unspeakable sorrow, for a long, long time. Ever so gradually the tightness and heaviness in my chest begins to lift. Then comes awareness of the pulsing of my heart, a surging in the midst of this weighty expanse of grief. Pain concentrates there. This is no ordinary human emotion, but a deep and enduring grief, wide as the landscape.

As my mind rises above the grief, I recall a recent conversation with a man whose pastime is playing internet war games, flying World War II (WWII) virtual airplanes in a squadron with other New Zealand flyers. Intrigued and puzzled by his passion for flying virtual bombers, I am vaguely aware of a gender gap at the level of imagination. Now that shadowy vagueness coalesces into something more explicit. A vast gulf stands between his way of relating to WWII air bombings, via internet games, and my way, through dreaming, receiving the grief of war in the cells of my body.

The dream presents a story at odds with the dominant cultural story of triumph that accompanies military victory. Beneath this heroic story lies another, hidden story that seems to reside in the recesses of bodily tissue. Wartime bombing brings a wound to the chest, a wound to the heart of the earth. Although the purported target of war is some human enemy, bombing involves a direct assault upon the earth.

Within the altered consciousness of the dream, a merging of human body and earth body takes place. My body, transformed into oneness with the earth body, absorbs the assault suffered by the earth into my own consciousness. In the gestalt of the dream, the human body becomes a conduit for the earth body. The interiority of the subtle body serves as a bridge to the interiority of the earth. My life feels strangely sacralized by the dream.

The dream evokes a topography where human body and earth body join in holographic relationship. Similar patterns, arising across vast differences of scale, generate a single field of participatory knowing. The patterns of the larger reverberate within the smaller, the planetary within the personal. In these fluid intersections between microcosm and macrocosm, interchanges of knowing between human and earth and are mediated through the organ of the subtle body.

The dream also catalyzes a shift in identification—from the culture of supremacy that drops bombs and plays war games, to the recipient of this action, the earth body. Under the spell of the dream, consciousness shifts from wartime actor to embodied receptor. Entering the standpoint of the earth receptively, one apprehends the speechless sufferings endured by the earth body.

The dream offers clues concerning successive shifts in consciousness necessary to restore psychic kinship with the earth. Implied as a first step is the releasing of our fantasy of violence as a game. A second step entails bending imagination to experience— from a receptive place—the impact of human violence on the earth, entering the other side of our aggression and violence, from the recipient's perspective and allowing this awareness to sink into the caverns of cellular knowing.

From these depths, a profound grief, locked within the human heart, opens. Surrendering to waves of grief awakens buried kinship feelings for the earth. With this awakening of affective ties to the earth body, it is a small additional step to relinquish our species' role as enactors of violence upon the earth.

Earth Healing Dreams

A third set of earth dreams, appearing more recently, move beyond entering into immediate perception the earth's destruction, providing intimations of healing energies that follow destruction. These dreams offer images of forces that effectively counter-balance destruction.

I moved from San Francisco to the Pt. Reyes Peninsula in 1996, a few months after the 1995 Mt. Vision fire ravaged the Inverness Ridge, the backbone of the peninsula. Twelve years later, the fire instead burns in my soul. I dream of fire burning out of control on the Point Reyes Peninsula, my beloved home for the last dozen years.

Standing in front of the Inverness Ridge, I watch the fire climbing the far side of the ridge, nearing the summit. Against a glowing bright orange background, darkened sticks of timber at the crest of the ridge succumb to the flames. Like a row of blackened pick-up sticks, each tree along the summit falls backwards into the orange mass of flames, dropping one after another, in a strange syncopated rhythm. I am horrified to watch this beloved landscape undergoing destruction. With all my being, I want to act, to do something, to halt the devastation.

In parallel with the dream, my body is undergoing the fiery ravages of menopause, my skin crawling with sensations of needles, pricking indistinguishably from inside and out. My treasured job of seven years is in jeopardy, the entire work environment spinning into chaos and upheaval. My blood boils in protest, pounding fiercely against the vessels meant to contain it.

Ironically, two months after the dream, I move my residence to a cottage situated directly beneath Mt. Vision, the site where the first sparks of the 1995 fire ignited. During these same months, I visit an old lover, who re-sparks my affections, casting my choices and commitments of the last quarter century up in the air. My life situation is summed up by the dream's stark and piercing imagery: the entire landscape I have inhabited for the last twelve years is undergoing rapid-fire destruction. The dream signifies a major transition ahead: my identity, constructed over the last dozen years, will succumb to sudden demolition.

Yet the fire dream is followed one week later by a dream of *retreating to the mountains for ten days, in order to "listen to the sound of the snow."* In this pair of dreams, extreme heat and rapid destruction are counterbalanced by the cool stillness and timelessness of the mountains, resting under a blanket of snow. Immersion in profound silence and contemplative solitude are shown as the means for restoring equilibrium following fire and chaos. While the snow dream offers practical guidance about how to balance the dynamics of overheating and burning within a single human life, it also suggests how these grand energies are balanced on vast scales within nature. In the pair of fire and snow dreams, the cool stillness and silence of the snowy mountains is offered as the balancing agent for restoring equilibrium following the fire's destruction.

The Ecology of Earth Dreams

In my twenty-year journey through the dream landscape, the earth dreams appearing along the path have led to the recovery of psychic kinship with the earth. The path, which began in dissociated fog, led to exquisite moments being of mirrored and met in the depths of my wounds by the Earth herself.

Then the path came upon horrific scenes of earth destruction, asking that I return the gift of mirroring, by witnessing and by feeling—in the cellular knowing of my body—the sufferings of the earth.

And finally, the path arrived at nature's secret: her amazing potential for reversal! The hot raging fire of destruction is followed by forces of reversal—the soothing coolness, stillness and silence of mountain snow.

In this series of earth dreams, the thematic patterns of earth communing, earth destruction and earth healing might suggest archetypal patterns of earth dreams appearing in our time. Dreams reveal that it is our intimacy with nature, our psychic kinship with the earth body, that can heal our planetary wounds. And this oneness with the earth body is reached through the humble doorway of the human body.

Earth communing dreams invite a deep feeling connection, or subjective re-enchantment, with the earth. Oozing with vitality, earth communing dreams evoke awe and fascination, commanding attention and respect. They also address gaps in the mirroring function of mothering, granting experiences of being seen in one's uniqueness by the Great Earth Mother. These dreams suggest that the initial step in recovering kinship with the earth is the subjective encounter with the earth's elemental life force. According to Brian Swimme and Thomas Berry,

> Without [the] entrancement...[that] comes from the immediate communion of the human with the natural world, a capacity to appreciate the ultimate subjectivity and spontaneities within every form of natural being...it is unlikely that the human community will have the psychic energy needed for the renewal of the Earth.[10]

Earth communing dreams bathe the dreamer in the same bath of animating energy that washes over the planet. Experiences of this participatory field serve to reawaken psychic kinship between dreamer and earth.

Dreams that weave us back into a soulful connection with the earth may serve as preparation for engaging with a more difficult type of dream: confronting destruction upon the earth. Such dreams feature cataclysmic events with massive destruction and upheaval. Sometimes the destruction pictured originates in the natural world; other times, it is manmade.

We may wonder about the deeper purposes behind earth destruction dreams, so let's consider this phenomenon further. Natural catastrophe dreams can assist us in sorting out our relationship to the great powers of nature. As Swimme and Berry remind us:

> Violence and destruction are dimensions of the universe. They are present at every level of existence: the elemental,

the geological, the organic, the human. Chaos and disruption characterized every era of the universe, whether we speak of the fireball, the galactic emergence, the later generations of stars, or the planet Earth.[11]

Dreams of massive destruction can help us to confront and accept this natural and inevitable part of the great drama of creation, even informing our actions in the face of it. The staggering emotions these dreams evoke speak to the reality of our interwoven relationship to the earth, that what happens to the earth happens to us.

Being in the presence of unleashed elemental forces, whether in waking or dreaming, can awaken a profound sense of awe, aliveness and participation. Boundaries between self and world dissolve when such elemental potency is loosened in the environment. Developing a felt relationship with these elemental powers ultimately allows one to feel more at home on the earth. Coming into a conscious, respectful relationship with the grand forces of the natural world is part of becoming a whole human being, capable of living authentically as a participant in the unfolding story of the earth.

Dreams of natural disasters often parallel cataclysmic changes happening in the dreamer's personal life, appearing during major life transitions, when our identity undergoes radical transformation. Upheaval and change in the human psyche is regularly depicted in dreams through tumultuous macrocosmic events.

Still we should not assume that all natural disaster dreams are necessarily or only psychological in their import. Some disaster dreams may be premonitions or preparations for actual events, and others may ask the dreamer to become a psychic carrier of prior catastrophes, to bear some of the psychological weight of historical collective events. Given that disasters, whether natural or manmade, carry widespread impact, they require a collectively-shared effort to be metabolized psychologically.[12]

Cultivating an attitude of respect and reverence towards powers greater than ourselves as revealed in dreams can aid our survival in the midst of an actual catastrophe, rendering our judgments more appropriate to the acute necessities of the moment. Facing these grand forces with humility, we become psychically open to receiving vital guidance from beyond in a life-and-death moment.

Witnessing cataclysmic events in nature often elicits terror in the dreamer. Earth destruction dreams ask the dreamer to come into relationship not only with overwhelming destructive images, but also with our human capacity for terror. To stay in conscious relationship with the energies of terror requires acquiring a capacity to metabolize the intense physiological and emotional states activated by the human terror response. Full-blown terror, associated with the responses of fight, flight, freeze and appease, has been estimated to be many times that of orgasm![13]

The process of learning to metabolize fear requires remaining present and aware amidst acute physiological arousal that tends to scatter awareness. It requires progressively overcoming dissociative tendencies that eject awareness from the body—by cultivating mindfulness and presence amidst the swirling of fear, akin to the calm center in the eye of a hurricane.

When one faces the data about the extinction of species, depletion of resources, destruction of habitats, and imminent global warming, planet Earth may seem doomed. But I have noted that dreams of the earth, when taken altogether, do not yet pronounce this outcome. While they do confront us with shocking and terrifying scenes of destruction, acting as a wake-up call, they also provide clues about processes necessary for earth healing. Earth destruction dreams may be accompanied by dream images that show what is necessary for healing our relationship to the earth.

A third category of earth dreams concerns healing the human-earth relationship. These dreams address questions such as: How can the tide of destructive energies—unleashed upon the earth by many generations of human beings, now reaching a critical tipping point—be turned towards healing? What do our dreams say about healing in relation to the planet? What elements are necessary for earth healing, from the perspective of dreams?

Earth healing is frequently portrayed as a matter of balancing opposing forces that have become grossly imbalanced. This principle of balance appears frequently in earth dreams. When burning heat meets cooling balm, coastal fire scenes shift to mountain snow scenes, a balancing of forces is implied. A dreamer floats on the surface of the ocean, directly above the depths, with an implicit expectation of bridging the two. These images affirm an ancient wisdom that opposing forces must be balanced in the creation and sustenance of life.

There are perhaps endless dream examples of a realignment that restores balance after the hyper-manifestation of one element that becomes inimical to the balance of the whole. Sky and earth, spirit and matter, fire and water, light and dark, solar and lunar, upper and lower, ascent and descent, masculine and feminine, north and south, hot and cold, surface and depths, form pairs of opposites forever being reconciled in our dreams. These same balancing principles figure prominently in dreams of the earth.

The principle of balance is profoundly understood by indigenous peoples, informing the ecological, cultural, and psycho-spiritual practices that enabled humans to flourish in harmony with the natural world for millennia. Apela Colorado of the Oneida tribe distilled nine tenets of indigenous science, highlighting the principle of balance:

> The purpose of indigenous science is to maintain balance...The end point of an indigenous scientific process is a known and recognized place. This point of balance, referred to by my own tribe as the Great Peace, is both peaceful and electrifyingly alive. In the joy of exact balance, creativity occurs, which is why we can think of our way of knowing as a life science...When we reach the moment/place of balance we do not believe that we have transcended—we say that we are normal. Always we remain embodied in the natural world.[14]

Ancient wisdom recognized balance as the deep and abiding principle that secretly permeates all of life, the dynamism behind the unfolding of the universe. Earth dreams return us to this ancient, healing wisdom of balance.

Endnotes

1 Stevens, Anthony, and Price, John, *Evolutionary Psychiatry* (Clifton, NJ: Routledge, 2000), p. 204.

2 Macy, Joanna, *Coming Back to Life: Practice to Reconnect Our Lives, Our World* (Stony Creek, CT: New Society Publishers, 1998).

3 Jaenke, Karen, "Ode to the Intelligence of Dreams," *ReVision,* no. 27(1): 2-9.

4 Stevens, Anthony, *The Two Million-Year-Old Self* (College Station: Texas A&M University Press, 1993), p. 30.

5 Freud and Jung both built their models of the psyche based upon keen observations of dreams, their own and others.' At the frontiers of human consciousness, our dreams, and other altered states, may well be our most reliable informants, guides and teachers.

6 Stevens, *The Two Million-Year-Old Self.*

7 Stevens, *The Two Million-Year-Old Self.*

8 Stevens, *The Two Million-Year-Old Self,* p. 36.

9 Located in the Mariana Islands group, at the southern end of the Mariana Trench, Challenger Deep is a relatively small slot-shaped depression in the bottom of a considerably larger crescent-shaped trench, which itself is an unusually deep feature in the ocean floor. "Earth Structure" [article on-line]; available from http://en.wikipedia.org/earth_structure; Internet; accessed 13 July, 2009.

10 Swimme, Brian, and Berry, Thomas, *The Universe Story: From the Primordial Flaring Forth to the Ecozoic Era* (San Francisco: HarperSanFrancisco, 1992), p. 268.

11 Swimme and Berry, *The Universe Story,* p. 51-52.

12 Herman, Lisa, "Engaging Images of Evil: An Imaginal Approach to Historical Trauma". *ReVision,* no. 31(1), p. 44-52.

13 Levine, Peter, *Waking the Tiger: Healing Trauma* (Berkeley, CA: North Atlantic Books, 1997).

14 Colorado, Pamela, "Indigenous Science and Western Science—A Healing Convergence" (Presentation at the World Sciences Dialog I, New York City, April 25-27, 1994), p. 1-2.

Karen Jaenke, MDiv, PhD, has taught qualitative research, dream studies, imaginal psychology, group process, and professional identity courses at various Bay Area graduate schools during the last dozen years. She is an executive editor of ReVision: Journal of Consciousness and Transformation, *where she has edited issues on Imaginal Psychology, Shamanism, the Wounded West, and Earth Dreaming, and contributed various articles on dreams, participatory knowing, evil, and shamanism. A graduate of Princeton Seminary and the California Institute of Integral Studies, her dissertation* Personal Dreamscape as Ancestral Landscape *explored the power of dreams to recover deep memory and indigenous ways of knowing. She founded Dreamhut Consulting (www.dreamhut.org), where she offers dissertation coaching, dream work and hypnotherapy consulting services from Point Reyes, CA.*

Things

Hush

this timepiece I carry
is not yet calibrated
to the movement of light on rocks
though I am learning

and each time a bird flies overhead
and the velvet fwap fwap of its wings
reaches down into my ears
and strums the lyre in my chest
I am that much closer
to knowing the precise moment
when frogs will start and stop speaking
and which leaf the wind will sing to first
and whether the clouds over there
are coming to meet the mountain behind me

slow and patiently won
is this jewel-toned art
of listening with the star-shaped ears of the skin
and tracing the inner linings of things
with soft brushes in the belly

for this classroom
of forest floor and wide sky
is a place we learn by waiting
as its inhabitants, ginger and wary
slowly fill us with music
and light the candles behind our eyes
and nudge us gently
this way and that
until we are moving
with the turning of the earth

—Catherine Baumgartner

"Between Honey and Pain": Colony Collapse Disorder and the Colonization of the Wild

Bonnie Bright

Control and colonization in the name of culture has led to a loss of soul and a disconnection from both inner and outer nature. Although the root of cultivate *means to tend, honor or cherish, our tendency to tame, control, and avail ourselves of the natural "other" takes us further from the wild potentiality of nature (and human nature) than ever before. Our pathological estrangement from wilderness has led to increasing objectification, colonization, and violence. Further, humankind's history with honeybees is a story representative of the western inclination toward objectification, domination, and enslavement of nature, animals, and even our fellow human beings: a story that may well end in crisis and an ultimate colony collapse of our own.*

Some say the world began long ago in ancient Egypt when the goddess Neith emerged from the primordial waters and gave birth to Ra, the sun, and then flew away in the form of a bee. She established her sacred temple, called the House of the Bee, in the middle of the Nile delta in Sais in Lower Egypt where it stands to this day.[1]

That bees would be connected to wild creativity, to sacred places, to wilderness itself, is appropriate. Pulitzer Prize-winning poet Gary Snyder defines wilderness as a "place where the wild potential is fully expressed,"[2] associating it with richness, energy, Eros, chaos, ecstasy, and the unknown. He quotes John Milton, who alludes to it as a place of abundance and "a wildernesse of sweets."[3] In the wild, Snyder so often contends, imagination and the body rise unbidden, wild and otherly in nature.

The opposite of wild is *cultivation*.[4] *Cultivate*, from the Medieval Latin *colere,* means to prepare and use for raising crops, to foster the growth of, to improve by labor, or to care for.[5] According to Snyder, something or someone that is cultivated has weeded out the wild from their nature. Our *culture* (based on the same root) considers this tempering of the wild a positive step, though it has not always been the ideal. It is a dilemma I know well, surfacing in bittersweet memories of raking the earth on the family farm of my childhood to rid it of wildflowers disparaged as weeds, and of befriending sweet baby calves or pigs as I fed them each day, only to see them turn up on the family dinner table.

Sometime in the Neolithic Age ten to twelve thousand years ago, the human animal first turned the earth with a sharp stick in order to plant large quantities of seeds, to deliberately *cultivate* them into fields of single crops, and wildness changed forever.[6] A distinction, a *division,* arose. Wildness became something *else*; something other than what we could predict, control, or manipulate. Just like the farm on which I was raised, what we could not control was labeled *wild*, was feared in its chaos and unpredictability. Wildness was not known, not familiar, not a friend, and therefore it became a foe. Wildness, wilderness, became *otherness* which we sought to improve, to control at all costs; even to colonize. Wild animals that could not be domesticated were fenced out, run off, or killed. Wild territories had to be conquered and tamed. No longer was wildness numinous, sacred, or inspiring of awe; instead it seemed foreign, frightening, and strange.

As human animals, we set ourselves apart from Milton's *wilder-*

nesse of sweets, separating human from nature and mind from body. Today, divided from ourselves and our natural place in the fabric of being, we fearfully observe and condemn the unexpected. Unconsciously and perhaps unwillingly, I, like many of us, stifle the wild, creative impulse, building instead a hierarchy where humans reign isolated and supreme: ultimately, a sinister trap. As diversity disappeared, so did wild power, passion, uniqueness, honoring of otherness and mystery. Thus, with the loss of wild, we also lost our awe of it, and a sense of its sacredness.[7]

The cultivation of the earth has had devastating results, converting it from a living force to a dead object that could be manipulated and controlled. Jared Diamond, another Pulitzer Prize-winning author, deems it "the worst mistake in the history of the human race."[8] Craig Chalquist points out that despite numerous benefits, the first systematic plowing of the earth also led to "a sense of separation from Home that over time has overdeveloped into pathological estrangement—pathological for us as well as for the planet."[9] Paul Shepard writes,

Wildness, pushed to the perimeters of human settlement during most of the ten millennia since the Pleistocene, has now begun to disappear from the earth, taking the word's otherness of free plants and animals with it. The loss is usually spoken of in terms of ecosystems or the beauty of the world, but for humans, spiritually and psychologically, the true loss is internal.[10]

That loss, Shepard asserts, "is our own otherness within."[11]

Colonization and Collapse

Honeybees preceded humans by nearly a hundred million years. In Africa and Spain, 25,000 year old rock art depicts humans gathering and eating honey from wild bees.[12] Honey was sacred to the Maya of Central America, as it was in Egypt, Israel, India, China, Greece, and Rome. It has long been valued for its medicinal and antiseptic properties. Additionally, honey was virtually the only sweetener available until the discovery and mass cultivation of sugar cane in the New World in the 17th century.[13]

Bees live in *colonies,* distinguishable localized populations within a species.[14] Ironically, the word *colony* stems from the same

Latin root as "cultivate": *colere* means to honor, cherish, worship, live in, inhabit, or till. Unfortunately, over time, cultivation has given way to colonization.

Queen Elizabeth commissioned Sir Walter Raleigh to establish an early European colony as a foothold in the New World. Founded in 1587, the colony of ninety men, seventeen women, and nine children of Roanoke was dependent on local Native Americans for supplies and food. When times grew lean, the British colonists resorted to manipulation, extortion, and threats to obtain what they wanted. Relations between the invading Europeans and the Native American Indians quickly became strained as worldviews and values clashed.[15] In one deplorable attempt to terrorize and control the "untamed savages," the British burned the Indian village Aquascogok; in response, the Indians disrupted and destroyed the colonists' fish and animal traps. All-out war broke out between the natives and the demanding newcomers. By 1590, when British ships finally arrived with supplies and fortifications, the colonists had vanished, leaving behind only a troubling mystery that was never solved.

Centuries later, an eerie parallel has arisen in yet another colony: this time one of bees. Like many species, honeybee populations have been declining steadily since the mid-1900s, dropping from six million commercial colonies in 1944 to only three million by 1980.[16] Researchers attribute these troubling decreases to disease, parasites, pesticides, and various alterations of the environment. Not only insecticide use, but housing and business development, deforestation, and depletion of natural resources have wiped out many native habitats and plants that bees visit to gather nectar and pollen. Our forays into genetically modified crops and insect-proof pesticides repel bees from plants that once were a staple. Overall, massive colonization of the earth has resulted in deforestation of natural habitats and the loss of many plant and flower species. Increased pollution coats leaves, petals, and the wings of bees and blocks the sunlight by which they typically navigate.[17]

Additionally, loss of genetic integrity among commercialized bees has also created concern. For example, Michael Schacker refers to a "genetic bottleneck" in which all commercial queens now come from fewer than 500 breeder queens, resulting in a dramatic decrease in biodiversity and therefore of immunity and resilience to new threats.[18]

In 2006, an new and inexplicable phenomenon found beekeepers removing the lids of beehives for routine maintenance only to find the hives empty except for the queen and a few of her attendants. The queen, the abundant stores of honey, and the developing brood had all been completely abandoned. The bees were nowhere to be found, seeming to have vanished as completely as the lost colonists of Roanoke.

The menacing absences spread. By the spring of 2007, one-fourth of beekeepers in the United States reported losing over 30% of all their honeybees. In early 2008, total die-offs reached 36% in the U.S. and 60% in France.[19] Within weeks of each other, Australia, Brazil, Canada, China, Europe, and other nations reported that honeybees were vanishing by the billions. The bizarre absence of even dead bees has led experts to believe that the bees are dying uncharacteristically far away and alone, widely dispersed from the hive.[20]

Termed *Colony Collapse Disorder* due to entire colonies dying out almost overnight, this disturbing mass exodus of the bees remains ominous and incomprehensible. It is hard to imagine what their disappearance might mean. In addition to providing honey, honeybees are responsible for one of every three bites of food we eat, pollinating the majority of our fruits and vegetables along with cotton and alfalfa, a primary food for livestock.[21] The growing loss of the bees leaves a roaring silence, a growing void in the ecosphere that threatens to swallow the agricultural world we know.

Colonization: A Cross-Species Disorder

This contemporary catastrophe has ancient roots. Across millennia, human beings learned to cultivate bees as they did much of the rest of the natural world. The earliest evidence of beekeeping was discovered in 2007 in Tel Rehov, Israel, dating from the 10th to early 9th centuries BCE. Nearly thirty cylindrical clay and mud beehives stacked one upon another were uncovered in an excavation along with pots for storing honey and fertility figurines, marking the site as sacred.[22]

Since then we have largely lost touch with the sacred aspect of *cultivation*, originally associated with tending, honoring, and cherishing the living thing we aim to develop. Methods of beekeeping from the Middle Ages show little evidence of tending or cherishing bees that provided sweet honey to satisfy human desires. In medieval Europe, bees were often suffocated, crushed, drowned in a tub of water, or poisoned to death in order to obtain their honey. In a brutal procedure called "brimstoning" practiced in Europe and elsewhere, colonies of bees were asphyxiated and burned in hives placed over a fire billowing deadly sulfur to leave the golden honeycombs free for the taking.[23]

Other aspects of nature fared no better. As industrialists systematically plundered the earth and its ecosystems in an ongoing thirst for *cultivation*, the quest to possess and improve advanced along with its harsh cousin *colonization*, the urge to occupy and dominate. With *slash-and-burn* farming, which eliminates native flora and heavily erodes and saps the soil,[24] and massive deforestation that has devastated up to 80% of wooded areas in Europe, China, and South America,[25] the destruction of native life through burning, drowning, disregard, and abuse advanced from trees and bees to humans.

As the desire to dominate and possess continued to grow, suffering increased, and an increasing fear of "other" swept the globe in the form of witch-hunts from the 15th to 18th centuries, mirroring the same unconscious cruelty and lack of regard for life with which honey was once harvested. Minorities and those at the margins of society—women, shamans, and medicine people who knew the old ways of herbs, rituals, and nature spirits—were accused, put on trial, and hanged, drowned, beheaded, or burned at the stake.[26] Even bees, because they provided a valuable and controllable commodity, likely fared better.

Fear of the "other" was not the only justification for violence and persecution. With the discovery of the so-called "New World," the insatiable hunger to command the wild, to tame, and to possess accessible resources multiplied as colonists set foot on previously unexplored territory and claimed it as their own, disregarding the indigenous inhabitants who had flourished there for millennia. These and later acts of colonization nearly always included exploitation, usurpation of land, rights, customs, and culture, and the wresting of profit from others.[27] Up to 90% of native peoples in Australia, Hawaii, and the New World were wiped out by violence, war, displacement, forced marches, and newly introduced diseases against which they had no immunity.

Wildlife and ecosystems also continued to suffer. The callous practices that, centuries before, had led to the extinction of bears in England expanded as European colonizers in the New World oversaw the decimation and displacement of the bison and of fifteen million pronghorn along with a good portion of the native soils and grasslands.[28]

Commercial beekeeping enterprises have continued to grow as mass crop production around the world steadily increases. In California, for example, the almond harvest has been lucrative for commercial beekeepers. Almonds, a two billion dollar industry in California, require intense cross-pollination performed primarily by honeybees.[29] An estimated 1.5 million hives, more than two-thirds of all the commercial colonies in the entire U.S., are needed every year in order to achieve this. Pallets of bees are crammed onto trucks and shipped up to three thousand miles over burning tarmac, in sweltering temperatures, and through heavy traffic fumes. Some beekeepers admit they expect to lose 10% of their bees on the trek, a forced march that is the bees' own trail of tears.

Once on site, in lieu of nutritious pollen they collect later in the year, bees are fed sweetened corn syrup to simulate an early spring, triggering them to reproduce prematurely to generate enough worker bees to pollinate the almonds. Malnourished and exposed to a heavy dose of pesticides from surrounding fields, nearly half the bees in the country are massed together without regard for their natural needs. As a result, parasites and diseases often spread rapidly between colonies. It was during the annual mass assembly of bees in the almond groves of California that the deadly *varroa* mite contagion was first reported. Within a few years it had spread to nearly every managed bee colony in the U.S.[30]

Colonized Labor

Treating bees as free labor sounds an alarming echo of other acts of colonization.

A few centuries ago, the quest to harvest something sweet had led to another forced journey. When Spanish conquistadors embarked at Jamaica in the 16th century, the island's native Arawak Indians inhabited the island. Quickly enslaved and forced into harsh labor, the Indians were rapidly decimated by disease and abuse. Many are said to have committed suicide in order to escape untenable living conditions; desperate mothers even murdered their children rather than see them enslaved.[31] With the extinction of their slave labor, colonizers rapidly turned to African slaves to maintain the intense labor demands of the sugar cane fields. At the height of its production, Jamaica imported five thousand slaves per year from western Africa by rounding then up like cattle, shackling them, and shipping them across the ocean in cramped, inhumane conditions without regard for their origins, tribes, customs, languages, health, or humanity.[32]

As for the bees, brutal exploitation of their labor continues. In medieval times they were used as a weapon of war, with whole hives dropped over ramparts onto the heads of an attacking enemy. Today, bees are trained to locate chemical explosives or unexploded landmines that riddle the once-sacred landscapes of war-torn nations.[33] Bees have also been turned into laboratory cocaine addicts to learn more about the nature of addiction in humans.[34]

Civilization Collapse Disorder?

The abrupt decline of the bees after such a long time on earth draws to mind images of the Classic Maya people of Central America who, after flourishing for over a millennium, suddenly and purposely abandoned their vast cities between 800 and 900 CE and vanished to parts unknown.[35] Like the vanishing of the bees, the mystery of the Maya remains unsolved, but increasing evidence suggests that deforestation played a significant role in their disappearance. As more and more trees were cut down to build enormous metropolitan areas and to clear land for farming, local ecosystems were deeply impacted, resulting in heavy erosion and drought. No longer able to sustain itself, their highly advanced civilization collapsed.

Myth has it that when Ra cried, his tears were bees.[36] If bees are tears, then our tears, perhaps along with our capacity for compassion, are drying up at an alarming rate as the primordial life-giving waters from which the goddess Neith emerged recede as well. Drought has set in on many levels as deforestation of the collective psyche takes its toll.

The devastating decline of the honeybees raises unsettling questions about whether the bees are acting as the proverbial canary in a coal mine, foreshadowing the imminent demise of the human race as we plummet toward a colony collapse of our own. In his recent book *A Spring Without Bees*, Michael Schacker muses on the mythical as well as biological implications of CCD, referring to it as a potential *Civilization* Collapse Disorder.[37]

Regarding the colonizer, Memmi declares, "To live without anguish, one must live in detachment from oneself and the world."[38] Yet the "hum" of a bee in flight is also found in "human" and connects to "humus," meaning "earth."[39] By listening in on the silence left by the vanishing bees, the bison, the trees, and the tribes that have been lost, by letting it echo inside the landscape of our own psyche to hear where it travels, how it moves, and what it wants, we awaken to our work. Bees gather nectar to make sweet honey, the *prima materia* that becomes liquid gold. "Nectar," comes from the word "nek," meaning "death," and "tar," "to overcome."[40] Overcoming the history we have wrought requires a homecoming, a reunification of action and place like the natural act of countless bees coming back to the hive after a long day's work.

Poet Mary Oliver describes how the taste of honey is composed of "everything lost that is found."[41] In a sonnet, Pablo Neruda reflected evocatively on an ongoing struggle, a journey "between honey and pain."[42] By facing ecological anguish and reflecting on it, we begin to address the parts of ourselves that have been left arid, deforested, scattered, and alone. In fully engaging, we discover a song in the silence, the hum of longing to cross-pollinate a reciprocal relationship between bees and bodies, peoples and plants, humans and humus. We find ourselves opening, like a flower, to the wild.

Endnotes

1 "On the Symbolism of the Bee in the Occult Tradition." Polaris. http://www.polarissite.net/page26.html

2 Snyder, Gary. *The Practice of the Wild*. Shoemaker & Hoard, 1990.

3 Ibid, p. 12.

4 Ibid.

5 Dictionary.com. *The American Heritage® Dictionary of the English Language, Fourth Edition*. Houghton Mifflin Company, 2004. http://dictionary.reference.com/browse/

6 Chalquist, Craig. "Mind and Environment: A Psychological Survey of Perspectives Literal, Wide, and Deep." Unpublished presentation given at JFK University, Pleasant Hill, CA, October 2006. http://www.terrapsych.com/mindandenvironment.html

7 Snyder, Gary.

8 Diamond, Jared. "The Worst Mistake in the History of the Human Race," *Discover*, May 1987, p. 65.

9 Chalquist, Craig.

10 Shepard, Paul. *Coming Home to the Pleistocene*. Island Press, 1998, p. 143.

11 Ibid.

12 Jacobsen, Rowan. *Fruitless Fall: The Collapse of the Honey Bee and the Coming Agricultural Crisis*. Bloomsbury USA, 2008.

13 Ransome, Hilda M. *The Sacred Bee in Ancient Times and Folklore*. Dover Publications, 2004.

14 Dictionary.com.

15 Markham, Edwin, ed. "Princess & Cavalier: The Age of Colonization 1570-1620." In *The Real America in Romance: An Authentic History of America. Vol. IV*. William H. Wise & Company, 1912.

16 Schacker, Michael. *A Spring without Bees: How Colony Collapse Disorder Has Endangered Our Food Supply*. The Lyons Press, 2008.

17 Fountain, Henry. "Supernavigator's Secret." *The New York Times*,ober 28, 2003, F3. What does F3 mean?

18 Schacker.

19 Benjamin, Allison and McCallum, Brian. *A World without Bees*. Pegasus Books, 2009.

20 Stipp, David. "Flight of the Honeybee." *Fortune* 156, no. 5, 2007.http://money.cnn.com/magazines/fortune/fortune_archive/200 7/09/03/100202647/index.htm

21 Kolbert, Elizabeth. "Stung." *New Yorker*, August 6, 2007, p. 52-59.

22 Friedman, Matti. "Archaeologists Discover Ancient Beehives." *Washington Post*, September 4, 2007. http://www.washingtonpost.com/wp-dyn/content/article/2007/09/04 /AR2007090400886.html?tid=informbox

23 Ellis, Hattie. *Sweetness and Light*. Three Rivers Press, 2004.

24 Diamond, Jared. *Collapse: How Societies Choose to Fail or Succeed*. Penguin, 2005.

25 Glendinning, Chellis. *My Name Is Chellis and I'm in Recovery from Western Civilization*. New Catalyst Books, 1994.

26 Pavlac, Brian A. *Witch Hunts in the Western World: Persecution and Punishment from the Inquisition through the Salem Trials*. Greenwood Press, 2009.

27 Memmi, Albert. *The Colonizer and the Colonized*. Beacon Press, 1965.

28 Mann, Charles C. *1491: New Revelations of the Americas before Columbus*. Vintage Books, 2006.

29 Kolbert. "Stung."

30 Ibid.

31 Floyd, Berry. *Jamaica: An Island Microcosm*. Saint Peters Press, 1979.

32 Ibid.

33 Jacobsen.

34 Belluck, Pam. "The Food Dance Gets New Life When Bees Get Cocaine." *The New York Times*, January 5, 2009, D3.

35 Diamond, 2005

36 Seton-Williams, M. V. *Egyptian Legends and Stories*. Fall

River Press, 1999.

37 Schacker.

38 Memmi, p. 26.

39 Online Etymology Dictionary. http://www.etymonline.com/index.php?search=hum&searchmode=none

40 Online Etymology Dictionary.

41 Oliver, Mary. "Honey at the Table." In *New and Selected Poems: Volume 1*. Back Bay Books, 1983.

42 Neruda, Pablo. "Sonnet XVII." In *Still Another Day*, edited by William O'Daly. Copper Canyon Books, 1984, p. 9.

Bonnie Bright is pursuing a PhD in Depth Psychology at Pacifica Graduate Institute in Santa Barbara, CA, having completed her Master's Degree in the same field at Sonoma State University. She is an active board member for AHBI, the Association for Holotropic Breathwork, and working toward certification as a professional facilitator. Bonnie has trained extensively in the Enneagram, a psycho-spiritual personality typology system, and is currently studying Dagara-inspired ritual and medicine with West African Elder Malidoma Somé. Her avid interest in the loss of species, habitats, cultures, and heritage led her to depth psychological fieldwork on an archeological excavation of a Classic Maya site in Belize in 2009. Bonnie offers research, writing, coaching, and consulting services for individuals and organizations using depth psychology through a new venture, Depth Insights.

From Ecopsychology to Terrapsychology: Tales Told by Corn

Craig Chalquist

Much has been written lately about the domination and control of food as a means to dominate and control entire human populations. As giants of agribusiness corner global markets and companies like Monsanto patent seed and plant genes to restrict their preservation and uses, ecopsychology, the study of the health and pathology of our relations with the natural world, stands ready to shed light on how the growing neocolonial control of food impacts social and personal well-being. Switching lenses, Craig Chalquist then offers a brief terrapsychological foray into how and why corn, one of the most profligate of nature's food offerings, came to be so ready an agent of human expansion around the planet.

A month after I traced a large circle in the soil with my finger and dropped in some corn kernels, I returned to the community garden in Walnut Creek to admire a green atrium of breeze-rustled columns standing higher than my head. Properly tended, a single ear of corn contains enough grains to grow several hundred new plants. Little wonder primal peoples revere the bountiful generosity of nature.

219

Like a child trained to repeat songs sung by cartoon characters selling cereals, this earthly generosity has been made to serve profit, colonization, and empire. The ecopsychologist cannot help noticing how our troubled, exploitive relationship to corn mirrors the pathology of our relationship to the natural world. Yet is this the entire story of corn? If corn could speak, what might it say about why it so graciously adapted itself to human needs?

I am often asked to clarify the relationship between ecopsychology and terrapsychology. When I coined the word "terrapsychology" to describe the deep study of how the places where we live reach into the human psyche, I fashioned my own version as an evolution of ecopsychology and depth psychology augmented by findings from Systems Theory and other fertile fields. Ideally, then, terrapsychology embraces ecopsychology. In practice, however, we should be wary of the limitations (and, frankly, the underlying motivations) of grand explanatory schemes, many of which prove less comprehensive over time than initially intended. Humanistic psychology was announced as a "Third Force" to include behaviorism and psychoanalysis, which it never quite did; the "Fourth Force" of transpersonal psychology covers even less actual territory despite its best aspirations. Safest, then, to describe terrapsychological approaches as outgrowths of ecopsychology and related disciplines and leave the rest to future scholarship.

This makes room for a more relevant question:

What is the difference between how ecopsychology and terrapsychology would examine a particular issue: for example, the human relationship to corn?

A Brief Ecopsychology of Corn

The prolific grass known as maize and corn was domesticated roughly nine thousand years ago in Mesoamerica, where it fed growing populations and acquired a spiritual significance; to this day traditional Navajo ceremonies celebrate a girl's coming of age with corn pollen blessings. From the Americas corn spread around the world to become by weight the largest global grain crop in production.

Corn mutated from its less edible ancestor, teosinte, at a time when hunter gatherers were giving ground to the world's first farmers. As the inhabitants of the Fertile Crescent struggled to find more game animals, they came up with the revolutionary idea of storing grains. Granaries led to single-crop agriculture, which led to writing, mathematics, new forms of transportation, centralized power, armies to defend villages wedded to immovable croplands, rising human populations, institutionalized religion, class stratification, early urbanization, and other massive mutations toward what we now think of as "civilization."[1]

For some among the original ecopsychologists, this agriculturally impelled expansion added up to a great collective mistake, a vast wrong turn in human history. According to ecologist and naturalist Paul Shepard, monocropping and animal domestication led to such profound dissociation between the human mind and the natural world that civilization in the West inevitably fosters psychopathic immaturity, omnipotence, insecurity, and warfare.[2] In full agreement with Shepard, psychologist Chellis Glendinning refers to an "original trauma" caused by humanity's psychological separation from nature and reinterprets the Fall from Eden myth to argue that we were wrong to leave what the Garden symbolizes: a preindustrial sense of healthy union with the world.[3] Ecofeminist historian of science Carolyn Merchant has written about modernity as "the death of nature,"[4] a knell also sounded by ecofeminist writer and scholar Susan Griffin.[5] Of the essays compiled in *Ecopsychology: Restoring the Earth, Healing the Mind*, nearly all emphasize the ecologically destructive impact of civilization and call for a return to premodern relations with nature.[6]

An ecopsychological analysis of corn would therefore emphasize its exploitation in the service of conquest, dissociation, and domination.

This is easily done. As journalist Michael Pollan has observed, corn enabled widespread colonization of indigenous cultures. Packing in hundreds of kernels per seed (compared to fifty for a wheat seed), corn is ready to eat, a source of fiber, twine, animal feed, and fuel, and highly adaptable to a wide range of climates because of its genetic variability. It is easy to transport, hard to destroy, and its use as a commodity allows the leap from a subsistence economy to a market economy.[7]

Mass production of corn benefited directly, as that of many crops did, from the invention of the Haber-Bosch process (1909) for fixing nitrogen to create ammonia useful for fertilizer, bombs, and poison gas. Bosch was its promoter, Nobel-winning chemist Fritz Haber its creator. After the First World War, nobody knew what to do with the leftover stockpiles of gas munitions, so they were turned into soil, a war on nature that accelerated plant growth at the cost of cropland exhaustion and pollution. (Some of the gas was recycled for use in German concentration camps. Having been made ill by exposure to its noxious fumes, Haber's wife used his pistol to shoot herself.) Uncoupled from any effort at sustainable education, the resulting quick-fix "Green Revolution" saved lives from starvation in the short term but ultimately fed further overpopulation, desertification, and soil exhaustion.

Today, more than half of industrially fixed nitrogen goes to corn crops, every bushel of which also requires a quarter to a third of a gallon of petroleum. Corn's has always been a hungry generosity. Billions in farming subsidies run into the coffers of huge companies like Cargill and ADM, which together buy roughly a third of all American corn. Much of it goes to fatten cattle on feedlots and chickens stuffed into gigantic factories. Most of the rest is converted into corn syrup and starch, adding whiteness and extra empty calories to breads, cereals, hams, hot dogs, frozen pizza, ice cream, low-fat salad dressings, citric acid, soup, soda, crackers, condiments, and deserts as well as plastics, gels, sugar substitutes, adhesives, pillows, comforters, wallpaper, chalk, crayons, various coatings, plaster board, and gasoline. Little wonder U.S. corn production is double that of any other crop and requires land space the size of New York State.

Corn's hungry generosity has been especially generous with the calories found in nearly all processed foods. As these calories have increased in density and use, so have obesity, diabetes, high cholesterol, and liver disease. In fact, high fructose corn syrup (HFCS) not only adds no nutrients, it robs the body of them while padding it in heart-straining fat.

In some cases HFCS introduces a heavy-metal poison. A 2009 study published in *Environmental Health* reported that nearly 50% of tested food products containing HFCS showed signs of mercury contamination from how they were produced.[8] Another 2009 study detected mercury in nearly a third of fifty-five popular foods and beverages produced by Quaker, Hershey's, Kraft, Hunt's, Yoplait, Manwich, and Smucker's, among others.[9] Mercury poisoning can cause a variety of diseases and ailments, including permanent brain damage in fetuses.

Heavy metals that flow from feedlots are so high in residues that the resulting waste is toxic. The runoff contaminates adjacent soils and nearby wells and aquifers. Additionally, factory farms breed antibiotic-resistant superbugs capable of pandemics like Mad Cow Disease and Swine Flu. Agribusiness lobbying in Washington and elsewhere prevents such public dangers from being effectively guarded against.

Corn: agent of colonization, child of warfare, consumer of subsidy, subsidizer of consumption, ingredient of obesity, oppressor of livestock, breeder of rampant disease. Corn: tool of alienation as industrialists and agronomists turn nature's plenitude back upon itself in the service of profitable scarcity, ill health, toxicity, and control. Corn: whitened metaphor of the rule of collective fantasies of empty purity over the wild world of matter; a sugary spiritualization, etherealization without end. No wonder we call something "corny" when it has no substance or soul left.

Is this the extent of the tale told by corn?

A Brief Terrapsychology of Corn

Ten thousand years ago, as Fertile Crescent hunter-gatherers contemplated a grim future without sufficient game or forage, they found themselves surrounded by a number of odd terrestrial coincidences. For example, theirs was the site of an unusually high abundance of what are now the world's most productive grasses, rare cereals, self-pollinating plants, and fast-growing annuals evolving to send their energy into dense seeds nourishing to humans instead of storing it in roots and rhizomes underground. The grassy ancestors of wheat and barley were likewise evolving. At the most opportune time possible, the Fertile Crescent was earning its future name by turning itself into an earthly cornucopia for its hungry inhabitants.[10]

Four of the five most agriculturally important animals lived there: the cow, pig, goat, and sheep, all easily domesticated. Inventive humans would combine their fur, sinew, and skin with metals taken from the ground and smelted to bring forth new technologies capable of supporting growing and wayfaring populations. Located in a trade crossroads, these forthcoming villages and towns sent their wares throughout Europe, a continent with a convenient east-west orientation that, unlike the Americas, whose natural verticality brought travelers quickly into new climates, encouraged wide transmission of agricultural techniques.[11]

As all this unfolded, corn's ancestor, teosinte, evolved in South America. Instead of remaining at the top of the grass stalk, what would become the cob traveled downward, away from the male tassels, to the middle, where the sheathed ear could capture more nutrients and enlarge its seeds. This was quite an evolutionary gamble: no human interest in peeling the husk to expose the seeds meant no reproduction and no more corn.

Corn's new arrangement also allowed humans to wipe pollen from one tassel and dust it on the silks of another, thereby creating an enormous range of useful variants. With this fast series of evolutions in place, corn could now involve humans directly in its sex life. In a single generation, corn could also learn what humans favor and provide it.[12]

Terrapsychology assumes an Earth that knows what it's doing. Just *how* it does it remains mysterious—manifestations of its latent animation? Emergent properties of natural systems?—but it is now clear that life here evolves into ever higher and deeper levels of complexity. Research in ethology, ecology, and other fields has made relegating sentience only to humans highly problematic, suggesting that living qualities like purpose and intentionality do not reside solely with big-brained naked apes.

Discarding the nature-reversing prejudice that planetary intelligence somehow derives from us like some traditionalist Eve projected from Adam's rib, we find ourselves free to fashion a terrapsychological thought experiment around the following question:

If Earth wanted a species to achieve enough interdependence to fulfill its own destiny, how might this best be arranged?

Ask this question and at once the "coincidences" fall together into a meaningful pattern. A wise human mother might sweeten the prospects for her children leaving the nest by making home life less comfortable while setting before them the benefits of faring forth into work, school, or new relationships. With no neocortex (yet) to sharpen her focus, the diffuse but purposeful panexperientialism of Terra had to make due with a drought, a depletion of large game, and arrangements of plant, animal, and other tempting advantages to lure the more daring of her two-legged experiments in consciousness away from the organic harmonies of Eden. Once they had gone forth to found new villages and plant new crops, settlers arrived to expand early centers of urban civilization.

Corn's reproduction symbolically reflects—parodies? foreshadows?—this passage. When fertilized by pollen, the nucleus in the silk tip divides into genetically identical twins. One, the wanderer, digs a tiny tube down through the silk thread to the flower waiting below. When the second twin, the settler, takes the path of its wandering kin and arrives at the same destination, it fuses with the egg to form an embryo. The first twin then penetrates the fertilized flower to form the starchy, nutritious endosperm component of the kernel. Which leaves one day to found more colonies of corn plants.

Corn has adapted not only to us, but to our machinery by growing in stiff, upright rows that increase its already astonishing yield. If anything, corn's profligate promiscuity and fertility are only enhanced by the oddity of its sexual organs suggesting each other's presence—phallic female cobs and flowered male stamens—despite their distance from each other along the stalwart stalk.

Taken together, all these remarkable "coincidences" coaxed the human appetite for single crops, surrounded us with useful and loyal animal friends, seduced us away from containment in nature's limitations, and freed us from strict obedience to Earth's wavering cycles of scarcity and abundance.

Since that distant time our meaning-seeking species has marched around the world through millennia of existential curiosity and geographic exploration. What have we developed along the way?

Religion, racism, sexism, tyranny, warfare, and mechanicality—but also spirituality, solidarity, egalitarianism, liberty, peace, and high technology, all the while dreaming restless dreams of an eventual homecoming as secure adults who have achieved a high degree of self-reflective responsibility.

Have the results been worth the risks as we have spread ourselves around the wide world like some immense crop of ever-adapting corn? An impossible question to answer without trivializing the misery and death that have befallen humans and non-humans alike down the gory centuries between us and the once-Fertile Crescent we now bomb from above with bunker-busters. For this grim harvest we can hardly blame Mother Terra, crops and corn notwithstanding. Every mother who pushes a child out the door takes the chance that child will return one day and, having failed to grow up, smash its own cradle.

If we replace judging the past ten millennia as a tragic mistake with diagnosing its shadows as symptoms of overdevelopment—for all new skills and strengths, collective as well as personal, carry the risk of overuse at the cost of other powers—we stand even so amidst global crises of our own making, the results of overextended adolescence bitterly mixed with the emotional immaturity, irrationality, and will to power which ecopsychology has warned us to outgrow or die from. Will we go on the evolutionary record as the first species to perish from willful denial?

Here at the edge of extinction with so many fellow creatures falling irrecoverably into the abyss, our as-yet unmanaged passions overheating the planet to its sobbing poles, we hold within fragile five-fingered hands the outcome of one of Terra's grandest experiments.

Endnotes

1 Chalquist, Craig. *Terrapsychology: Re-engaging the Soul of Place*. Spring Journal Books, 2007.

2 Shepard, Paul. *Nature and Madness*. The University of Georgia Press, 1998.

3 Glendinning, Chellis. *"My Name is Chellis, & I'm in Recovery from Western Civilization."* Shambhala, 1994, p. 60-63.

4 Merchant, Carolyn. *The Death of Nature: Women, Ecology, and the Scientific Revolution.* HarperOne, 1990.

5 Griffin, Susan. *Woman and Nature: The Roaring Inside Her.* Sierra Club Books, 2000.

6 Roszak, Theodore, Gomes, Mary, and Kanner, Allen, eds. *Ecopsychology: Restoring the Earth, Healing the Mind.* Sierra Club Books, 1995.

7 Pollan, Michael. *The Omnivore's Dilemma: A Natural History of Four Meals.* Penguin, 2007.

8 Dufault, Renee et al. "Mercury from Chlor-Alkali Plants: Measured Concentrations in Food Product Sugar." *Environmental Health*, 2009, 8:2. http://www.ehjournal.net/content/8/1/2

9 Wallinga, David, et al. "Not So Sweet: Missing Mercury and High Fructose Corn Syrup." Institute for Agriculture and Trade Policy, January 2009. http://www.healthobservatory.org/library.cfm?refid=105026

10 Chalquist, *Terrapsychology.*

11 Diamond, Jared. *Guns, Germs, and Steel: The Fates of Human Societies.* W. W. Norton, 2005.

12 Pollan, *Omnivore's Dilemma.*

River of Uranium: A Geologic Passage through the Underworld

Matthew Cochran

From the author: "Uranium and its extracted nuclear form can put us in touch with the deeper agility and force of psyche, revealing elemental ways of being led by the landscapes in which we dwell. There is no doubt that the geologic soul of the American Southwest is elemental or that it sources from water and reverberates from uranium."

Opening

Isolation. Disconnection. Severance.

These words describe the modern fate of humanity and its breach of relationship in all directions. Yet this is how an Initiation or an Underworld experience typically begins (as it did with me), feeling like a myth lost, a soul gone wayward, a spirit vanished, a scapegoat separated from the herd, an apocalyptic dream. Then we are forced to sink down into the primal depths, into the darkness, deep into the *prima materia*, the matter of earth, to suffer the fallout, the dismemberment, the complete breakdown, only to decay into the fertile core of an elemental ground zero.

We only have to look around us today to see innumerable signs: cracks in the veneer of the people we know, in the "business as usual" about us, visible in the eroding social structures, relentless in the punctuated and fast-creeping ecological changes—there deep in the knowing twilight of ourselves. Stories are everywhere: poetic whisperings, weeps and rages, in the intelligent weeds preparing the damaged soil, in the repatterning migrations of animals, within human transcendent denial and those eyes that veer away if you look too close. The Global Economic Machine is not only a very real and complex violence but also a simple monstrous abstraction from direct living.

How do we fire the forgotten synapse, live from the vitality of the senses, acting from common sense? And where do we go after all these powerful fabricated distractions have been broken? Perhaps the opening to the Underworld is an implosion, a force that knocks us inward hard enough to generate an outward awakening—something that sets the World Soul booming. "The well tempered character can only result," notes Bachelard, "from explicit and repeated confrontations, through proper understanding that tempering involves struggle and triumphs in an elemental combat at the very core of matter."[1]

Wandering Activism

Yet to be something ecologically real, a person beyond "the shield on which the whole world is engraved,"[2] we must first expose ourselves to the truth and redress the Earth wounded by centuries upon centuries of literal war. Rather than react within the bounds mapped by society, we could be carefully scouting the actual ground and responding courageously for Others' sake in whatever way they call for. To stay insulated in the "civilized" human context remains within a barbed wire agreement to stay diminished, passive, near the surface. A far-ranging deep freedom is a unique relationship that forges us with the molten blueprint of Earth. Why not be a forceful ecology that shatters ownership?[3]

This awareness leads to an underworld awareness, a chthonic geography or archetypal geology that is a doorway best found through a wandering praxis and a tracking psyche: immanent through the ecological heritage we all carry, this innate ember tended from the tens of thousand of years our species were hunter/gatherers. This evolved ancestral skill is the fusion of all our senses in attunement with the "World behind the World,"[4] an extensive full-body glow catalyzed through honed instinct, a mind in alliance with Nature's laws. At best wandering activism reweaves ecological unraveling, locating the passageway to the lost soul of geology.

Geologic Soul

Western Civilization's acute disconnection is betrayed by its sustained war against Nature as humans are now a geologic force.[5] From space we see the imprint of this in places like the Nevada Test Site, in war zones the world over, in clear-cuts of the Pacific Northwest, in the checkerboards and pivot circles of Agribusiness, in the strip mining of the Appalachians, or simply in the extreme makeover of a vast metropolitan area. Yet ironically, it is through a geologic awakening (a natural catastrophe), a foundational shaking, that an ecological rage, grief, or despair may erupt, and through its personal erosion we may begin to work our way back down through the surface cracks, fissures and joints to travel into the bone marrow of the earth. Here is one pathway back into a grounded witnessing that recognizes sacred limits. Uranium and its extracted nuclear form can put us in touch with the deeper agility and force of psyche, revealing elemental ways of being led by the landscapes in which we dwell. There is no doubt that the geologic soul of the American Southwest is elemental or that it sources from water and reverberates from uranium.

Geologic soul is that permeable border or breathing boundary that fuses psyche and landscape. It is the human soul heated deep by the soul of earth and forged in a unique expression that gives the unforgettable particularity to a place. It acts as a touchstone where Human and Other connect, much like a petroglyph. It has a cutting edge and could be argued as the underworld foundation of ecopsychology and terrapsychology.

The American West's "frontier" towns in many ways are the scars of settlement and extractive industry—marks of an initial geologic violation; and the subsequent wounding invisibly trickles through everyone who lands in them.[6] These regional towns and their outlying areas in Utah, such as Moab, Blanding, or Bluff are no different from each other in their exile as presences of place or in their distinctive ecological degradation. They all came into soul-scarred being because of the prospect of what they each harbored: an overlying relationship to the matter below, now called uranium.

One could say geologic soul also seeped out of ancestral Europe through the tricky middle life that so shaped Jung and crystallized many of his seminal ideas around archetypes and the collective unconscious. "The first imaginations and dreams were like fiery liquid basalt; out of them crystallized the stone that I could work."[7] When he was breaking from establishment but not fully self-defined, he called his emerging psychology "prospective psychology" before he renamed it "complex psychology."[8] As something looking toward the future or as something with potential, "prospective" also reflects his Swiss mountain character, the geologic steadiness and grounded nature that caught many intellectuals off guard. "Prospective" was also one of the many geologic metaphors used throughout his work. The places I will speak of reflect an unconscious prospective *geology* (not yet a conscious complex geology), the frenzy of rooting out uranium, the very matter that, once extracted and refined, was made into the seed of annihilation as used in atomic detonations. Here matter mirrors energy,[9] and what is found through uranium's story is an expression of the unearthed human psyche. The original prospective geology has yielded a complex psychology.

To "prospect" also reminds us of the analytic hour, of the digging into depths through psychoanalysis. Modern techniques of geological prospecting search for "trace elements." This is done through detecting radioactivity (symptoms), searching for variations in density through composition of the underlying rock (case history) through electric currents, magnetic readings, and seismic surveys that are well-placed detonations that create sound waves (triggers). These "remote sensing" techniques are deemed safe yet only hint at what truly lies underneath (the complex). Much of modern psychology has gone to the same lengths as exploitation geology by *remov-*

ing the very source elements that are so valuable from the body of the soul by working through or eliminating the symptom, numbing the pathology through pharmaceuticals, even stealing the client's vitality through the practice of bad therapy.[10]

Meanwhile modern geology still practices soul theft, soul removal, and soul violence on extreme levels primarily through its ubiquitous disconnective behavior with land and the oblivious belief that places have no soul. To consider the sentience of Earth is tragically beyond our imagination, and therefore the Earth's imagination is beyond us, the wellsprings of memory untouchable. Through the fault of prospective geology comes the fracturing of the geologic soul.

Many towns of southeast Utah were *literally* founded by this mindset. In the following story, by archetypal geologic passage, we attempt to follow the situation through the underworld river of uranium.

Uranium Bound

> *Oh! The light play of this heavy mass...*
> *Oh! To feel the rough lines of my*
> *Most cherished torment flow like a river.*[11]

Before uranium was named uranium, it was something else.

The source of matter is usually negotiated by water, a geomorphic elemental, and deserts although arid are no exception to this signature. Desert uranium now divorced from this element was river-born, abandoned to water as so many first-borns are in myth.

Water as river meanders, wandering a path of least resistance, eroding landforms, softening or sharpening them, carrying sediment, depositing, following gravity where it leads to ocean or alkali plain. But it also carries more than water, it carries life: insects, leaves, sticks, woody debris, life that has faltered, falling into its medium in some way. As a river stretches side to side over time, curving its way through a place, it erodes away banks by speeding along the outer curves and undercutting incisively; on the inside it slows, lazily setting down its load in crescent-shaped moons called point bar deposits. Here the organic material, the scattered life of the water, piles up to become the *prima materia* (alchemical formless base of all matter) of a potential mineral. Then the animation wrapped up within this river is covered over and made invisible as these point bars become buried by flood sediment, mudslide, migrating sand dune, or volcanic ash, thereby preserving these weaving channels with their sediments far beneath the surface.

Time passes inexorably, inexplicable to the human psyche. The land fractures and faults, buckles and moves over millions of years. These old sinuous channels of porous river sands and point bar deposits are compressed and heated, intensified under the weighted layers of earth above. Through the fractures, hydrothermal blood of a deeper magmatic realm travels upward and out following the old snaking permeable pathways of the buried riverbed. These hot, deeply mineralized fluids infiltrate the concealed point bars, mixing with the local ground water and intensifying the organic matter. Everything begins to transform. Naturally alchemical in this strange underground vessel, this age-old interaction can create cherts, agates, petrified woods, red vanadium, and uranium as yellow carnotite or grey pitchblende.[12] This vast array of complex and colorful minerals brings the present desert its vibrancy (as seen in Arizona's Painted Desert) and is the gift of this elemental geomorphic and geologic meeting ground concentrated in the new moon point bar deposits. This is a 240-million-year-old interaction far from over, although today a few of these hidden pockets have been re-exposed through erosion, outcropping visibly to the eye of the world.

These matters were all "uranium" before it was found or named. It is harmless in its quiet contract with the earth, still in a state of deep becoming, as yet untouched by human hands. What it *is* becoming, what its true name is, remains a mystery...and yet "it is human beings who awaken matter; it is the contact of the...human hand, a contact imbued with all our tactile dreams, that gives life to the qualities slumbering in things."[13] But what kinds of hands have touched it? And what might matter awaken in humanity?

Because uranium gained a different energy as soon as it was displaced from its natural place, stripped from its ecological context and unearthed, something else was wrestled from it. Its essence was extracted, isolated, refined, and manipulated into a terrible force. That terrible force is a result of human hands and is now beyond our grasp as an out-of-hand geologic power.

Native Echoes of Knowing

After discovery coolly snowballed the heated alchemical process, a different sort of attention was given to uranium, and a much quieter one, before Western civilization unearthed it all. As bright colors of places draw life to them, we know that the Ute and Navajo nations met these natural outcroppings of the West and began to use their colors (yellow uranium, red vanadium) as ceremonial war paint, decorating their bodies for combat.[14] Something small and sacred beyond mechanized mass destruction was honored here. Because early people's way was careful use of what was given by the earth, the scale of warfare also remained a more natural balancing act, enacting much more than needless death:

> Coming in actual personal contact with the enemy by touching him was the bravest act that could be performed...to count coup on—to touch or strike—a living unhurt man and to leave him alive, and this was frequently done...to go into battle carrying no weapon that would do any harm at a distance. It was more credible to carry a lance than a bow and arrows; more credible to carry a hatchet or war club than a lance; and the bravest thing was to go into a fight with nothing more than a whip, or a long twig.[15]

This fighting intimacy is vastly different from the extreme distancing of modern warfare, with its remote devastation by sniper rifle, missile, stealth bomber or predator drone. Those faceless virtual battles are disconnected from the visceral violence inflicted.

But what did native tribes actually recognize in the colors of this apparent matter? Why uranium and vanadium specifically as a power in warfare display? Did warriors sense something deep in the essence of these minerals? The power of the sun, lava and water? Uranium is now used as the explosive core of the nuclear bomb, while its sibling vanadium adds to the tensile strength of steel used for armoring military helicopters, tanks, and warships. It seems the tribes knew something of uranium from stories, myths or dreams, sources perhaps revealed through deeper relationship with place, ancestors or otherworld:

> The Navajos...were warned about the dangers of uranium. The people emerged from the third world into the fourth and present world and were...told to choose between two yellow powders. One was yellow dust from the rocks, and the other was corn pollen. The people chose corn pollen, and the gods nodded in assent. They also issued a warning. Having chosen the corn pollen, the Navajos were to leave the yellow dust in the ground. If it was ever removed, it would bring evil.[16]

In mysterious proximity to uranium's places in southeast Utah, atop the underground riverbeds that harbor it, is evidence of even earlier cultures, both their dwellings and their innumerable petroglyphs. Today, near Moab at Moonflower Petroglyphs along the Colorado River, at Newspaper Rock further south along the tributary of Indian Creek, and out to the Bighorn Sheep panel on the tributary of the San Juan River near Bluff (not to mention the extensive scattered sights everywhere in-between), we see ancient cultures' markings, soul on stone, along the waterways. As well, myriad dwellings perch in the cliffs of high canyons, while Great Houses, Pueblos and Kivas pattern the land in sophisticated archetypes, their dwellings aligning to natural cycles of equinox, solstice, sun, moon and stars. All these named and unnamed, found and unfound, concealed and revealed sites are extensions of Chacoan culture, a once-flourishing and long-enduring ancient people. Though their vanishing (1200-1300 CE) is still an enigma, although some research indicates they too surpassed ecological limits seven hundred years ago.

There is, then, a curious, even ominous, and certainly eerie relationship marking uranium, native cultures, and our present culture through the echo of forgotten knowing. The landscape of extracted uranium is marked, the ancient places are marked by petroglyphs, our culture is marked by our actions. This triad of wounding targets a forgotten story about similar fates.

"Uranium Capital of the World"

As to uranium's distinctive expression we only need to look at Moab's history to understand more deeply the weeping wounds of something prematurely unearthed.

The face of Moab is an intricate pattern of outlandish geographic beauty, of colors (red rocks, green valleys, blue skies), shapes and relationships defined not only by the sheer erosion acting as sensuous shaper and mad sculptor but initiated as well by its geologic body below, a transformative blueprint for a sentient architectural gothica, a cathedral of the soul.

The long north-south trending valley bordered by castle walls of red rock are a result of twin faults like dry moats paralleling each side. The valley between is a dropped fault block known as a graben. Crosscut perpendicularly through these walls runs the Colorado River, once fed by the Ancestral Rockies' ancient water flows. The wind is apparent in the extensive cross bedding of the Triassic red rock, an ancient desert environment of migrating sand dunes much like the modern Sahara. Interspersed are mudstones and siltstones evidence of intercontinental visits of oceans and paleo-environments of delta regions, the oscillating borders of land and sea. Underneath, as in nearby Paradox Basin, are massive salt domes from old seas that evaporated, making the place an ocean of wildness (the fins and arches of Arches National Park were created to some extent by the upheaval of salt domes).[17] The labyrinthine canyons, the hoodoos and needles, are all recent erosive effects of water or wind. This land is defined by these two elements, apparent in its curves, meanders, swells and pour-offs. Uranium, of course, was bound to be here, in crescent moon deposits along the old underground river channels.

Early Mormon ranchers tapped into the Colorado River and led water down the greening valley, but it was the yellow color of uranium oxide that fully populated the place. Uranium began to be removed in much greater quantities on the Colorado Plateau when sought after as a dye for ceramic glazes of porcelain; it was then shipped to the burgeoning china trade out of London. In the early 1900s in Europe, the Curies, famous chemists, were increasingly interested in radium, thinking that the isolated radioactive element might cure cancer.[18] But it wasn't until a Texan geologist named Charlie Steen drilled through sandstone into a massive point bar deposit of uranium that Moab exploded, thereby advertising forever the rags to riches myth.

Moab still feels like a Boomtown. Cycles of boom and bust and the frenzy of construction eat up its fringes. The manic motorized activity of ATV's, Jeep Safaris and mountain bikes scream across dirt roads originally carved by prospectors. The infrastructure of uranium exploration radiated future pathways into the landscape. Climbers knock bolts through petroglyphs, chalking up lichen and cracks to conquer rock. Using land is the name of the game. No one remembers how to listen: traffic, loud motors, the ugly hum drown the quiet of the steady red rock. A late-afternoon desperateness lingers in the air. There is an energy here powered by the geology but intensified by uranium's history: a fighting *neikos*, a vibrating restlessness, a fury of sold out activity. Many people reenact the wounds of a place; the frenzy from the early mining days has translated into an accelerating technological overuse called "recreation," with the economic myth of the Uranium Capital remade into the Adventure Capital.

The legacy of Charlie Steen's lucky uranium gamble is everywhere: the Uranium Building on main street and the well-named Atlas Mill bearing the burden of immense uranium tailings piled beside the Colorado River; sprinklers dampen the flying radioactive dust even as it leaks into the passing waters. I found myself exhausted here, overwhelmed, disoriented, my body fatigued. The body's extensive nuances relate the presence of place and can speak its subtleties. What exactly is the wound though? What has uranium's unearthing caused?

Conversations in town led to stories of contamination: for example, a woman's father who worked in the mines, the childhood memory of him returning home from work when his uranium badge turned red from too much exposure. Or a transplanted New Yorker remarking that the energy was the same in Moab as in the Big City and that's why he liked it (the Manhattan Project: the clandestine creation of the world's first atomic bomb, fueled by uranium).

At Moonflower Petroglyphs (snake symbols and spirals) on the Colorado River, just downstream from the defunct Atlas Mill, I found an escape chute one hundred feet up through a chimney of rock deep in a crack. Built with rudimentary ladders of juniper by the ancient culture that also carved the rock, it allowed them to ascend from the canyon bottoms quickly and invisibly. From up high it was much easier to track what was encroaching or endangering them.

I could see the whole length of the river and the breadth of the town like a geologic maze through red rock. The entire body of Moab was silent from this perspective, safer, although the overall degradation was easily seen in a glance, the make-over extensive and the wounding deep in the shadowed canyons where this reckless population had landed, living there on the tailings of extraction for the promise of fast money.

Yet...the frenzy was engulfed in winter silence. Cottonwoods stood in wind along quiet rivers; straight sun, blue, blue sky. The land still standing too, though hollowed out, its guts bored out, rusting parts sprinkled between junipers. Wind moved in the spaces rock makes. (*They have forgotten us* came to mind like a geologic voice.) This well crafted land, this meandering rock. We die forgetting, marveling at the landscape we overran, overlooking the fragmentation of our unearthed souls. We miss the openings to enter back into quiet contract with Earth. Back down the chimney I went.

But what if we come to terms with the hidden wounds of place? What is the character beneath the wound and what transformation occurs in reconnection? A geo-desire to be led by the land, to be fused with its consciousness, is the longing that leads me. I suppose environmental clean-up, green technologies, sustainable living and so on are attempts at this, but their appropriation by mainstream business and the global economic machine perpetuates a separate consciousness and a consciousness of separation.[19]

The evidence of uranium's unearthing wasn't just in Moab. In wandering all over the Southwest there were signs of its energy: in the hundreds of abandoned mines on remote washes and streams between Blanding and Bluff, at White Mesa Mill, which refines uranium even while 93-mph winds blow around its toxic tailings. Diné miners in New Mexico and Arizona die of cancer. It was from this greater plateau region that uranium began to be displaced, extracted, exploited, mined, and sent across the earth, supporting an industry of prospecting and removal through conquest by "radioactive colonization."[20] Knowing now that uranium hosted by Earth is nature's quiet alchemy, I realized that the ungrounded energy here resulted from ripping uranium from its source.

It began to occur to me that uranium was something other than we imagined—that we've displaced our state of disconnect into it: civilization and psyche torn from the earth and refined so completely that we've isolated the deadliest part of ourselves and made it into a weapon of geologic destruction.

Three Rivers and Trinity

The Tularosa Basin in southern New Mexico is a place I've spent more time wandering and living in than southeast Utah—particularly because of Three Rivers petroglyphs.

Many years before the presence of uranium carried me away, I came across this humble basalt ridge like an abandoned oasis in the barren Chihuahua Desert. There is a lost ecology of petroglyphs here: insects, reptiles, amphibians, fish, plants, humans, and a diverse array of peculiar geometric symbols: opening butterflies, a man inside a fish, a coiled snake inside a thunderbird, two deer touching nose to nose, a bighorn sheep with two arrows, turkey tracks, the feet of a tiny child, a spiral inside of an open hand, hands with six fingers, faces, thunderstorms, and circles of all kinds. But beyond what I could see was an indescribable intensity that I felt as an unbearable tension in my body. I found out later that the petroglyphs mirrored what this energy was.

The evening sunsets there are spectacular as they can only be in the Land of Enchantment; in fact they fleetingly reminded me of a nuclear bomb going off with the immense thunderheads piling upward underlit by a red sun already below the horizon. One day while wandering about twenty miles away (as a raven flies) a terrible grief broke through me as I noticed the gated entrance to Ground Zero of the Trinity Site: the place of the first atomic detonation, the bomb fueled by uranium.

All the images of the petroglyphs at Three Rivers: the weeping faces that I thought had to do with rain, the nested circle patterns like the targets of ground zero, the thunderbirds like stealth fighters that flew across the White Sands Missile Range, the double spiral symbol on a rock cracked perfectly in two, the whole ecology of petrified species witnessing. All these markings were here a thousand years before July 16, 1945: past, present and future. Three Rivers Petroglyphs instantly became the "fiery liquid basalt out of which the crystallized stone was worked."[21] And I was part of it, marked too by the fearful flash of human destructiveness and the blinding tragedy of lost connection.

Not surprisingly, displacement is a both a cultural and historical theme that runs through the Tularosa Basin. The Jornada Mogollon, ancient inhabitants of Three Rivers, vanished in the 13th Century after seven hundred years of dwelling there as evidenced by their pit houses, remnants of ornate pottery, and their generations of petroglyphs. Later, the Mescalero Apaches were displaced by migrating Mexican ranchers and forced onto reservations by the U.S. Government. Texas settlers eventually displaced the Mexican ranchers—and then Trinity. What does a nuclear explosion displace?

After Trinity the military moved in, appropriating the Tularosa Basin and forcing out residents to establish "proving grounds" that are now the White Sands Missile Range (incorporating Holloman Air Force Base and the military town of Alamogordo) to further test the explosive nature unleashed here. Nearby, the town of Las Cruces (The Crosses), advertises itself as the heart of space exploration[22] (uranium is used to fuel much of its rocketry experimentation). So here we have it, a region dedicated to Displacement, played out through destruction and subsequent abandonment—the dark unrealized aspects of amplified disconnection: destroying Earth in order to leave it, the ultimate use of a "resource." Apocalypse incarnate and literalized resurrection (Lift Off). One petroglyph at Three Rivers burned into my soul from the very first visit depicts a cross inside a circle, this circle ringed by a larger circle of dots: a target, the crosshairs, ground zero; the cross of crucifixion circled by witnesses; the Wheel of Life, the Four Quarters, no quarter within this old symbol bearing tension and bordered by wholeness.

What was the chthonic geography, the archetypal geology? Underneath the surface disruption, what was going on here? The names alone indicated a poetic resonance. Trinity had exploded within the Jornado del Muerto—the Valley of Death as the conquistadors named it—and the nearby Malpais (Bad Country) lava flow had been renamed the Valley of Fire by the Bureau of Land Management when it established a recreational site in the black lava beds. The Tularosa (Red Reeds) Basin is an ancient evaporite depression where water from the 11,000-foot Sierra Blanca and encircling mountains vanishes into the ground much like the Jornada Mogollon had. Hence the White Sands, brilliant gleaming sand dunes of sun-baked gypsum, the evaporative remains of what was once a vast ephemeral alkali lake.

Beneath this geography lurk eerie parallels to Moab. The Tularosa Basin sits in an extensional fault zone created by opposing tensions: faults that reach deep into the mantle of the earth, the source of Malpais lava and Three Rivers basalt. The basin was once an anticline: an arched layer of rock whose middle collapsed, leaving the depression it now is, a fallen arch.[23] While Moab is the land of upheaval, intact arches and extracted uranium, the Tularosa Basin is the land of depression, a fallen structure where chain-reaction unchained uranium to leave widespread fallout.

My visceral reaction to Trinity was so potent and present that I was forced out of Three Rivers as if from the blast itself. I suffered symptoms of acute displacement: separation anxiety, confusion, disorientation, indecisiveness, a basic loss of wits. Three Rivers and I were fused in a flash. It took me weeks of wandering through the wild country of the Inner West back north before I could return to my home in Montana. In the Grand Tetons of Wyoming, amidst gentle geo-thermals and young, life-giving, creative geology, wildflowers, and profusions of life, I came to my senses.

Uranium Unbound

We knew the world would not be the same. A few people laughed. A few people cried. Most people were silent. I remember the line from the Hindu scripture, the Bhagavad-Gita...Vishnu...is trying to persuade the prince that he should do his duty and to impress him takes on his multi-armed form and says: "Now I am become Death, the Destroyer of Worlds." I suppose we all thought that, one way or another.[24]

These are the words a dignified Robert Oppenheimer uttered with quiet tears. Known now as the "American Prometheus," he set the stage for a strange re-deification fueled by uranium, with Trinity is now a mythic event. The image of the blast is indelibly burned into nature and culture, alive in people's nightly dreams, daily fears and moral anxieties. It was Prometheus who stole fire from the gods to give to the human race; in punishment he was chained to a rock where each day a great vulture ate his liver, and each night it grew back—like the cancer that gradually killed Oppenheimer.

The ripples of the blast at Trinity keep going like a tsunami from an earthquake. Weeks later, bombs dropped on Hiroshima and Nagasaki killed tens of thousands in a matter of seconds, wounded hundreds of thousands, and obliterated the land. Nuclear testing in Nevada, the South Pacific, Alaska, and other places added up to over one thousand more detonations by the close of the millennium.

The Cold War came and went with its insane premise that the capacity to destroy the world infinite times over with nuclear fire would somehow keep us alive. Since then, Chernobyl, Three Mile Island, and now Bruce Power. Nuclear power fuels military aircraft carriers and Trident submarines. Depleted uranium has been used in bullets and missiles since the 1980s. This echoes America's early tactics with native tribes when ecocide (eradicating buffalo herds) was used as a foundation of genocide. Many think Gulf War Syndrome is related to the handling of depleted uranium ammunition.[25]

If Earth mirrors psyche, then by looking at uranium, this 240-million-year-old element, we can track a cultural alchemical failure and trace a human breach in nature. From extraction through refinement, we too are unearthed and transformed, poisonous and immensely destructive. An incandescent mirror has come to life. How long must we stare into this mirror before we begin to see ourselves?

Yet there was one thing created at Trinity. It was Trinitite: a beautiful green-glass stone fused against the solid earth by the immense heat of the blast.

Green Goddess Unveiled

And what is the face that is staring at us from the bomb?[26]

Although manipulated into a ruthless tool of war, uranium holds Life, Desire and Death like the Three Streams of Celtic lore "reminiscent of instructions to the soul, not in this case of the soul after death, but the soul seeking to enter birth."[27]

The word "uranium" comes from the Greek god Uranus. In astrology, Uranus symbolizes explosiveness and revolutionary awakenings. In myth, Uranus is father of the Titans, beings with whom we associate modernistic-technological hubris (Prometheus was a Titan).

But Uranus was castrated by his own son at the instigation of Mother Earth. Under Uranus and patriarchy lies the much older matriarchy that mothered it; "Uranus" was appropriated from Urania, who goes by many names: Mother Earth, Our Lady of the

Summer, the Mountain Goddess, Queen of the Winds, and the Heavenly One.[28] *Ur* is a prefix that echoes "Earth," uranium was carried by waters from the ancestral Rocky Mountains, Trinity was detonated at mythic midsummer, nuclear fallout rides the winds, and a nuclear bomb sends rocks to the clouds, bridging earth to Heaven. Full circle. Bachelard again: "Nothing changes shape like clouds, if not the rocks."[29] Yet Venus Urania, the Guardian Queen, was the most destructive aspect of the Triple Goddess.[30] What to make of all this?

Myths say that those who witnessed the Goddess Unveiled were blinded by her brilliance—just as on the day of the blast, a blind woman saw it from miles away. Witnesses of the Goddess were dismembered violently, eaten by their own dogs, and cast to oblivion. Just as a forceful ecology shatters notions of ownership, so the dark matter glowing inside Trinity is transforming the world. The heat of Her eyes gleams like green glass at Ground Zero.

Initiatory Energy

Although this essay might feel like despair and doom, it celebrates the desire for initiation into deeper mysteries and offers praise for Uranium, who shows us a way through destruction to the creation nested inside. Severance destroys, but it also opens the first stage of the tripartite journey into the Underworld in search of initiation. In deep rites of passage we become a moving geology.

I believe we can heal our ongoing nuclear experiment by making it into a personal praxis.

The incandescent mirror of Trinity reflects a type of enlightenment which can only spring out of the darkness. Within its heart, the praxis of moving inner energy has been guarded in secret circles for ages, bits of it embering through Yogic, Taoist, Cabalistic, Hermetic, Celtic, Pagan, and Native traditions, to name but a few. Circuits of force and elemental energy can be moved inside the body, a fact described metaphorically through opening chakras, arousing the Serpent, lighting up the Tree of Life, animating the subtle body, and circulating the microcosmic orbit (the alchemical Circulatio). These inborn patterns of energy recall the swirl of water on a stream, the twist of a tree branching up and rooting down, wind wandering as a dust devil, storms tracking across the ocean, Earth turning, lunar revolutions and galaxies spiraling—and nuclear forces hidden in uranium.

Uranium with its many names remains a mysterious force, a primal energy and purely elemental. Trinity's blinding light may mirror an inside darkness, but this is where creative restoration catalyzes. When the power of nuclear consequence is felt and tended between us all, the outer darkness may come to reflect an inner light.

Joanna Macy addressed our nuclear inheritance with a Nuclear Guardianship Project that dares to imagine communities living and tending radioactive waste sites while educating future generations about the history and significance of such places. Places of nuclear detonation such as Trinity might become well-tended shrines, verdant temples, places of prayer and contemplation, sanctuaries of awakening, and sites of a geologic ethic honoring both an outer place and an inner condition.

In the courage to face our most destructive acts of creation and our most creative aspects of destruction we might find a willingness to give back to the Earth what we have taken too soon or carelessly forgotten in our haste to avoid the fear of a planetary consciousness.

Endnotes

1 Bachelard, G. *Earth and Reveries of Will*. Dallas, TX: The Dallas Institute Publications, 2002, p.118.

2 Graves, R. *The Greek Myths*. London: Penguin Books, 1960.

3 Morales, A.L. *Medicine Stories: History, Culture and the Politics of Integrity*. Cambridge, MA: South End Press, 1998, p.103.

4 Meade, M. *The World Behind the World: Living at the Ends of Time*. Seattle, WA: Greenfire Press, 2008, p.14.

5 Berry, T. *The Great Work: Our Way into the Future*. New York: Bell Tower, 1999, p.3.

6 Chalquist, C. *Terrapsychology: Engaging the soul of Place*. New Orleans, Louisiana: Spring Journal Books, 2007, p.39.

7 Shamadasani, S. *Jung and the Making of Modern Psychology: the Dream of a Science*. New York: Cambridge University Press, 2003, p.113.

8 Giegerich, W. The Soul's *Logical Life: Towards a Rigorous Notion of Psychology*. Frankfurt: Peter Lang, 2001, p.61.

9 Bachelard, G. *Earth and Reveries of Will*. Dallas, TX: The Dallas Institute Publications, 2002, p.17.

10 Chalquist, C. Personal communication, 2010.

11 Bachelard, G. *Earth and Reveries of Will*. Dallas, TX: The Dallas Institute Publications, 2002, p.77.

12 Baars, D. *The Colorado Plateau: A Geologic History*. Albuquerque, NM: University of New Mexico Press, 2000, p. 137-141.

13 Bachelard, G. *Earth and Reveries of Will*. Dallas, TX: The Dallas Institute Publications, 2002, p.17.

14 Ringolz, R. *Uranium Frenzy*. Utah: Utah State University Press, 2002, p.5.

15 Jensen, D. *Endgame: The Problem of Civilization*. New York: Seven Stories Press, 2007, p.183.

16 LaDuke, W. *All Our Relations: Native Struggles for Land and Life*. Cambridge, MA: South End Press, 1999, p. 97.

17 Chronic, H. *Roadside Geology of Utah*. Missoula: Mountain Press Publishing Company, 1990, p. 77-79.

18 Ringolz, R. *Uranium Frenzy*. Utah: Utah State University Press, 2002, p.5.

19 Lynn, C. Personal communication, 2010.

20 Churchill, W. *From a Native Son: selected essays on Indigenism*. Boston, Massachusetts: South End Press, 1996, p.147.

21 Giegerich, W. *The Soul's Logical Life: Towards a Rigorous Notion of Psychology*. Frankfurt: Peter Lang, 2001, p.61.

22 Sonnichsen, C.L. *Tularosa: Last of the Frontier West*. Albuquerque: University of New Mexico Press, 1980.

23 Chronic, H. *Roadside Geology of New Mexico*. Missoula: Mountain Press Publishing Company, 1987p.114-117.

24 Else, J. (Director/Producer). *The Day After Trinity: J. Robert Oppenheimer and the Atomic Bomb* (DVD ID 1479PIDVD). Image Entertainment, 1980.

25 Jensen, D. *Endgame: The Problem of Civilization.* New York: Seven Stories Press, 2007, p.61-64.

26 Giegerich, W. *Technology and the Soul: From the Nuclear Bomb to the World Wide Web.* New Orleans, Louisiana: Spring Journal Books, 2007, p.107.

27 Stewart, R. J. *Merlin: The Prophetic Vision and The Mystic Life.* Arcata, CA: RJ Stewart Books, 2009, p. 114.

28 Graves, R. *The White Goddess.* Farrar, Straus and Giroux. New York, 1948.

29 Bachelard, G. *Earth and Reveries of Will.* Dallas, TX: The Dallas Institute Publications, 2002, p.142.

30 Graves, R. *The White Goddess.* Farrar, Straus and Giroux. New York, 1948, p. 374.

Matthew Cochran's degrees are in Geology, Surveying and Mapping and more recently, a Masters in Depth Psychology from Pacifica Graduate Institute. Yet true wisdom and real life skills have been learned by wandering in the wild as well as through the painstaking work of simplifying his life from the complexity and inherent disconnection of western civilization. He now lives in southeast Utah finding vitality and contentment in alliance with a remarkable place and community adapting and changing in accord with nature as best he can.

Dreaming with the Stones:
The Rock Art of Ometepe Island

Ryan Hurd

Intuitive ways of knowing can complement empirical investigations of landscape and history. In 2006, Ryan Hurd investigated prehistoric rock art in Nicaragua using nature observation and dream tracking methods to reveal hidden site-specific properties. He shares a method that can be practiced anywhere, from backyards and city parks to historic lands and sacred sites.

Section I: Investigating Ancient Art

I run my fingers over the flat boulder. The tropical sun bears down, and sweat is dripping off my glasses. My fingers seek what my eyes cannot see. Then I feel it: the rough stone is suddenly smooth, and my fingers follow a slight depression in the basalt. The depression curls around in an invisible tight circle. Suddenly my eyes can see: a large spiral motif materializes on the flat stone like a concentric ripple on a still pond of water.

I see it plainly now: a pecked design that is over a foot wide, and hundreds of years old.

Moments before my trained eyes had detected nothing, but not until my flesh made contact with the ancient rock art design was I able to see it. I photographed and recorded the pecked rock art—a petroglyph—in my field notebook. Then our team began the long hike back to the lower slopes where we were staying on Ista Ometepe, a volcanic island in the middle of Lake Nicaragua.

That night, I realized that the manner of this field discovery had occurred in a dream ten days before. In the dream,

I see a pecked petroglyph—a long meander that I follow with my gaze. It's not on a rock, just an image of a line that snakes around, coming into being as I follow it. Also, there is a strong feeling of texture, as if I am tracing it with my finger. But there is no dreambody—best I can describe it is as if I am 'seeing' the texture, or feeling the vision. It is synesthesia.

Widening the Focus

Whenever an event repeats itself, that's a signal to pay attention. This time I was given a lesson on how to become a better archaeologist. The message seemed to be "Don't look with just your eyes...make contact with all your senses." We had been recording petroglyphs on the island for weeks now, but this moment was the first time I glimpsed the multi-dimensionality of ancient art in the field. It seems my nightworld self knew it long before my dayworld self caught on.

To investigate prehistoric sites such as rock art locales, we have to relearn how to see the world. Our inherited techno-militaristic worldview has a laser focus but ricochets off into space before it can account for the depth of the earth. At the same time, our method of science hides the qualitative aspects of our decision-making, and sweeps under the rug data from sources other than the rational mind. So we are doubly blind as we miss out on many sensory clues. We are not trained to recognize those we do "see" because the world is overlaid with our own projections and assumptions.

When I investigated the prehistoric rock art of Ometepe Island, I was unaware of Craig Chalquist's work with terrapsychology.[1] But my investigations dovetail into Chalquist's call for a psychology of place that values the imaginal realm as much as the outer dimensions of the landscape. This chapter is a case study that explores how intuitive inquiries can enhance traditional data recovery methods for anyone who wishes to explore the depth and cognitive significance of human ruins and ancient sites.

By way of example, this chapter describes practices that widen the focus of the analytical gaze so that we can account for our psychological projections, making room for a true dialogue with place to begin. These methods can break down the illusion of objectivity and allow for anomalous data from non-rational sources to emerge. By balancing sensing with intuition, we can account for biases more easily and, at the same time, discover novel information about the place we are investigating. Most importantly, for our communities and the world at large, these techniques can help break modern isolation so we can start belonging to this land again.

Before I describe these practices, let me frame the topic of rock art on Ometepe Island.

Rock Art as a Cognitive Artifact

Prehistoric rock art is a special kind of artifact. Paintings, carvings, and pecked designs in caves, in rock shelters and on boulders are found all over the world. The oldest date to the Upper Paleolithic, or the end of the last Ice Age. These mysterious artifacts scattered around the globe reveal how people long gone envisioned the cosmos. More so than heaps of trash and crumbling palace walls, rock art exposes symbols and mental constructs that lay behind the day-to-day business of living. In this way, rock art gives us a unique glimpse at the structure of prehistoric minds.

The problem, of course, is interpretation. How can we understand how a radically different culture saw the world when its images and artwork invoke so many of our own personal associations? Rock art has also proved resistant to the traditional inquiries of chronological dating, which is expensive and, until recently, destroyed the art in the process.[2] While science has largely turned its back on the mysteries of rock art, we still have an opportunity to learn what these ancient stones have to say.

The Rock Art of Ometepe Island

Our crew arrived in Nicaragua in January 2006.[3] We traveled by bus to the shores of Lake Nicaragua. Even from a distance, Ometepe Island cuts an impressive profile across the horizon where its two enormous cone volcanoes jut out of the lake. From above, the island is a double spiral, with a small spit of land connecting the two volcanic slopes. The northern volcano is still active, and occasionally erupts smoke, ash and debris onto the cloud forest below. We stayed on the more docile and unpopulated southern half, in a town on the lower slopes of the Volcano Madera.

Many tourists know Isla Ometepe as dramatic place to stay for a few nights before heading off to Costa Rica. But Ometepe is more than a backdrop to the burgeoning ecotourism industry; it also boasts one of the densest collections of undocumented petroglyphs in Central America. The island has been occupied by human groups for two thousand years. The little archaeology that has been done cannot yet connect the petroglyphs to a specific culture.[4] No doubt several cultural groups are represented. Contemporary inhabitants have little cultural continuity to pre-Columbian times even though they are engaging in a similar horticultural lifestyle as practiced two millennia ago. Christianity has built tall steeples in Nicaragua like in most of Central America but in the shadows of the tropical canopy are remnants of a different time.

The rock art of Ometepe consists of petroglyphs, which are deeply grooved designs hammered into the large basaltic boulders that dot the forested volcanic slopes. The designs include human figures, animals and insects, although the largest portions of them are abstract designs, meandering lines, whorls and swirls. No wonder Ometepe is also known as "the island of spirals."

The entire island can be considered an archaeological site and much of it is legally protected, but the petroglyphs are still endangered from commercial agriculture. Ometepe has entered the world economy and locals clear ground by burning vegetation for coffee, bananas, and dry rice farming. The fires damage the stones, causing the top layers to exfoliate and peel off, taking the ancient art with it. As a result, the volunteer-led Ometepe Petroglyph Project[5] seeks to record as much of this vanishing cultural heritage as quickly as possible.

I traveled to Ometepe to contribute to this cause, but once on the island, my own interests in ecopsychology and dream research came into focus. I wanted to go deeper into my experience of the rock art on Ometepe. During my time off, I augmented official archaeological duties with multiple visits to a prehistoric rock art site of my choosing. These extended site visits convinced me that the landscape holds stories, and wants these stories to be told.

Site Description of La Eternidad

The site I chose to visit has been previously recorded as N-RIO-58 and is known locally as La Eternidad (Eternity). The site is a dense boulder cluster consisting of over twenty basalt stones. Twenty-three petroglyphs have been pecked into the boulders and still survive. Sitting on the lower slopes of the Volcano Madernas, the site is now located in a young stand of mixed deciduous trees with a dense understory of saplings, low brush and vines. The area around the site has burned before, as is visible from several blackened stumps as well as some severe rock exfoliation.

The majority of the petroglyphs at La Eternidad are curvilinear and spiral designs. There are also two zoomorphic (animal-like) designs and one anthromorphic (human-like). Another interesting feature of the site is the dozens of cupules, which are small rounded indentions in the rock. These cupules are formed by repetitive wear, similar to ground stone mortars but not wide enough to be useful for processing grain. The top of one stone has an unusual splay of 19 small cupules clustered together. This is the stone that became my entranceway into the "inner life" of the site.

Section II: The Practices

Archaeologist Paul Devereux suggests that observations of ancient sites "can only be made by the observer becoming immersed in the sites, their positioning and their ambient topography."[6] Places are not just spaces filled with dead objects—they are an arena of action. We have to make time for the action to unfold, whether we are trying to glimpse a rare bird or divine the purpose of ancient art. This action also unfolds in our own minds, and is dynamically displayed in reveries and each night as we dream.

In order to get closer to the rock art site on Ometepe Island, I held numerous extended site observations at La Eternidad and also incubated dreams about rock art. These two practices are the core intuitive exercises that balanced my rational observations. Taken together, these methods draw attention to not only the "exteriors" of rock art (the designs themselves, their topographical relationships, the geology underlying them) but also the "interiors" of my perception of rock art. How does the site showed up in my own consciousness? The question exposes biases and ignites potential for new observations.[7]

This next section briefly explains each method. Then I will briefly flesh out the narratives that were exposed through day-world/nightworld intuitive practices.

The Practice of Nature Observation

Drawing inspiration from Devereux's idea of site immersion, I crafted a practice that combines a nature observation with intuitive body awareness.

First, I adapted psychologist Eugene Genlin's[8] *focusing* technique to become more attuned to my body's non-rational sensing modalities. This method allows us to consciously bring up those vague discomforts that we all carry. By inviting these feelings forth and naming them, a felt shift sometimes occurs that can be likened to a discharge of energy. Just a few minutes of this attention can produce a clearer frame of mind that cuts through emotional residue. Akin to a "check-in" at the beginning of a group meeting, this exercise can minimize inappropriate mental projections while clearing the path for more authentic responses that co-arise in communication with others (human and non-human). I would do this after taking a seat somewhere at La Eternidad, facing the boulder cluster so petroglyphs were always in view.

In the second step, I shifted my attention to include the setting around me. This practice of nature awareness is adapted from the indigenous practices of Native American Haudenosaunee (Iroquois) tradition as described by naturalist Jon Young.[9] The recommended posture is sitting down comfortably with alert eyes but a soft gaze that takes in peripheral movements. Hearing, smell, and minute bodily reactions are also important to scan along with emotional responses and spontaneous mental imagery.

In each session I took copious notes of my observations, thoughts, emotions, and bodily reactions. The sessions of observing, noting and observing more lasted about forty-five minutes to an hour. By waking up my full sensing capabilities, the stage was set to observe rock art in its "natural habitat," which includes a human participating in the environment. This sounds strange, but it's important to feel welcomed to a site, and that takes time. For me, I knew I belonged when the huaracas, loud jay-like birds, stopped alarming me when I arrived at the site.

What separated this practice from an open-ended nature meditation is that my attention always returned to the rock art. I often focused on a large spiral motif directly across from my sitting location. This "entrance stone" made a good seat, and later I realized it was the only design that is oriented to the south.

The Practice of Lucid Dreaming Inquiry

I complemented my observation of the rock art site by incubating dreams about rock art during the night. Dreaming is a reliable state of consciousness that comes to most us with regularity.[10] Dream content is not randomly generated,[11] but rather closely follows the preoccupations of the dreamer.[12] Like all imaginal spaces, dreaming is a participatory mental event between the conscious ego and the autonomous imagery of the mind (i.e. the "unconscious"). Dreams can be incubated successfully to focus on an issue or creative problem, and they have been cited as inspiration and scientific breakthrough for eons.[13]

I incubated dreams in which I realized I was dreaming, and then focused on the concept of rock art while still dreaming. The value of heightened self-awareness during such dream activity, known popularly as *lucid dreaming*, is that one can make conscious choices in the dream landscape. Unfortunately, lucid dreaming is often depicted as "dream control," but as lucid dream educator Robert Waggoner asks, "Does the sailor control the sea?"[14] Another advantage of lucid dreams is that they are clearly recalled upon awakening, making for a rich data source that can be plied with any number of creative explorations.

For me, lucid dreaming comes spontaneously when I am shaken out of my routine life, especially when I am sleep- deprived, not sleeping at home or working through a socially intense situation. All three of these conditions were met on Ometepe Island. In other words, culture shock makes for a reliable stepping-stone to lucid dreaming.

For six nights while staying on Ometepe Island I encountered prehistoric rock art in the dreaming landscape. Within these dreams I tried to maintain a phenomenological attitude to accept what comes. This involves becoming aware of one's beliefs coupled with an attempt to suspend these beliefs in order for observable phenomena to arise.[15] Practiced in the dream, phenomenology is an active meditation that requires patience and a strong sense of trust in the unknown.

What comes up in the dream space? What emerges? In an ecopsychological context, these dreams are more than just a "simulation" of my perception of rock art, but rather, real moments in time that reveal the shared imaginal space between the landscape and my embodied presence.

Section III: Biases and Anomalous Perceptions

Several interlocking themes arose in my nature observation notes as well as in my lucid dreams during this period of site observation at La Eternidad. These meta-themes transgressed waking life to appear in dreams and back again. In this section I will present some of these imaginal narratives and how they impacted my perception of La Eternidad.

Defocalizing Western Vision

I have alluded to the first "aha" in the introduction of this article, when a spiral petroglyph came into view only after my fingers had made contact with the smooth parts of the stone. *Don't just look with your eyes...*This lesson came in many forms, including one of the first dreams on the island:

I am standing on a boulder and I see a rock art design out of the corner of eyes, but it disappears when I focus on it. Then I think I see another, a small spiral design, but it too disappears when I look directly. I notice what's happening, that the designs are everywhere, all over the rocks, but only at the periphery of my vision. They blip in and out of existence at the edges of my visual field as I scan the rock face—an amazing effect.

The lesson here was that to see correctly, I must defocalize my vision. Stop looking so hard, and start seeing. Defocalization is crucial to the practice of nature awareness as well. Naturalist Jon Young calls such defocalized sight "owl vision." It is difficult to do at first. We are accustomed to a hard monocular focus, but clarity comes at the expense of the fluttering multiplicity all around us. To break free of this way of envisioning the world, we must lose focus so we can gain ground.

Biases Revealed

The smooth texture of the spiral glyph also revealed one of my unchecked biases about rock art: that it is *visual art*, meant to be seen. This is a Western perspective rooted in centuries of history. Rock art is not necessarily even "art," something to be admired as a final product, and from a distance. As Ernst Grombrich suggests, "There is really no such thing as art. There are only artists."[16] Instead, perhaps the act of making the petroglyphs was most important and its continued presence merely a reminder of ritual celebration, a memory in stone.[17]

Another bias that was quickly revealed was the idea that the rock art of Ometepe Island might depict visionary encounters or altered states of consciousness. This bias was laid bare in the following lucid dream:

I enter a completely dark space, falling steadily. I wonder what will emerge and remind myself not to expect anything. There is a texture of sound, rich deep tones or vibrations, some heavier tingling, but no light whatsoever. Then thin, white filaments of light emerge in a loose cluster in the center of my vision. These lights are curlique filaments that slowly shift around as if suspended in some (fluid) medium...I have the thought that this resembles the long meanders of some rock art, but made of light and three dimensional.

At first glance this dream illustrates one of my pet theories of the time, that the rock art of Ometepe Island, specifically the abstract designs—swirls, spirals, and meanders—at La Eternidad, may have been produced to depict shamanic visionary imagery from dreams, entheogens or other techniques of ecstasy.

While this may be a valid, testable hypothesis,[18] I needed to reclaim this projection so I could participate more fully in the mystery of Ometepe's rock art. These notions, and any preconceived notion that we bring with us to an ancient site, must be made fully conscious so we can properly weigh their merits in light of evidence. If we do not account for these biases, we will miss the subtle intuitive hits that the site actually does provide in the moment.

Boulder Sites as a Field of Sound

As it turned out, this dream also revealed an anomaly that I had not yet consciously noticed. In the dream of the white filaments, I also encountered "a texture of sound, rich deep tones or vibrations." Interestingly enough, this dream was mirrored in waking life three days later. I was sitting in rock art observation at La Eternidad when I noted a peculiar sound. The sound was an unknown insect, a call low in pitch, deep rumbling and intensely vibrational. The sound filled the air like a cloud rather than coming from a specific source.

Twenty minutes later, I finally admitted to myself that this unique sound was not directly from an insect,[19] but actually the reverberation of an insect's call echoing off the boulder cluster. I wrote three notes trying to rationalize away the reverberation as a "persistent mosquito" before acknowledging this anomaly. In fact, I had noted a "humming" the first time I sat in observation, but I had forgotten completely about it (which is why good field notes are imperative!). Perhaps the dream had loosened my mind to pay attention to this bizarre perception the next time it occurred.

I felt this reverberation effect on four different days. Each time the field of vibration was located in a new place, depending on the singing cicada's location as well as on my own. However, all these encounters occurred within the confined space of the boulder cluster with petroglyphs close at hand. Within the three dimensional sound-scape, the vibrations seemed to be inside my head. The effect was strong, creating a calm horizon in my mind. In the journals, I wrote, "the hum continues, it is very entrancing. I feel quiet."

Acoustic Archaeology and Sacred Topography

This unique feature of La Eternidad poses the question: What is the significance of acoustics in relationship to rock art boulder sites? The question has some precedence in the literature. In fact, *acoustic archaeology* is a subfield that studies how sound profiles of sacred sites can create unique effects and even consciousness modulation for participants. Rock art from the Paleolithic era has been shown to be associated with high resonance areas of caves: the locations with the strongest musical resonance are consistently marked with paint-ings.[20] Acoustic mapping at Stonehenge has revealed that the place-ment of the large Heel stones dramatically improves human voice resonance within the monuments.[21] Closer to Ometepe, acoustic mapping has shown some promise in Mayan temple sites, and on decorated cave stalactites which are thought to have been struck like bells.[22]

Given the presence of numerous small cupules (or cup-marks) at La Eternidad, perhaps the boulders enhanced the rhythmic pounding of the stone with a hand tool. These unobtrusive features are usual-ly interpreted as domestic—or ignored completely—but could also be artifacts of trance-inducing activities or group musical events. I find it interesting that I ignored these cupules too, even after I sat across from the "entrance stone" for several weeks.

So my bias towards "altered states of consciousness" was turned inside out thanks to these intuitive practices, paradoxically revealing a testable hypothesis that some of Ometepe's petroglyph boulder clusters may have been chosen for their ability to make "standing wave resonance focused echoes," as archaeologist Aaron Watson puts it in his *Introduction to Archaeoacoustics*. The social critique of science has shown that we will never be free of our worldviews and biases; our scientific integrity therefore hinges on taking responsibility for them by making them fully conscious so they do not secretly pollute our reasoning.[23]

During my stay on Ometepe I was lucky enough to interview Nicaraguan archaeologist Rafael Gonzales, who wrote his dissertation on the rock art of Ometepe and has spent countless hours wandering the slopes discovering new sites. His passion for the mysterious swirls, spirals and animal designs is obvious. Toward the end of my trip I asked Gonzales what he thought about the significance of the abstract geometric designs. Officially, he told me, we still cannot say because the archaeological work on the island is so limited. But he told me that an island-wide study of the distribution of the rock art images revealed an interesting pattern. On the lowest slopes of the island, where most of the indigenous people made their homes by the shores of Lake Nicaragua, many of the rock art designs are humans and animals such as monkeys, birds, and crocodiles. But the higher up the volcanic slope you go, the denser grows the concentration of abstract geometric design elements. This detail is a reminder that although we know so little about the people who lived here in prehistoric times, there is a multidimensional language pecked into their landscape, waiting to be rediscovered.

Conclusion: Stones, Boundaries and Beyond

The practices described in this brief case study demonstrate ways to invite a conversation with the populated landscape. My studies of the rock art of Ometepe Island has shown me how muddled are the boundaries between my perception of the landscape and the shared myths of the land that communicate via stones, dreams and topography. Philosopher Irene Klaver notes that stones and rocks have always marked boundaries for properties. These boundaries are territorial, and, like gravestones in our cemeteries, can demarcate the threshold between the living and the dead. "Boundaries," she writes, "are places where different entities, different modes of being, different ontological domains meet, interact with one another, give and take from another."[24] Similarly, cognitive archaeologist David

Lewis-Williams suggests that prehistoric rock art was cross-cultur-ally created as a boundary between this world and the imaginal world.[25] In this way, my dreams and sittings at La Eternidad helped my imagination blend with this special place on the island, to cast images onto the stones. In the end, I felt welcomed by the stones and invited to travel further.

To take the next step into this passage, we must set aside pre-conceptions and walk in the sensing and intuitive realms simultane-ously. This doubling can only enhance our understanding of the world, a humble understanding strengthened not by objective dis-tance but by courageous participation.

Endnotes

1 Chalquist, 2007.

2 Callahan, 2003. Carbon dating is less destructive today, but still expensive; spectral chronometry requires a particle accelerator. In a few cases, ethnography makes valid cultural insights, but most of the world's collection of rock art is not connected to a living group.

3 I volunteered as part of the Ometepe Petroglyph Project, began by archaeologist Suzanne Baker, and assisted by Nicaraguan archae-ologist Rafael Gonzales.

4 Baker, 2002. Only two major archaeological excavations have been undertaken in the last century, the most recent was Wolfgang Haberland's work in the 1960s. The earliest human settlement on Ometepe may be around 2000 BCE.

5 http://culturelink.info.

6 Paul Devereux, 1992, 68.

7 Keep in mind that these explorations were meant to compli-ment the usual archaeological field methods of recordation, such as photography, map making, GPS recordation, and a structural analy-sis of rock art figure types. Intuition may be under-reported in the social sciences, but it still needs to be balanced with the quantifiable aspects of our shared reality.

8 Ecopsychologist Andy Fisher (2002) is the first to use Genlin's work (1978) in an ecopsychological context.

9 Young (1996) is a student of Tom Brown.

10 While there are still strong fissures in the field of dream research as to the function of dreaming, most researchers agree that when it comes to meaning or significance, dreams reveal more than they conceal. A state of mind ruled by the cholinergic memory system, dreams are emotional, strongly visual and tend to blend long-term memories and value structures with current events.

11 This is a confusion stemming from Hobson's early physiological work (1977), which empirically shows that REM dreams are instigated by strong electric pulses emanating from the brainstem. The pulses themselves are "randomly" timed, but this does not equate to "random" dream narrative structure, which Hobson himself has clarified more recently (2002).

12 Domhoff, 2003

13 Barrett, 2001

14 Waggoner, 2009. Dream manipulation is possible to a greater or lesser extent, but it is an unreliable practice for beginners and may produce strong resistance from the dreaming world in retaliation. A more inclusive view of the possibilities of lucid dreaming is that it combines the best of both worlds: the imaginal properties of dreaming consciousness (horizontal memory access, strong emotionality, and dynamic visual symbolism) and the stabilizing properties of waking consciousness (ability to focus attention and keep an observational attitude). Also see Hunt 1989; Winkelman 2000.

15 Depraz, Valera and Vermersch, 2000.

16 As quoted in Lewis-Williams 2002, p. 45.

17 The theory that some rock art creation is related to altered states of consciousness is explored in Lewis-Williams 2002.

18 Jeremy Dronfield's (1995) work with Irish megalithic tomb art presents a testable method for interpreting rock art imagery as endogenous visual phenomena—but that's for another field season, or perhaps another lifetime...

19 A cicada, a large winged insect common to the tropics. Cicadas, which is Latin for "buzzer," makes loud buzzing sounds by a special modification of the exoskeleton.

20 Scarre, 1989.

21 Watson, 2001.
22 Lubman, 1998; Devereux 2001.
23 Wallace, 2000.
24 Klaver, 2003, p. 163.
25 Lewis-Williams, 2002.

Bibliography

Baker, Suzanne. *The petroglyphs of Ometepe Island,* 2002, http://culturelink.info/petro/ (accessed 5/18/10).

Barrett, Deidre. *The Committee of Sleep.* New York: Crown Publishers, 2001.

Callahan, Keith. *Current Trends in Rock Art Theory,* 2003, http://rupestreweb.tripod.com/theory.html (accessed 5/18/10).

Chalquist, Craig. *Terrapsychology: Reengaging the Soul of Place.* New Orleans: Spring Journal Books, 2007.

Depraz, Natalie, Frances Valera and P. Vermersch. The Gesture of Awareness: an Account of its Structural Dynamics. In *Investigating Phenomenal Consciousness,* ed. by M. Velmans, 121-136. Amterdam: John Benjamin, 2007.

Devereux, Paul. *Earth Memory: Sacred Sites – Doorways in Earth's Mysteries.* St Paul: Llewellyn Publications, 1992.

Domhoff, William. *The Scientific Study of Dreams.* Washington DC: American Psychological Association, 2003.

Dronfield, Jeremy. Subjective Vision and the Source of Irish Megalithic Art. *Antiquity,* 1995, (69): 264, 539-550.

Fisher, Andy. *Radical Ecopsychology.* Albany: SUNY Press, 2002.

Genlin, Eugene. *Focusing.* New York: Bantam Books, 1978.

Hobson, Allan and R.W. McCarley. The Brain as a Dream State Generator: an Activation-Synthesis Hypothesis of the Dream Process. *American Journal of Psychiatry,* 1977, 134, 1335-48.

Hobson, Allan. *Dreaming: An Introduction to the Science of Sleep.* Oxford University Press, 2002.

Hunt, Harry. *The Multiplicity of Dreams.* New Haven: Yale Press, 1989.

Hurd, Ryan. Dreaming of Rock Art on Ometepe Island, Nicaragua. In the *Annual conference for the International Study of Dreams in Bridgewater*, MA, June 20-24, 2006.

Hurd, Ryan. Nature Observation as a Field Technique: The Relevancy of the Ecological Self for Anthropologists. In Paper the *Annual Proceedings for the Society of the Anthropology of Consciousness,* New Haven, CT, 2008, March 19-23, 2008.

Klaver, Irene. Phenomenology on the Rocks. In *Eco-Phenomenology,* ed. Charles Brown and Ted Toadvine, 155-169. Albany: SUNY Press, 2003.

Lewis-Williams, David. *The Cave in the Mind.* London: Thames and Hudson, 2002.

Lubman, David. *Archaeological acoustic study of chirped echo from the Mayan Pyramid at Chichen Itza,* 1998, http://acoustics.org/press/136th/lubman.htm (accessed 5/18/10)

Scarre, Chris. Painting by Resonance. *Nature,* 1989, 338, 382.

Waggoner, Robert. *Lucid Dreaming: Gateway to the Inner Self,* Needham: Moment Point Press, 2009.

Wallace, B. Allan. *The Taboo of Subjectivity.* New York: Oxford University Press, 2002.

Watson, Aaron. *Introduction to Archaeoacoustics, 2001,* http://www.monumental.uk.com/site/research/ (accessed 5/18/10).

Winkelman, Michael. *Shamanism: the Neural Ecology of Consciousness and Healing,* Westport: Bergin and Garvey, 2000.

Young, Jon. *Seeing Through Native Eyes: Understanding the Language of Nature,* Owl Media, 1996.

Ryan Hurd is a consciousness researcher and dream educator, editor of DreamStudies.org and author of Sleep Paralysis: A Dreamer's Guide.

Lessons from Home

Kathryn Quick

We spend much time watching out for the houses we own, cleaning, maintaining, repairing, and improving them. Is it possible, however, that they watch out for us as well?

> Every man [woman] should have his [her] own plot of land so that the instincts can come to life again. To own land is important psychologically, and there is no substitute for it...we need to project ourselves into the things around us. My self is not confined to my body. It extends into all things I have made and all the things around me.—C.G. Jung.

There is a house that watches over me, and being here with it has taught me many things. It found me through kind friends when I asked for a safe place in which to raise my children. We made a deal: the house would serve my needs by providing a home for my family and a workplace for me, and I, in return, would take good care of it.

When my house found me I was looking for security. I was reassured that I was going to the right place the week before we moved in, when the Loma Prieta earthquake hit but the house was not damaged in any way. The fossil-filled sandstone layers which lie beneath the shallow clay soil here are stable, or at least they were during that particular shaker. I have always said that I wanted to live in the woods and work in the National Parks. While I haven't quite made it there yet, the subdivision I moved into is known as "The Woods," and the surrounding streets have names like Glacier, Rainier, Sequoia, Olympia and so forth, so I guess it's a good idea to be careful how you word it when you ask for something.

The house's location atop a large hilly area provides it with a view of the surrounding valley, and from the front porch you feel like you can see or hear what's coming up next. Its high perch also keeps it safe from major winter floods, although it tends to sit and stew in its own little puddle when the rains hit hard and heavy. When storms blow through the hills, the doors of the house slam shut on their own, as though the house were angry or trying to protect itself from the intrusion.

A house is more than just four walls and a driveway. It is attached to the land it sits on and is affected by the location of the place where it was built and the elements that bombard it, just as we are. Without care it will no longer function efficiently and will eventually crumble to the ground from which its materials were originally made. When given the care it needs, it usually enjoys a lifespan as long as or longer than those of the humans who work for it. Its inhabitants may come and go, but the house endures, surviving the changes made by each new resident, just as we survive the changes we undergo when we move from one house into another. Their walls protect us and even guard our secrets, but if they could talk, their stories would be endless, just as our own become in time. A new chapter in our story begins for us whenever we move.

Fertile Beginnings

I moved into my house from a much smaller one located in the valleys of Contra Costa County. That first house was the one where I began my married life and which taught me about beginnings and fertility. I gave birth to my two children during those years, and I tended the most fertile and productive garden there nourished by the deep, rich valley soil on which it stood. In that first little house I became an adult, and I learned the basics of nurturing and caring for growing things while being introduced to the work and the upkeep that every house requires.

After moving to my house in the "woods" I worked hard to keep my end of the bargain, watching over the house as well as working at home so I could watch over my children. It kept us safe and secure as we worked together, and for many years we seemed very happy, my house and me. But there were also moments when I felt trapped. It required a lot of attention, and sometimes I felt like its prisoner. Things broke; things were fixed or replaced; but some things I was unable to repair on my own.

The security that a house affords can be deceiving. Perhaps during those early years I took it granted and assumed that the stability of the house meant that life was also stable and secure. I forgot that there are other things that need work. When my husband left our house for greener pastures, I felt deceived and abandoned and blamed the house. Unable to bear the pain of loss sustained here, I, too, abandoned the house, moving out as soon as I could.

But the house did not abandon me. It sat patiently waiting and suffered through a year of careless renters while I figured things out. During this time, in other houses, I learned that I could be strong on my own, survive, and even grow wherever I landed.

Although I thought I would be content to leave the painful memories of this house behind forever, my teenage children were definitely not. It was for the two of them that I returned. They longed for the protection and stability that the house had always offered them, and they needed a safe place to recover, not only from their father's abandonment, but from mine, of the home they had known for most of their childhood.

It didn't take me long to realize that I needed and missed the house as well, although we would both require a lot of repairs to recover. In order to return, I had to face the pain of the abandonment and rebuild the life we had together. Luckily for us, the house reclaimed me as I was and continued to keep us safe while we healed and built a different kind of life here than the one we had known before. Some houses adjust readily to change when they have to. We all changed together as the house itself became a different sort of place, with its many rooms put to good use as we expanded our definition of family and sheltered as many other housemates as the place would hold.

Over the years I have dreamt of many houses, ones that were familiar and ones that were not. In my dreams I often find myself opening up the doors of new rooms that I hadn't known were there. As a dream image, houses are often seen to represent the self. What we do in the dream, what room we are in, or how the house appears can represent where we are in our own growth or what part of our self needs work. Each time I left the house, I was opening up and exploring other parts of who I was and what I was becoming, and each time I returned, I was staking my claim to and becoming more comfortable with those new parts of myself.

After a few years of coming and going, I began to feel that I no longer needed the house. Its care had become overwhelming for me, and I longed for something simpler to manage as I focused on myself and my education. As my family here grew up and became ready to get out on their own, so had I. We all moved out, and I gave the house a complete remodel to prepare it for sale. I felt good about giving it a face lift, repairing and replacing its worn out parts, and spent time reflecting on all the house had been to me. I finally appreciated how the house had protected me, and understood how we had undergone transformation together. I loved the house, but I was ready to let it go.

Finding Nature Downtown

So I left my house again, with the certainty that it was for the last time, and moved into a smaller house in downtown Martinez. My zip code hadn't changed, but the feeling of the place where I lived certainly had.

Famous for being the hometown of John Muir, the birthplace of baseball player Joe DiMaggio, and the place where the Martini was invented, Martinez retains the feeling of a small community. Lying on the northern edge of Contra Costa County, in its own little valley alongside the tidal estuary area of the San Joaquin and Sacramento Rivers, Martinez has undergone many changes since it was formally established in 1847. It is a town of many firsts, including the first ferry service in the Bay Area—an essential service during the gold rush years—and the first town big enough in Contra Costa to qualify as the county seat. It was one of the first to establish electricity, water treatment, and telephone services in the county, the first to publish a successful daily newspaper, *The Daily Press*, and the first to have a bank. Home of the founder of the California Public School System, John Swett, it contains many of the first public parks established in the county and still has the largest percentage of park and open space land of any town in Contra Costa.

It is also, unfortunately, the home of the first oil refinery built in the United States by the Shell Corporation. This installation remains the second largest refinery in the Bay Area, casting a shadow of particulate pollution and visible blight that still goes on but is largely ignored by its residents. All in all, things just seem to start here in downtown Martinez, become *refined*, and then move on.

My little downtown house demanded much less of my time to care for, so I was free to finally explore, in a deeper way, the town now outside my door. I located and became thoroughly acquainted with the closest parks, the marina, and the nearby Alhambra Creek. My studies in psychology were focusing more and more on our relationship with the natural world, and as I adjusted to my new place, I began to realize that as I tuned into Nature, it was making unexpected appearances right outside my door. A few nights after I moved in, for example, I realized I had uninvited company under the house when a mother raccoon about to give birth growled at me thru a gap in the wall. Her fierceness made it clear that she did not wish to be messed with. The next day I heard babies squeaking underneath the bathtub. That night we made a deal. She could stay until her babies were old enough to get out on their own so long as they stayed under the house and never entered it. She kept her end of the bargain, and I spent that winter and spring learning more about raccoon life than I ever intended as I felt and heard the creatures living under my floorboards.

One night mother raccoon and I unexpectedly found our selves face to face on the front walkway as she was returning to her young. We both held our ground and calmly looked in each other's eyes as

I told her it was time to go. They all left early the next morning, and as I replaced the broken vent they had used as a doorway, it was with a little sadness. Sometimes we all need a temporary safe place in which to regroup, to grow and to learn new things. The masks that raccoons wear teach us about our own. We can learn to try on new masks that transform how we see ourselves, show us how to heal, or even show us the face of what we can become.

In the weeks and months that followed, Nature continued to command my attention in many ways as I deepened my relationship with my community. Each time I drove in and out of town, I was reminded of the important role of one of nature's most eloquent spokesmen as I passed the house of John Muir, now a national historical site. At a conference on "Nature and Human Nature" in Santa Barbara, I dreamed of millions of ladybugs rising up from the ground around the tent where I was sleeping. When I returned home, the wild grasses in my yard were covered with ladybug larvae, so grass cutting got postponed that year until they all flew away home.

That spring, Martinez again became the site of another Bay Area first (at least since the 19th century) when a pair of beavers reclaimed Alhambra Creek and built a dam and a lodge right where the water passes through downtown. Beavers are known for their ability to build a community, and as I joined others who showed up to sneak a peak, I realized this was happening here. People gathered from all over town to share this new experience, smile at one other, and compare stories of beaver sightings. When the town council met to discuss the beaver "problem" and the hazards of a dam on the creek, the townspeople got together and protested the planned removal, so the beavers became permanent residents of Martinez.

It is said in folklore that beavers teach us about building our dreams and about how we have to act on them and work together to make them real. As I began to formulate my own dreams for the future, I was reminded that when given a place, our connection to the natural world can find a home in our lives. I learned that the more I tuned into Nature and to the places where I lived, the more they had to teach me. My appreciation for both of these lessons was deepening.

Back to the Woods

I continued to tend to my little house, and to my self as a part of the community, as the spring of that year turned into summer. The house only required a few repairs, and for fun I built a new brick walkway and remodeled the front porch, giving the house a new mask with which to face the neighborhood. I was leaving a permanent mark on the house, just as what I was learning there was leaving its mark on me.

Meanwhile my house had been sitting alone, for sale and empty all these months, as if it knew I would have to return and was again patiently waiting. I suppose I could blame the fact that it never sold on a crumbling real estate market, but perhaps it knew all along that I would need it again. Or maybe it needed me. When it became clear that I would have to move back in order to avoid losing it completely, I returned.

My children needed to return as well, and for a while we once again lived together as we continued to refine, or redefine, ourselves as a family. I am not really sure who was letting go of whom when it comes to my house, but I came back again, so I guess it was meant to be mine.

Eden is that old fashioned House
We dwell in every day
Without suspecting our abode
Until we drive away.—Emily Dickinson

The best part about coming back to my home in the "woods" was being able to reclaim my garden. It was always a challenge getting things to grow in the shallow clay soil, but I worked hard on it anyway—moving rocks, building raised planting beds, hauling in manure, and composting the prolific spring weeds that tried to overtake the garden every year. My garden was glad to have me back, and as I began to tend it again, it rewarded me with the most productive year ever. Maybe it is true that we can grow wherever we are planted, but when our roots have time to grow deeper they can also produce more visible growth.

Sometimes, however, you have to pay attention and tend to what is not so easily visible. Upon our return the plumbing lines under the house began to back up. Some deeper investigation revealed that the roots from the ash tree I had planted in the front yard had broken into the lines. Over the years, the tree had grown from a skinny seedling into beautiful shade tree that protected my house from the hot summer sun. By tree standards it was still a baby, but it now towered 40 feet above the ground and, like my own roots here, had become well established. The problem was soon repaired, but it occurred to me that, like the research I was doing for my master's thesis, sometimes you have to dig a little deeper to clearly understand the things that are holding you back.

I never expected to live here for as long as I have, but even while I was doing so, my house taught me many things: the joys of accomplishment, the rewards of claiming new parts of myself, the need for continuous repairs, the benefits of adjusting to change, the knowledge that comes from engaging with places in a deeper way, and the painful realities of letting go. My house also taught me the importance of becoming connected to a place and to a community so that we can understand our own place in the web of our earthly existence.

These days my house is still hanging on to me, and I am hanging onto it as well. Like many Californians, I struggle through a difficult economy and challenging job market. The safety and security of a house is no longer something I take for granted, and I continue to develop a deeper appreciation for what I have here. The work that we do on ourselves and on our houses happens simultaneously, whether we plan it that way our not. Our sense of self truly extends into the places where we live and into the work that we do while we are there. We may think we are the ones taking care of our houses, but our houses also take care of us.

Whether or not we have a house to call our own, there are lessons to be learned from every place in which we find ourselves: lessons about our place and about ourselves. By engaging more deeply with our surroundings, we are finally able to come home.

After moving back to her house, Kathryn Quick earned her Master's Degree in Depth Psychology, graduating from Sonoma State University in May of 2008. She continues to write about and research the psychological importance of connecting with the natural world and with the places that we live and visit. She has worked as a counselor to teens in the foster care system, and has mentored many young adults making the transition into adulthood. She is an advocate for change and for the incorporation of outdoor education, gardening, and other methods of ecopsychology into the current mental health care system. She is an experienced organic gardener and an artist who enjoys exploring myth and symbolic meaning thru earthen clay sculptures. And she would still like to be a Park Ranger when she grows up.

methods

Painted

my white hands
these lines on my body
are the places where Mystery has touched me
left its indelible mark
I belong to the land now
crawling along its story lines
recovering pieces of my lineage

for these layers waiting in the rocks
are where all things began
the wise ones knew this
it is why they stood before the stones
joining their palms to the humming
letting it fill them
orienting to the threads
that reach across the space we cannot see

we are strung
with the pull of broken lines
wanting to be whole again
the call is in us, reaching from the darkness

let it shiver you
let it loose all of the remembering
let it open up a space again
where dinner can be cooked in you
to feed you *and* the world

let the stones you've been carrying
drop back into the hands of the earth
so that you can be empty
and the light will pass through you
painting you full of magic

yes, magic

—Catherine Baumgartner

Longings, Travels, and Heartbeats: Wandering Nature in Search of Soul

Adrian Villasenor-Galarza

Soul and nature appear to have been crafted from the same clay, and learning to "read" its connecting tread yields potential for transformation. Reflecting on his travels around the world, Adrian Villasenor-Galarza explores how nature, psyche, and myth intertwine and conspire in complex ways to make evident the presence of the soul of the world within humans and the natural world.

I have always been deeply attracted to nature. The fondest memories I have of my family are intertwined with the natural places that we used to travel when I was a child, especially the coast. On our trips outside the city we would often go to the coast of Jalisco, Mexico. Having learned to swim early on, I would lose myself in the freedom of the waters of the Pacific Ocean. In my memories of those days, the tropical dry forest, the turquoise green ocean, the golden-sand beach, and the open skies, play as much of a role as my father, mother, and brother. Feelings of salty expansion, freedom, and connection fill my memories. When I go back there as an adult, I cannot help but feel the ancient bond of my other-than-human family.

Driven by a feeling of being at home in nature, I decided that I wanted to become a biologist. Ironically, however, it was mainly through undergraduate education that I was taught how to sever the connecting thread between nature and myself, between the workings of the soul and my conscious awareness. It took time and travel to reweave the thread.

In the following, I will explore, from a personal perspective, how land and psyche are grounded in the same soil, and how the search for soul can be understood as a deep longing for a healthy reconnection with nature.

The Land Down Under and the Ecologically Repressed

As soon as I finished my undergraduate studies I went to the other side of the world: to Australia to pursue graduate studies in marine ecology. It was there, in what was once named the "unknown land of the south," and in the company of the Great Barrier Reef, that a life-shattering event forced me to get more in touch with the sources of my existence.

During my searches I stumbled upon a book (Capra's *Web of Life*) that opened a new landscape of possibilities for my professional life. Becoming acquainted with all sorts of ideas related to the emerging "new paradigm" that sees the world as an interwoven matrix of subjects, I began to question my future as a marine scientist. It was in this period that my world set sail to previously uncharted territories and the whispers of the soul became more like the rumbling sounds of the blue whale, the loudest animal on Earth.

Apparently I had to go to the "land down under" in order to precipitate the upsurge of the unconscious contents of my psyche. This is not a coincidence, I believe; "When people inhabit a particular place, its features inhabit their psychological field, in effect becoming extended facets of their selfhood."[1]

Historically, Australia has been a continent rich in myth. Its aboriginal tribes have been dreaming with the land for more than forty thousand years. James Cook mapped the continent's eastern coast and claimed Australia in the name of Great Britain in 1770, and an English penal colony settled in Port Jackson (now Sydney) in 1788. However, the aboriginal tribes preceded Cook by millennia, and the high numbers of endemic species, the great diversity and richness of forms of life, and an inverted (to a Northern Hemispheric perception) passage of the seasons and the stars invited a reversal in my domesticated way of being. This in turn enabled a return of the repressed ecological unconscious or "world unconscious"[2] that allured my attention to previously ignored natural cycles and events around me and their influence in my psyche. Perhaps Jung was referring to these qualities of the Australian landscape when commenting on his own experience: "You feel free in Australia...There is a great relief in the atmosphere, a relief from tension, from pressure. But what then?"[3] When he says "you feel free in Australia," perhaps the "you" that he refers to is not the skin-encapsulated ego, as Alan Watts would call it,[4] but the world unconscious to which he alludes.

The "great relief" of "pressure" bestowed upon me by this emerging sense of the world unconscious paralleled the development of an illness. I fell ill because of my rational mind's constant efforts at total control. Once in the land down under, conditions were appropriate for the healing properties of the unconscious to manifest, but not without a mortal fight from my rational mind. In such precarious circumstances the mind surrendered, since it knew that the only way to health was by means of contact with the world unconscious.

The gradual process by which I integrated its transformative powers took me many months. Little by little, a sense of depth and a mighty reverence for the world came to life in my insides.

The last part of Jung's comment, "But what then?" meant for me a need to embark on a more conscious journey of soul-retrieving by sailing uncharted territories. James Cook claimed Australia's ownership by Great Britain, but I felt the need to reclaim my birthright as a son of soul.

Celtic Nature and a Growing Heart

"If we would recover the imaginal we must first recover its organ, the heart, and its kind of philosophy."[5]

On my way to England I stopped in Berlin at my stepfather's house to regain my health. After a month of forced introspection, I arrived at Devon, in southwestern England, the county that watched Darwin depart on his epoch-making travels on the *Beagle* in 1831. Living in a small community in direct contact with the land while engaged in transformative holistic education was the kind of endeavor that spoke the same language as my inner yearning to reconnect.

Upon my arrival I had written the following: "I am now beginning to realize that I am here...in this wider reality that I am beginning to explore, to catch glimpses of." This wider reality was the dawning of the possibility of conducting my life, in all its dimensions, informed by the workings of the soul, for which it is necessary to relearn the language, thought, and perception of the heart, as archetypal psychologist James Hillman so aptly puts it.[6] The relearning Hillman speaks of translates into a deep restructuring of everyday lives— relationships, feelings, deeds, and thoughts— informed directly by something other-than mind.

In the darkness of my room, however, I would notice that my heart would palpitate oddly, a condition that is medically known as cardiac arrhythmia. My heart would beat irregularly, going faster and then slower, beating so loudly that I would hear it clearly. It was as if my heart wanted to make a statement; to be fully recognized by my mind and to reclaim its primacy. I was convinced that it was literally growing. As I told this to a friend, I grabbed her hand put it on my chest and said: "Feel." She looked back at me, unable to hide her surprise, and said, a little alarmed, "Oh yes." I associated that strange phenomenon with my recent work on Goethean phenomenology and his "exact sensorial imagination,"[7] the inward exploration that surfaces underlying features and dynamics of the phenomenon under study by means of intuitive inquiry.

Hand in hand with my growing heart, it dawned on me, as to fellow students at the school I attended, that something special characterized the land there. Visitors and students alike commented on the "field," "presence," "magnetic attraction," or simply the "magic" of the place. It was said that the presence of so many influential leaders who came to Schumacher College to teach had created a palpable—and palpitational—subtle structure that informed the present participants. The house of James Lovelock, a developer of Gaia

Theory, stood not many miles away; one of his courses inaugurated the renowned college in 1991.

I often wondered what about the land and its *genius loci*, its spirit or soul, made it possible for us to be there in community with a shared intention. After all, we were in the territory of the Dumonii, one of the many Celtic tribes that spread throughout Europe. The Celts held animistic and polytheistic views of a cosmos deeply connected to the living earth. They enjoyed a strong connection with the archetypal Great Mother Goddess, the natural elements, and the spirits that governed them. Sylphs, nymphs, salamanders, fairies, elves, gnomes, and undines inhabited their world.

There in the magical land of Merlin, King Arthur, and his knights, I found myself involved in some sort of quest for the Holy Grail. At school I was taught how the imagination could be an organ of perception, and how we could actively participate in the perennial growth and death of natural events. By contemplating the seed/plant/decay/seed cycle with our soul's eye, we began to understand how to read the text of the world.

This was music to my insides. For Goethe, the dynamic and holistic contemplation of nature led to the archetypal and mythical. To apprehend this required a knowing of the heart. In the words of Hillman, "This intelligence takes place by means of images which are a third possibility between mind and world...[the] "intelligence of the heart" connotes a simultaneous knowing and loving by means of imagining."[8] I had been exercising my heart, both as a muscle and perceptual organ, and its abilities were showing up in the dancing images and the expansive feelings that accompanied the cardiac episodes in the darkness of my room.

It is said that the Grail could be found only by the pure of heart. The task on which we embarked at the college, a task conjured by the land itself, was to surrender our awareness to the deeper ground of the heart, mediator between psyche and world, and let ourselves be infused by the soul of soil, which would take us closer to a purity of the heart found in Percival, one of the achievers of the Holy Grail. For me, this movement toward purity of the heart came as an expansion, as though the growth of my heart were mimicking the great explosion of life in the Devonian period (named after Devon) when fish evolved legs and were able to explore the land as a radiation of plant groups caused the greening of terrestrial ecosystems. This explosion of life may well be imaginally registered by our hearts in those lands, perceptible by "dwelling deeply in places through knowledge and love that strengthen over time in continual interactions between the human and the non human."[9]

Dionysus by the Bay

"Myths matter because they are the collective dreams that wed inner and outer, people and places, known and unknown. Myths image deep structurings of the human experience of the nonhuman."[10]

After finishing my studies I returned to Guadalajara, Mexico with high hopes and great intentions. I was excited with the idea of applying what I had learned and felt completely renewed.

Instead, I became more and more alienated from the people that had seen me grow up. I was extremely hermitic and depressed by the lack of empathy and understanding that I felt all around. I felt alone fighting against a Goliath-like society that seemed to stand for all the wrong values—like a hyper-objectivism that allowed an industrial growth system to take a destructive toll on people and planet alike. I longed for my previous travels: Europe, Africa, South East Asia, and India, each holding messages for my soul and learnings necessary for my growth and development. After two years in Guadalajara I realized that my wanderings were not finished, but perhaps just beginning.

San Francisco is a vortex in which an upsurge of unconscious material is perpetually enacted and reenacted in the everyday lives of the area's inhabitants: material touching largely on the bizarre, innovative, erotic, and idealistic. The resulting stage-like performance unfolds as the functioning core of the small, densely packed city.

Named after St. Francis of Assisi, the patron of environmentalists, San Francisco hosts natural landscapes that actively and strongly participate in the lives of its inhabitants, as is evident in burgeoning environmental initiatives in the city and adjacent areas and in an overall awareness of "eco," sustainable, or "green" living. With the water surrounding it on three sides, the city of Neptunian earthquakes remains in close touch with oceanic depths while transmitting their impulses all the way to the top of its many steep hills and even beyond, with the spreading fog as one of the vehicles. This unconscious/conscious vertical movement is filled with a celebratory Dionysian mood that may well originate in Hades itself. A clear example of this dynamic plays out a few steps away from my current home.

The Mission District and its sunny microclimate are well known as a hub of multicultural activity. Referred to by the city planning department as the "heart of San Francisco," the "inner Mission" is the oldest settled area of the city and has long been a home for the working class. The Mission is also a center of Latino culture and an incubator of counterculture. The relatively flat valley in which the Mission sits is surrounded by rolling hills that keep out ocean winds and fog. The valley's natural features and accessibility made it ideal for the Yelamu Ohlone peoples to settle here two thousand years ago. Today, they let me and my bike avoid the temperamental hills.

On Mission Street and parallel to it runs an imaginal fault that allows for a clear communication between worlds. Between Earth and the Underworld, a tributary of the river Styx flows imaginally through the Mission to feed its dark carnival atmosphere. From at least the 16th street BART station to Sycamore, this fault's Dionysian-Hadean surge is enacted by ever-present pimps, prostitutes, junkies, gang members, and homeless people that dwell in that stretch of two blocks as if contained by an invisible field. All this illegal activity is usually allowed, as if the city needed an arena for the repressed to shine through. As a therapy patient letting go of recalcitrant and unhealthy habits enjoys the resultant psychic healing, the Mission and its Underworld surge provides equilibrium and health to the city and its bioregion while retaining the presence of soul.

Perpendicular to Mission Street, another archetypal dialogue is taking place. When you walk down Valencia Street to the west of Mission Street and further in that direction, you enter a new realm. The trash in the streets, the loud Mexican music, all the noisy extravagance of the immigrants (return of the repressed) give way to a trendy hipster feel with its core in Dolores Park three blocks away westward. This is evident in the overall "retro" look of the bypassers, the revolutionary conversations that fly around in cafes and streets, and the trendy establishments and paraphernalia one encounters. It is remarkable how different microhabitats can coexist in such a small geographical area. My house stands precisely in the transitional zone between Valencia and Mission, reminding me of the border between Tijuana (Mission Street) and San Diego (Valencia Street), a borderland I enter merely by walking east or west.

In conclusion, I have come to believe that the *genius loci* speaks directly to my psychological, spiritual, and physical state of being. The felt essence of a place and its natural features, whether conveyed by ancient geological faults and movements or recent human accomplishments or catastrophes, finds its way through me, often by such a gracious path that I am unable to detect a solid boundary between it and me. Places invite me to reflect on the importance of the liminal in my life, and how much the in-between has influenced my personal search for soul during my wanderings. For now, longings, travels, and heartbeats all come together under the roof of my current home.

Endnotes

1 Chalquist, Craig. *Terrapsychology: Reengaging the Soul of Place*. Spring Journal Books, 2007, p. 7.

2 Roszak, T. *The Voice of the Earth: An Exploration of Ecopsychology*. Phanes Press, 2003.

3 Tacey, D. *Jung and the New Age*. Routledge, 2001, p. 161.

4 Watts, A. *The Tao of Philosophy*. Tuttle Publishing, 1999.

5 Hillman, J. *The Thought of the Heart and the Soul of the World*. Spring Publications, 2007, p. 6.

6 Ibid.

7 Bortoft, H. *The Wholeness of Nature: Goethe's Way of Science*. Floris Books, 1996.

8 Hillman, p. 7.

9 Chalquist, p. 52.
10 Chalquist, p. 76.

Adrian Villasenor-Galarza holds a bachelors degree in ecology and a master's in holistic science from Schumacher College, U.K., and is currently a PhD student of Philosophy, Cosmology and Consciousness at CIIS, where he studies ecology, shamanism, holistic science, and western esotericism. He has given many lectures and workshops in Mexico. He is deeply interested in a relational "bioalchemy" exploration of invisible avenues between ecology, psychology, spirituality, and education.

Tracking the Voices of the Land

Sarah Rankin

For Sarah Rankin, the simple but meaningful practices of walking, sitting, altar-building, and ceremonial work bring the many voices within us—whether luminous, shadowy, instinctive, or ancestral— into alignment with each other in an activated context of listening in on ancient landscapes and their nonhuman inhabitants.

Who are you, the one within, the whisperer behind my sleep, the dream guide in the traveling down and in? Who are you, ancient grandmother, here, small and old, sitting by the fire, wrapped in a thin blanket, and now, a solid presence over my right shoulder, always showing me the way? Who are you, word maker, the one whose voice desperately tries to find her way to air? I want to know the curves of your faces, the cadence of your voices in the spring air, and the rolling gait of your slow and easy walking across the land...

To the land I return as often as possible to find communion and solace with these entities that are at the same time the fullest expression of the deepest parts of myself and the reflections of the voice of the land, who is speaking through me at all times and asks for my participation.

287

How do I listen to the voices of the dreamer, the grandmother, the shape-shifter, the animal spirit, the guide? By walking, sitting, altar-building, and ceremony.

Many times, because of the circles I run in from day to day and the human-made structures that frame my everyday planes of perception, my entrance into the wild spaces can feel like fleeing, running way. But when I do take the time to slow down and honor my passage from what I see as my normal life to the one in which the wild ones play, these practices take on a feeling of ritual and deep participation. Bill Plotkin, founder of Animas Valley Institute and author of *Soulcraft* recognizes this entrance into enlivened space as the crossing over of a threshold. He recommends marking the entrance into sacred space and the return to the middle world in order to define the edges of a container that holds numinous experiences.[1]

In honoring the threshold, I like to draw a line in the dirt, say a little blessing of intention, if there is something specific within my psyche that I seek help with, or of gratitude, when time on the land on that particular day celebrates something new coming to life, or of openness, if my intention on that day is simply to receive. Something shifts in my awareness when I do this. I understand that whatever happens during my time on the land and in the company of the plants, animals, elements, and spirits is of mythical importance, meaning that the stories I encounter on this day are not my stories alone, but the ancient stories of the land and all who came before me.

Walking

One of the easiest and most accessible practices towards what one might see as Earth Soul encounter is the practice of walking. There is a loop I like to walk in the valley where I live that takes me down to what my partner Ryan and I have named the Meadow and into what we have named Yucca Pass. In the winter months we snowshoe this loop.

As I left my house one day, forgetting the art of intentional walking, I held no awareness of crossing a threshold. I was tired and stressed and I wanted so badly to write something meaningful, full of universal truths and grand ideas. The place of my head was much bigger than the place of my heart. In his essay "The Ecology of Magic," David Abram recognizes this sort of mentalistic departure as a retreat to a world of mind-based, artificial reality:

> When the animate presences with whom we have evolved over several million years are suddenly construed as having less significance to ourselves, when the generative earth that gave birth to us is defined as a soulless or determinate object devoid of sensitivity and sentience, then that wild otherness with which human life had always been entwined must migrate, either into a supersensory heaven beyond the natural world, or else into the human skull itself—the only allowable refuge, in *this* world, for what is ineffable and unfathomable.[2]

In my carefully shuttered reality I was blind to my environment, to the crystal clarity of the snow-covered morning, to the feeding of the small birds in the bare bushes. This changed when I returned to my senses and found myself so infused with the landscape that some small birds didn't know I was there. One even bounced off my leg, as I noted in my journal:

> *My mind does not need to lay down the tracks of some ancient wisdom. It does not need to make tidy connections that clean up the edges of the unknown. It is enough to be here, on the top of this threadbare hill, amidst the grasses that cling to their withered seed pods. It is enough to watch these plump, furry thrushes chatter and balance on the tips of these grasses. Tiny, squeaky conversation that sounds like plastic on plastic and delicate jumps from sprig to sprig. It is enough to leave my own awkward, basket-thatched, snowshoe prints among those of the wild turkey, elk, deer, moose, coyote that crisscross my path.*
>
> *As if recognizing my calm, half-smiling surrender to this snowy sunset and my place within it, the thrushes dive and clutter and chatter in closer, surrounding my legs. In a rush*

to claim the next pod, one bird glances off my leg. I watch as
another hangs from the end of the sprig of grass and clutch-
es the pod between his tiny feet. He then plunges his beak into
the pod, searching for seeds. Thrushes dance around my legs,
still squeaking, and then wash on with the wind, all except
this determined one, still searching. I wait a while and first
whisper, then speak in my most gentle voice that he had bet-
ter move on before he loses his friends. He squeaks and then
flits away to the shelter of a nearby pine.

I turn toward the downward-slope of the hill and slowly
walk out of the darkening forest, leaving my clumsy tracks
behind me. My frozen breath against the falling dusk is
enough.

I share this with you because perhaps you too become over-whelmed by the hugeness of the endeavor of deep listening. To know yourself as a listener to the land means that your ears must be attached to a great being, a being spacious enough to comprehend the voices of the forest. In that comprehending, you might feel, as I sometimes do, that the responsibility becomes so great that it is eas-ier to simply walk.

I recommend trying to let go of the intimidating grandness of the idea. Your attention, presence, and awareness are all that are required of you. The rest is just falling into a natural way of being, a way that is a part of your core as a human, a way that is retrievable every time you walk. To walk under the sky in the presence of the quiet forest is enough. It is participation that is called for, not the production of a tangible, universal truth that can justify the wander-ing.

Sitting

Another practice is sitting. This one is sometimes more difficult for me because walking allows me to feel more deeply in my body the crossing over to a different means of perception, whereas sitting requires full-bodied stillness and staying with the moment.

As with the practice of walking, I find it meaningful to cross a threshold by holding an openness to be called in by a particular spot in the wilderness, greeting the place that has chosen me, taking some time (usually with eyes closed) to mentally or verbally voice my intentions for the shared time, and then opening my senses to whatever happens. The following is a piece that I wrote during a sitting practice.

The Meadow

> Silence settles over the meadow
> Like warm breath on a pillow
> Time holds still
> Here is a plow with its rusted blades,
> Long forgotten in its death furrow
> There is the family home
> Log timbers now collapsed
> Gaping holes like teeth
> And everywhere lies the sound of secret
> Eyes that still watch
> Follow us on our religious walk
> That carefully and silently traces
> The forgotten boundaries of the meadow
> Far above, a bald eagle
> Cuts the winter air with its snow-tipped wings
> The meadow sleeps

Here there is a slowness more apparent than in the walking piece. To come into closer relationship with a place like a still and peaceful meadow with a collapsing farmhouse, perhaps it is appropriate to become like the meadow, watchful and unmoving. In such times, because the slowness of sitting allows the space for it, I like to write about the things I see and hear and feel as I sit.

Altar-Building

I have played in and built things in dirt for as long as I can remember. In the marshes of Indiana, my childhood friend Heidi and I would trample down the long grasses to make rooms and hallways and tunnels. Later, when my family moved to New Mexico, my brother Josh, my sister Hannah, and all the neighborhood kids and I would get together to build a city named Gladeville. An irrigation stream ran through our miniature town. Each of us constructed the house we lived in. Mine was at the northernmost end of town. It was built of twigs and had a pebble path that led to a bridge to my own island. In front of the stucco jail, our largest structure was Bob Boulder, a rock that we covered with captured ants. And then just yesterday, with my soon-to-be niece, Maya, we built a little house that she filled with all the necessary parts of a home: a door, a window, a kitchen, and a family consisting of a Mom, a Dad, and a little girl.

Even while growing up I understood these times of play to be just that. Now I look at them as necessary interactions with the places I live and have lived. Building these houses and getting dirt under my fingernails, smearing mud across my face, and molding the dirt with small hands brought closer contact with my self and the land. When Maya chose the things to build and fill her home with yesterday, I got a glimpse into what she sees as central to her three-year-old life: a way to move in and out, a means of seeing out, sustenance, and family. When I build and play now, it is within a field of ritual participation.

There is a mesa top on the edge of Chokecherry Canyon on the outskirts of Farmington, New Mexico, that I have returned to for the past ten years. Each time, often in the company of my little sister, I run up the edge of the canyon, down and around smaller canyons, making one big loop back to the starting point. I am on the lookout for the stone I will take with me that day.

When I return, I go back to the small scraggly twig that had dreams of becoming a tree, in a row of others like him, and I squat to dig up the rocks from all of my other times out on the mesa top. I arrange these rocks in a mandala-like circle with my new rock in the center. The northern rock is aligned with the La Plata mountains, visible from the canyon top, and the direction of my home in Durango, Colorado. Starting in the South, I call in the six directions, including the fifth, down into the earth, and the sixth, up into the sky. I end with my new rock in the center and a blessing for whatever it is that is present in my life at that time or whatever it is for which I ask assistance.

I have been enacting this ritual for over a decade, the last time in the company of a new oil well only feet away. Its steady whine pulsed through the earth and into my ritual. Something had changed and there were warnings of destruction and development in the air. Now I was fearful that my rocks might not always be there. I understood that these small ritualistic acts of gratitude and conversation are more important now than ever, and that the ritual must adapt and change in response to the needs of the land.

There are many meaningful ways to construct natural altars or structures of sacred space. My circle of rocks in Chokecherry Canyon is meaningful to me because it acts as a kind of symbolic holder of my life's transitions and rites of passage. Playing in the sand with Maya was meaningful for the pure joy of play and as a kind of symbolic representation of the psyche.

Expanding the idea of ritual, farming can be seen as one of the most meaningful ritualistic practices. As I write this, my brother Pete and my partner are out near the San Juan River clearing brush for a waterway and digging furrows for a grow garden that our family is fortunate to be a part of. Ritually turning over, feeding, and nourishing the soil also allows it to do the same for us.

Ceremony

I hesitate to write this section because of the magnitude of the idea of ceremony. Ceremony means something different for each of us and can depend on our spiritual upbringing and practices of faith. For me, ceremony takes place outside, in the air and on the land; is enacted very selectively, just when it is required, in deep reverence for the spirits that surround me; is carried out in the presence of my ancestors and the ancestors of the land; and is defined by a clear beginning, a clear intention, and a clear ending.

Last October, under the dizzying beauty of the Grand Tetons in Wyoming, I embarked on a solo walk with the guidance and support of Animas Valley Institute and my fellow soul wanderers. My intention was to walk to a place that felt edgy, a place that held a boundary of worlds so I could carry out a ceremony marking my transition from a place of emotional adolescence and wandering spirit into a place of womanhood, where I begin to embrace my gifts.

As I walked away from the cabins, I marked a clear threshold in the sand and stepped forward. I was met a few moments later by a crow who called down to me.

The crow calls her in
She calls back in her cracking human voice
And does something only a human would do:
She tosses almonds in the air, an offering
And listens as they hit the pavement,
Hoping the crow notices

Later, after the big-muscled uphill hike,
The slip-sliding down mud,
And the tracing of the bugling elk through the trees,
She turns toward the cold mountains
And bravely lifts her open face to the mystery
The tunnel of trees pulls her in
And the darkness swallows her

With each step,
She knows,
She understands in the watery, thudding,
Full-blooded pull of her ancient heart
That as the trees close behind her,
She will never return to the home she knows so well
The stories ride the turns of her veins,
But their pull to source has changed:
Home is a different house
With the same door

The bugling of elk
And the calling of crow
Have fallen away
Leaving static-edged fear
And heavy-big bear presence

It's memory that keeps her walking,
Following the elk trail through the gnarled trees

When the tree bends in the wind and screams
She halts her steps in the still mud
And knows she has found her stillness
After gathering loud-cracking twigs
She kneels as so many have before her
And builds a fire

She tends the wet fire
With patient hands and a soft heart
Feeding it bare, wet branches,
Curled moss that burns only smoke,
And her own blood from a small cut,
That drips, once, into the fire

Fear has left the soft, pink beds of her new heart
And a deep-breathing, soft-eyed attentiveness remains
This fire is new
This fire is hers and not hers
Even as the twirling, dancing first
Snowflakes of winter fall,
She knows that this fire
Will not go out

After this ceremony, completed by words spoken into the fire about my desire to open into my own womanhood and closed by the disassembly of the fire, I returned to the group and my everyday life more whole and sure of myself than I had ever been.

When I returned to Durango after this trip, Ryan and I found a beautiful home together on the outskirts of town. A month later, I was pregnant with our first child, now five months old in my womb, swimming and softly poking me as I write this.

Who are you, the dreamer, the grandmother, the shape-shifter, the animal spirit, the guide within? Where did you come from and what is it that you ask of me? When I hear your voice on the wind, is it the voice of my soul? Is it the voice of my unborn child? Is it the voice of my ancestors? Is it the voice of the forest itself?

Although I don't know the answers to these questions, I do know that what you ask of me is to listen, to get up every day and walk to the woods, to look for your voice in the shadows behind things, and to follow the paths of my own footprints, already laid out in the sand.

Endnotes

1 Plotkin, Bill. *Soulcraft: Crossing into the Mysteries of Nature and Psyche.* New World Library. Novato, CA, 2003.

2 Abram, David. *The Spell of the Sensuous: Perception and Language in a More-Than-Human World.* Vintage, 2003, p. 306.

Sarah Rankin is a teacher who holds a master's degree in Depth Psychology from Sonoma State University.

The Family Tree of Terrapsychology: History and Method

George F. Kohn

Looking at the lineage of terrapsychology in the fields of geography, biology, philosophy, ecology, and depth psychology reveals the flow of questions, answers, and unresolved problems at the heart of this ongoing research. Terrapsychology involves not only the examination of a new specialized topic, but a new way of seeing as well. The history and development of both the topic and method is the object of this study.

Things outside you are projections of what's inside you, and what's inside you is a projection of what's outside. So when you step into the labyrinth outside you, at the same time you're stepping into the labyrinth *inside*. Most definitely a risky business.
—Haruki Murakami and Philip Gabriel

Man is only an extension of the spirit of place.
—Lawrence Durell

Introduction: Call and Response
In the year 2000 I was "called" to be the priest-in-charge of St.

James Episcopal Church in Monterey, California. Clergy speak of being called by congregations, by the Church, most often by God. All three, on the surface, I believe, were true in my case as well. But in addition to that, I distinctly felt that I was called by the place itself. Before I even knew that there was a ministry opening at St. James, before my Bishop had authorized my seeking a position after six years away from active ministry, I drove by St. James and felt an attraction, a relationship of some sort, though I had never been there before. There was something familiar there on the hill, overlooking the Monterey Bay, like the cathedral in Iowa where I had been ordained and married, on a hill in Davenport overlooking the Mississippi, or the houses where I had lived in, in Iowa City and Muscatine, both on hills over water. I realized that places had always been central to the callings of my life, the topographies of childhood or my studies in Montreal, Varanasi, and New York City. Places, rather than people, have defined my sense of belonging.

My interest in place is a family tradition. My father was a professor of geography, chair of the department at the University of Iowa, and president for a time of the American Association of Geographers. His focus was primarily on geographic education, but he helped to move the field, during the 1950s and 1960s, in a more quantitative direction. My experience of the call of a place would be too subjective to fit into my father's academic discipline. It requires psychological and spiritual interpretive categories that must be sought elsewhere.

Those categories came into focus for me through the study of the tradition of hermeneutic phenomenology, particularly as expressed in the writings of Martin Heidegger and those who followed him. I had what amounted to a kind of conversion experience when, following some reading in the works of Medard Boss[1] I came to see myself not as a body that had a life, but as a life that had a body. My identity, first and foremost, was to be found in the world, which was no longer seen as something outside some inner me.

Geography, Place, and Depth

The field of geography deals with the interface of people with places, but the relationship between geographic and psychological theory has rarely been explored. In the 1950s-1960s the relational nature of this interaction was minimized by a conception of space as a "neutral container, a blank canvas that is filled in by human activity."[2] Within this paradigm geographers sought to restyle geography as a positivist spatial science, seeking to construct theory or 'spatial laws' on the basis of statistical analysis. I can remember asking my father, a leader in geographic education and theory at the time, about psychology. His response was that he didn't "believe in it."

Reacting against this exclusively objective type of analysis, some geographers took inspiration from psychology. One early psychologically aware effort is found in *Behavior and Environment*, edited by Tommy Garing and Reginald Golledge. Examining the approaches of geography and psychology under the influence of a fully behaviorist model, Golledge points out that although psychology assumes an individual actor in an external environment or situation, geography often focuses on "some higher-order unit,"[3] often seeing a concentration on the individual as "dismissed as being unscientific."[4] The environment is understood as a stimulus, the study of which has "waned in some psychological subdisciplines [with] the exception of environmental psychology." This field, Golledge states, has "highlighted the narrowness of the common conceptualization of environment in psychology as a stimulus or psychical energy impinging on the individual to which his or her senses are capable of responding."[5] Subsequent chapters exploring both geographic and psychological perspectives include a discussion of problems of spatial cognition, the interiorization of cognitive maps, the perception of environmental hazard, and studies of "shopping behavior,"[6] or "leisure environments" and "nature experience."[7]

This approach has little in common with a depth understanding of either place or psyche. It treats each as an object available for scientific testing, remaining on the surface where "meaning" has no meaning beyond conscious or instinctive behavioral intention.

The work of the more phenomenologically oriented geographer, Yi-Fu Tuan, goes somewhat deeper. Rather than staying inside the limitations of a stimulus-and-response model, Tuan allows for "an insider's view of human facts," and for questions that concern how "people attach meaning to and organize space and place." [8] This meaning, for Tuan, comes from within. "Place is a special kind of object. It is a concentration of value, though not a valued thing that can be handled or carried about easily; it is an object in which one can dwell."[9] The value of a place comes from an individual's experience of that place. "The given cannot be known in itself. What can be known is a reality that is a construct of experience, a creation of feeling and thought."[10] Place, for Tuan, "is created and maintained through the 'fields of care' that result from people's emotional attachment."[11] At its most creative these fields become manifest in "mythical space and place."[12] "Our imagination constructs mythical geographies that may bear little or no relationship to reality."[13] Even so, this approach, while quite expressive of the experience of psychological relationship with place, still persists in dividing "mental" life from "reality."

Depth psychology makes its geographic debut in the writings of David Sibley. They provide one of the first attempts by a geographer to explore the role of the psyche in socio-spatial process.[14] Sibley writes that

> Freud's psychoanalytical writing provides a starting point for an examination of relationships between the self and the social and material world. This is the field of object relations theory, which, for Freud, referred to the infant's relationship to the humans in its world, but it is a theory which has been generalized to include non-human aspects of the object world, a wider environment of human and material objects, and extended beyond infancy.[15]

Silbey speaks of places as taking on the identities of either an "ecological self" or an "ecological other,"[16] external boundaries dividing the good and comforting from the bad and dangerous:

> Self and other, and the spaces they create and are alienated from, are defined through projection and introjection. Thus, the built environment assumes symbolic importance, reinforcing a desire for order and conformity if the environment

itself is ordered and purified.[17]

Melanie Klein, Erik Erickson, and, especially Michel Foucault and Julia Kristeva are all cited in support of this dualistic interface of object relations, psychology and geography. The "subject" and the "object" are understood as separate entities which retain an objective status as things to be manipulated and used.

A Biological Perspective on Place

An alternative and quite interesting take on the relationship of psyche and place is presented by biologist Rupert Sheldrake. Combining insights from both physics and biology, Sheldrake applies field theory to the study of the bio/psycho/social milieu. As he sees it, fields are formed by, and exert influence on, the activities of the life within the field. "It might make sense," Sheldrake writes, "to think of the laws of nature as more like *habits*; perhaps the laws of nature are *habits* of the universe, and perhaps the universe has an *in-built memory.*"[18] The idea of such "morphogenetic fields*"* is presented as "an alternative to the mechanist/reductionist approach" of evolutionary theory. Memory is understood as a "tuning in" to these fields, rather than an accessing of information stored within the organism.[19] "The morphic fields that organize our behaviour are not confined to the brain, or even to the surroundings in which it acts [but] involve a conception of holistic patterns of organization which embrace the body and the environment."[20]

Sheldrake makes a significant connection between his theories and those of Carl Jung:

> Jung thought of the collective unconscious as a collective memory, the collective memory of humanity. He thought that more people would be tuned into members of their own family and race and social and cultural group, but that nevertheless there would be a background resonance from all humanity...It would not be a memory from particular persons in the past so much as an average of the basic forms of memory structures; these are the archetypes...*Morphic resonance theory would lead to a radical reaffirmation of Jung's concept of the collective unconscious.*[21]

Further linking the work of Sheldrake to a Jung-based, depth psychological perspective is the work of David Hill on the *Soul's Body*. Working with Robert Romanyshyn and Rupert Sheldrake, who were both on his dissertation committee, Hill asks "in what ways might Rupert Sheldrake's hypothesis of morphic fields and morphic resonance amplify psychology's concepts of soul and soul-making?"[22] Drawing on the work of James Hillman, Henri Corbin, and Roberts Avens, Hill focuses on the "imaginal" nature of the psychic/environmental interface in Sheldrake's approach as well as in processes which make it difficult to draw literalistic boundaries between psyche and environment. Places are seen in this respect more as an actual part of our lives than as a set or stage for them. We, in turn, are integral to our places. "Soul" is not something we have inside us, but a perspective on the whole of life that includes the places we live as well as all other relationships.

Philosophy and Place

Whatever is true for space and time, this much is true for place: we are immersed in it and could not do without it. To be at all—to exist in any way—is to be somewhere, and to be somewhere is to be in some kind of place.[23]

In *Getting Back Into Place* Ed Casey explores place as integral to our "being-in-the-world."[24] In *The Fate of Place* he traces the overcoming of place by an abstract "space" from the time of Plato (and even before) up to the modern era, when place began to reassert itself in the work of Martin Heidegger and Maurice Merleau-Ponty. "The anonymous subjectivity of the lived body is continually confronted and connected with the intersubjectivity at stake in public places."[25] This idea of intersubjectivity, discovered in philosophy, is essential in extending psychological discourse to the field of place. It recognizes in place an equal partner in the *relationship* of emplacement. It pays respect to the *Anima Mundi* (Soul of the World) that Hillman and others had found so significant when dealing working in the area of psyche, of soul. "Just as place is animated by the lived bodies that are in it, a lived place animates these same bodies as they become implaced there."[26] As Sheldrake did in biological language, Casey develops the philosophical basis for questioning the hard and fast boundaries that keep us psychologically alienated from our environment.

Complementing Casey's extensive work are Jeff Malpas's books *Place and Experience*[27] and *Heidegger's Topology.*[28] He too looks at the intersubjectivity of one's being within the surround, and, as Casey had done before him (perhaps reading back through Merleau-Ponty), points out the shift in Heidegger's later work from a discounting of place, in favor of time, to a view giving pride of place to place itself.

Gaston Bachelard too has made significant contributions to the phenomenological approach to space and place.[29]

These philosophical interpretations of the significance of the place/world for human beings remain central to understanding the importance of place for Jungian depth psychology. "With the introduction of the term psychoid archetype 'the rigorous separation of the psyche and world is abolished.'" Roger Brooke goes on:

> The human psyche is not ontologically separate from the world; in a profound sense, it *is* that open place in which the earth-world can realize herself. Human consciousness, for Jung, is Nature conscious of itself. This is the deepest implication of Jung's consistent attempt to think of psychological life as an expression of Nature. It is also his way of thinking through human bodiliness to a non-Cartesian, non-dualistic ontology.[30]

People never appear apart from some place. There is always a *Da* ("there") implicit in *Dasein* ("human being"), a philosophical insight which must not be ignored in psychological study or psychotherapy.

Jung himself resisted the philosophical implications of his own work, being devoted to a Kantian worldview and insisting (as had Freud) on the scientific credibility of his empiricism. As Graham Parkes points out, however, Jung "was prepared—perhaps as a result of his early studies of psychic phenomena—to take the idea of 'second consciousness' more seriously than his predecessor,"[31] and that the

> goal of Jungian analysis can be...to move the 'center of gravity' of the psyche away from the I in the direction of the unconscious, thereby diminishing the I's control and shifting the balance of power toward the autonomous complexes and the archetypal figures of the collective unconscious.[32]

This broadening of the Self could include a place for place, even though Jung does not specifically identify this. Medard Boss, a close associate of Heidegger, wrote that "Jung, as no psychologist before him, clearly recognized the artificiality of the mental separation of human reality into subject and isolated external objects."[33]

Debra Smith Knowles, in her exploration of conflict and concordance between Jung and Heidegger,[34] shows that, while Jung did not understand or did not like the ideas presented by Heidegger, there is much within Heidegger's thought that allows a space for Jung and creates the possibility of moving Jung out of his own philosophical limitations with respect to psyche and place. In Heidegger's own words,

> Man is never first and foremost man on the hither side of the world, as a "subject," whether this is taken as "I" or "We." Nor is he ever simply a mere subject which always simultaneously is related to objects, so that his essence lies in the subject-object relation. Rather, before all this, man in his essence is ek-sistent into the openness of Being, into the open region that lights the "between" within which a "relation" of subject to object can "be."[35]

We do not stand separate over and against our environment. The environment is always an aspect our identity, and we are always an aspect of the environment in which we live.

Ecopsychology

In *The Spell of the Sensuous*, David Abram draws the connecting line between phenomenological hermeneutics (the descriptive and interpretive philosophical approach of Heidegger) and ecology by noting that perception involves "the ongoing interchange between my body and the entities that surround it. It is a sort of silent conversation that I carry on with things, a continuous dialogue that unfolds far below my verbal awareness."[36] Our world is built, therefore, in relationship with all that is around us, the "things" we relate with, and the places that contain them and us. This kind of ecology studies the vital relationships among all the actors involved, including those we have previously considered "inanimate."

> The singular magic of a place is evident from what happens there, from what befalls oneself or others when in its vicinity. To tell of such events is implicitly to tell of the particular power of that site, and indeed to participate in its expressive potency.[37]

Theodore Roszak used the term "ecopsychology" to refer to the effort "to bridge our culture's long-standing, historical gulf between the psychological and the ecological, to see the needs of the planet and the person on a continuum."[38] Reflecting on ecopsychology, James Hillman points out that "an individual's harmony with his or her 'own deep self' requires not merely a journey to the interior but a harmonizing with the environmental world."[39] He sees the investigation of *Anima Mundi*, the world as ensouled, as a next step as psychology moves beyond intrasubjective individualized therapy and intersubjective group dynamics.[40] Ecotherapists like Linda Buzzell have devised ecopsychological interventions to bring the environment into the treatment of stress and depression and psychological insights into the areas of urban development and environmental planning.[41]

Archetypal Aspects

Jung used the concept of archetypes to speak about the deepest structural formation of the psyche. These universal patterns and motifs manifest in complex images discerned in dreams, in mythology, in cultural expressions such as alchemy and astrology, and in *personae*, the imaginal "persons" who populate our "inner" and "outer" lives. Hillman extends this work by calling for a "polytheistic" psychology not tied to the idea of a central ruling self.[42] Exploring archetypes that structure experience as they emerge in the lives of people who interact with a place over time offers clues about what might be needed for healing, growth, and transformation in that place.

The focus on archetypal psychology is at the heart of much of the research being carried out at Pacifica Graduate Institute, some of which is relevant to an understanding of the "soul" of a place. Archetypal reflection plays a dominant role in Elizabeth Perluss' dissertation, *Landscape Archetypes: Islands, Valleys, Mountains, and Deserts*,[43] as it does in Paul Jones' *City and Psyche: An Exploration into the Archetype of the City.*[44] Laura Mitchell connects ecopsychology and the philosophical approach of Merleau-Ponty in her study *The Eco-Imaginal Underpinning of Community Identity in Harmony Grove Valley: Unbinding the Ecological Imagination.*[45] She also creates a model for using such insights for ecopsychological community action. Rosemarie Bogner presents an overview of the psyche/place interface as an introduction to a film project.[46] George McGrath Callan uses ecopychological and alchemical concepts along with the archetypal to look at place in *Temenos: The Primordial Vessel and the Mysteries of 9/11.*[47]

Finally, Craig Chalquist has developed a cross-applicable method, which he calls variously "locianalysis" and "terrapsychology" in his dissertation[48] and in his book *Terrapsychology: Reengaging the Soul of Place.*[49] These works describe archetypal metaphors that link topography, ecology, and the lives of occupants, although from the psychotherapeutic view used in Chalquist's dissertation, the place often takes the role of the traumatized victim, with the original European colonizers and developers seen as narcissistic abusers. For many of the authors cited above, the transference between the researcher and the places studied is taken into account, not as something to "bracket" and exclude as much as possible from undue influence, nor as a hindrance to analytical objectivity, but as evidence of a kind of "call" of the place to the researcher in question to attend and to learn from its archetypal depths.

The works mentioned above offer theoretical or applied models for the emerging discipline of ecopsychology. Study of a place is greatly informed by such concepts even when it does not hold an environmentalist agenda. Such work forms part of an ongoing paradigm formation that includes biological, archetypal, philosophical, psychological, and terrapsychological referents.

Method for Exploring the Presence of Place

The study of the "soul of a place" cannot be adequately covered by the methods of my father, the social science traditions of academic geography, or even by their intersection with psychology in its behaviorist manifestation. As was the case with Jung's own work, such a study of necessity must have recourse to "the realm of the mother": the depths of imagination.[50]

For philosophical justification, deep study of places must turn to the tradition of hermeneutics most completely laid out in *Truth and Method* by Hans-Georg Gadamer. Gadamer clearly and extensively traces the Enlightenment separation of knowledge from lived experience, particularly in the study of historical texts, from the biblical hermeneutics of Schleiermacher through the historical studies of Ranke and Dilthey down to the phenomenological work of Husserl and Heidegger. [51] At the core of his quest for meaning and understanding in the human sciences, Gadamer draws on a relational model for understanding a work of art rather than on the objectivist model of the natural sciences.

Essential for this method is the "hermeneutic circle," which grasps the whole in relation to its parts and the part in relation to the whole. As Heidegger had pointed out in *Being and Time*, we are "thrown" into an encounter with text or event (or place?) with a pre-understanding, a "foreknowledge" that is then refined and tested, further refined and tested within the evolving relationship.[52] Acceptance of "prejudice" and a willingness to be transformed are both essential to the inquiry. The reality inquired into is never simply "there to be found," as is assumed in the scientific model, but always a provisional combination of intersubjective "outer" and "inner" realities that are never truly separate.

A person who is trying to understand a text is always projecting. He projects a meaning for the text as a whole as soon
as some initial meaning emerges in the text. Again, the initial
meaning emerges only because he is reading the text with
particular expectations in regard to certain meaning. Working
out this fore-projection which is constantly revised in terms
of what emerges as he penetrates into the meaning is understanding what is there.[53]

Of Schleiermacher's participatory approach, Gadamer says that
"it is ultimately a divinatory process, a placing of oneself within the
whole framework of the author, an apprehension of the 'inner origin'
of the composition of a work, a re-creation of the creative act."[54] Of
Ranke he says that "all individuation is itself already partly characterized by the reality that stands over against it, and that is why indi-
viduality is not subjectivity, but living power."[55]

The historian does not investigate his "object" by establishing
it unequivocally in an experiment; rather through the intelli-
gibility and familiarity of the moral world, he is integrated
with his object in a way completely different from the way a
natural scientist is bound to his.[56]

This kind of participation is crucial for deep research on the psyche of a place. The researcher is in the place, and the place (in terms
of understanding and meaning), is in the researcher. Both researcher
and place involve psychic components; both researcher and place,
from a Jungian perspective, are also in the psyche. My own research
into the soul of a place in one city block in Monterey, California
reaffirms a "creative depth" found in that city by Craig Chalquist.[57]
Only by standing overlooking the bay with its mile-deep canyon and
walking the land with an Ohlone descendant have I been able to
sense a psychological dimension to the place, a dimension reaf-
firmed in discussions with those for whom Monterey has long been
an important part of their lives.

Gadamer concludes his work by emphasizing the importance of
language in interpretive efforts. It is "the medium of hermeneutic
experience."[58] Use of language in scientific and social scientific

discourse defines its parameters and limits. As an example, moving to a first person perspective when discussing people, events, or places opens up their relational qualities. Likewise, development of archetypal language opens up the depth dimension of research, with the imaginal qualities of a place on a par with its objective features.

Possibilities of Autoethnography

Autoethnography originally represented a move away from the domination of the outsider, even colonialist, perspective on indigenous and oppressed people. It sought out the indigenous voice as the truly legitimate expert on the culture under examination. More recent examples of this sort of writing are found in *Auto/Ethnography: Rewriting the Self and the Social*, edited by Deborah Reed-Donahay,[59] and Ruth Behar's *The Vulnerable Observer: Research that Breaks Your Heart*.[60] It has been employed anthropologically in feminist and liberationist writing.

Carolyn Ellis, a leading teacher in this field, writes about a number of autoethnographic methods in her work *The Ethnographic I*, which demonstrates the technique of autoethnographic writing even while she explains it. Ellis deals with "indigenous ethnography," which she sees as "written by researchers who share a history of colonialism or economic subordination, including subjugation by ethnographers who have made them the subjects of their work."[61] She then broadens the idea of autoethnography to promote it as a way of writing about being part of any sub-group to which one belongs. In *Personal Narrative* "researchers view themselves as the phenomenon and write evocative stories specifically focused on their professional and personal lives,"[62] while in "reflexive" or "narrative" ethnography the focus is

> on a culture or sub-culture, with researchers using their own life story in that culture to look more deeply into the self-other interactions. This approach offers insight into how the researcher changed as a result of observing others—as Dilthey says, the I is discovered in the Thou. The researcher's personal experience is also important for how it illuminates the culture under study.[63]

This approach is used on a "continuum ranging from starting research from one's own biography," to what Ellis terms "confessional tales" which are completely taken up within the researcher's personal encounters.[64]

Style as much as topic marks autoethnographic work. Much of it is written in the form of a story. It is as much an art as a science. Ellis' book itself presents a "methodological novel" with an appendix that contrasts the impressionistic/interpretive and the realist approaches that autoethnography attempts to balance: story and theory, meaning and data, creativity and objectivity, the concrete and the abstract, etc.[65]

When discussing the history of autoethnography or interacting with her students, Ellis looks at the question of the "scientific" legitimacy in the use of this method. In anthropology the personal has always been a part of the ethnographer's work. Bronislaw Malinowski kept diaries for observations that he felt were too subjective to be included in official publications.[66] At least one student mentioned in Ellis' narrative (fictional or not) comes from a sociological, statistical understanding legitimacy in research, expressing the view that autoethnography is entirely subjective. Yet the point is that such subjectivity is inherent in research. To deny or hide it behind an illusory objectivity cannot help but be distorting.

More kinds of understanding and more depth of understanding in all but highly structured and artificial situations can be achieved and conveyed only when the researcher consciously includes the subjective dimension in the research and communicates results in a form that encourages empathy as well as objective assent. In my own research in Monterey I find the place echoing much of my biography: in explaining my intuitive mother to my scientist father, in struggles with addiction in the many Twelve Step groups that meet there, in the blending of Buddhist and Christian thought and practice as the place hosts generations of spiritual seekers. All this tells me about myself, which in turn illuminates Monterey.

The Wounded Researcher

Autoethnography takes a depth psychological turn in the writing of Robert Romanyshyn in *The Wounded Researcher*. Romanyshyn uses his own psychological experience (in his case woundedness and mourning) much as Ellis does, as a window into the "gaps" between researcher and topic. Re-search is "deepened, re-figured, and reflected through the things of the world."[67] "Soul is not inside us. It is on the contrary our circumstance and vocation. It surrounds us, and we are called into the world, as we are called into our work, through this kind of epiphany."[68] This work is grounded in the perspective of a phenomenology that

> situates one between the two extremes of subjectivism and objectivism. For a phenomenologist, the world that we perceive and as we perceive it is not already an object complete in itself waiting for its laws to be discovered and explained by a conscious subject who is apart from it and not a part of it, a subject who floats, as it were, above or beyond the world, like some disembodied spectator mind. On the contrary, phenomenology begins with our entanglement with the perceptual world, the world that makes sense as we sense it.[69]

Romanyshyn, again like Ellis, seeks a new language of research in "metaphor," the equivalent of Ellis' "story." He sees the depth psychologist as somewhat of a "failed poet"[70] and speaks of poetry, mythology, astrology, and alchemy as various approaches that psychology has tried in order to tell its insights from a deeper perspective than that offered by scientistic objectification. He draws much on the myth of Orpheus to detail "six Orphic moments in re-search with soul in mind." The six moments are: 1) being claimed by the work, 2) losing the work, 3) descending into the work, 4) looking back at the work, 5) being dismembered by the work, and 6) letting go of the work (which he terms "mourning as individuation").[71]

The method he advocates is both imaginal and relational. Research into soul is a "part" of one's own soul means that dreams, synchronicities, and other imaginal activities inform the research. "Transference Dialogues" draw on therapeutic insight about the relationship moving back and forth between therapist and patient: a model for the relationship between the researcher and the subject of the research. The Dialogue begins by "opening a space/making a place" because this kind of research "calls for a process that specifically acknowledges [the] dynamic field between the [researcher and the researched] and establishes procedures that attempt to make this unconscious field as conscious as possible."[72]

> When the researcher allows himself or herself to let go of the work, he or she is making a space that can be a place for playing with the possibilities of the work, that is, with the aspects of the work of which he or she is ignorant.[73]

At that point the researcher engages in what Jung called "active imagination." From within a state of reverie, imaginal figures are invited in. Romanyshyn recommends engaging with these figures on a personal level, a cultural-historical level, a collective-archetypal level, and an eco-cosmological level. "In this moment, one has to learn to wait without desire of any sort" for an entrance into that "intermediate landscape between the world of sense and that of intellect"[74] which Henri Corbin termed *mundus imaginalis* (imaginal world), a surrender that calls for "an attitude of 'negative capability.'"[75] For example, I have engaged in imaginal dialogue with a teacher of Theosophy who died in my office on the hill in Monterey. I have also opened myself to wounding in common with the Christian/Dionysian/Orphic archetypal sacrifice as well as to a gratitude for wounds which may remain unhealed but that make us who we are. None of this conforms to double-blind research criteria, but it has brought me much more truly to the sense of soul that resides in that place.

Conclusion

Terrapsychological research builds on solid traditions of geographic and psychological exploration by combining these disciplines in new ways in new areas of focus. It is also developing a unique and exciting way to overcome the subject/object split and to involve deep psychological dimensions of researchers in the creation of wisdom that could help to heal the world.

Endnotes

1 Boss, M. *Psychoanalysis and Daseinsanalysis.* Basic Books, 1963.

2 Hubbard, P., Kitchin, R., et al. *Key thinkers on space and place.* Sage, 2004, p. 4.

3 Gärling, T., and Golledge, R.G. *Behavior and Environment: Psychological and Geographical Approaches.* North-Holland, 1993. p. 4.

4 ibid., p. 5.

5 ibid., p. 6.

6 ibid., pp. 342-399.

7 ibid., pp. 400-487.

8 Tuan, Y. *Space and Place: The Perspective of Experience.* University of Minnesota Press, 1997, p.5.

9 ibid., p. 12.

10 ibid., p. 9.

11 Hubbard, Kitchin, & Valentine, 2004, p. 259.

12 Tuan, p. 85-100.

13 ibid., p. 86.

14 Hubbard, Kitchin, & Valentine, 2004, p. 259.

15 Sibley, D. *Geographies of Exclusion: Society and Difference in the West.* Routledge, 1995, p. 5.

16 ibid., p. 11.

17 ibid., p 85.

18 Sheldrake, R "Mind, Memory, and Archetype." *Psychological Perspectives, 1987,* 18 (1), 9-23, p. 12, italics original.

19 ibid. p. 22.

20 Sheldrake, R. *The Presence of the Past: Morphic Resonance and the Habits of Nature.* Vintage Books, 1989, p. 198.

21 Sheldrake, 1987, p. 25, italics original.

22 Hill, A. David. *Soul's Body: An Imaginal Re-Viewing of Morphic Fields and Morphic Resonance.* Unpublished dissertation 1996. ProQuest Digital Dissertations database. (Publication No. AAT 3002403). (UMI Number 3002403). p. 3, italics original.

23 Casey, E.S. *The Fate of Place: A Philosophical History.* University of California Press, 1997, p. ix.

24 Casey, E.S. *Getting Back into Place: Toward a Renewed Understanding of the Place-World.* IN University Press, 1993.

25 Casey, 1997, p. 241.

26 ibid., p. 242.

27 Malpas, J.E. *Place and Experience : A Philosophical Topography.* Cambridge University Press, 1999.

28 Malpas, J.E. *Heidegger's Topology: Being, Place, World.* MIT Press, 2006.

29 Bachelard, G., and M. Jolas, trans. *The Poetics of Space.* Boston: Beacon Press, 1994.

30 Brooke, R. *Jung and Phenomenology.* London: New York, Routledge, 1991, p. 81.

31 Parkes, G. (1994). *Composing the soul: reaches of Nietzsche's psychology.* Chicago, University of Chicago Press, ibid., p. 366.

32. ibid., p. 367.

33 Boss, M. *The Analysis of Dreams.* Philosophical Library, 1958, p. 52.

34 Knowles, Debra Smith. *Along a Path Apart: Conflict and Concordance in C.G.Jung and Martin Heidegger.* Unpublished dissertation, Pacifica Graduate Institute, 2002. UMI Dissertation Services. (Publication No. AAT 3065324). (UMI Number 3065324).

35 Heidegger, M. *Basic Writings: From Being and Time (1927) to The Task of Thinking (1964).* Harper & Row, 1977, p. 299.

36 Abram, D. *The Spell of the Sensuous: Perception and Language in a More-Than-Human World.* Pantheon Books, 1996, p. 52.

37 ibid., p. 50.

38 Roszak, T. *The Voice of the Earth.* Simon & Schuster, 1992, p. 14.

39 Hillman, J. "A Psyche the Size of the Earth." Roszak, T., Gomes, M., & Kanner, A. (eds.). *Ecopsychology: Restoring the Earth, Healing the Mind.* Sierra Club Books, 1995, p. xix.

40 Hillman, J. *The Thought of the Heart and the Soul of the World.* Spring, 1992.

41 Buzzell, L., & Chalquist, C. *Ecotherapy: Healing with Nature in Mind.* Sierra Club Books, 2009.

42 Hillman, J. *Re-Visioning Psychology.* Spring, 1975.

43 Perluss, Elizabeth. *Landscape Archetypes: Islands, Valleys, Mountains, and Deserts.* Unpublished dissertation, Pacifica Graduate Institute, 2004. UMI Dissertation Services. (Publication No. AAT 3155818). (UMI Number 3155818).

44 Jones, Paul F. *City and Psyche: An Exploration into the Archetype of City.* Unpublished dissertation, Pacifica Graduate Institute, 2003. UMI Dissertation Services. (Publication No. AAT 3119796). (UMI Number 3119796).

45 Mitchell, Laura. *The Eco-Imaginal Underpinnings of Community Identity in Harmony Grove Valley: Unbinding the Ecological Imagination.* Unpublished dissertation, Pacifica Graduate Institute, 2006. UMI Dissertation Services (Publication No. AAT 3211955). (UMI Number 3211955).

46 Bogner, Rosmarie. *Places: An Exploration of Physical Environments and Their Influence on Intrapsychic Processes.* Unpublished dissertation, Pacifica Graduate Institute, 2002. UMI Dissertation Services. (Publication No. AAT 3060747). (UMI Number 3060747).

47 Callan, George. *Temenos: The Primordial Vessel and the Mysteries of "9/11."* Unpublished dissertation, Pacifica Graduate Institute, 2002. R UMI Dissertation Services. (Publication No. AAT 3113900). (UMI Number 3113900).

48 Chalquist, Craig. *In the Shadow of Cross and Sword: Imagining a Psychoanalysis of Place.* Unpublished dissertation, Pacifica Graduate Institute, 2003. (Publication No. AAT 3119806). (UMI Number 3119806).

49 Chalquist, C. *Terrapsychology: Re-engaging the Soul of Place.* Spring Journal Books, 2007.

50 Jung, C.G., and Jaffe, Aniela, ed. *Memories, Dreams, Reflections.* Pantheon Books, 1963.

51 Gadamer, H.G. *Truth and Method.* Crossroad, 1989.

52 Heidegger, M. *Being and Time.* SCM Press, 1962.

53 Gadamer, 1989, p. 269.

54 ibid., p. 186.

55 ibid., p. 204.

56 ibid., p. 213.

57 Chalquist, 2007, p. 115.

58 Gadamer, 1989, p. 385.

59 Reed-Danahay, D. *Auto/ethnography: Rewriting the Self and the Social.* Berg, 1997.

60 Behar, Ruth. *The Vulnerable Observer: Anthropology That Breaks Your Heart.* Beacon Press, 1996.

61 Ellis, C. *The Ethnographic I: A Methodological Novel about Autoethnography.* AltaMira Press, 2004, p. 46.

62 ibid., p. 45.

63 ibid., p. 46.

64 ibid., p. 47.

65 ibid., pp. 359-363.

66 ibid., p. 50.

67 Romanyshyn, R. *The Wounded Researcher.* Spring Journal Books, 2007, p. 8.

68 ibid., p. 9.

69 ibid., p. 88.

70 ibid., p. 10.

71 ibid., pp. 63-80.

72 ibid., pp. 135-136.

73 ibid., p. 137.

74 ibid., p. 147.

75 ibid., p. 149.

George F. Kohn is a doctoral candidate in depth psychology at Pacifica Graduate Institute in Carpinteria/Montecito, CA. He is an ordained Episcopal Priest and rector of St. James Episcopal Church in Monterey, CA with special interest in philosophy, comparative religions, and mental health. He holds a Masters of Divinity from the General Theological Seminary in New York City, and a Masters of Arts degree in Religion and Health from the University of Iowa. His proposed dissertation, from which much of this work originated, is on Hunukul Hill: Archetypal Dimensions of the Soul of a Place.

Enriching the Inquiry: Validity and Methodology in Terrapsychological Work

Craig Chalquist and Sarah Rankin

Since the call went around for a "terrapsychological" approach for tracing the deep connections—whether conscious or unconscious—that bind the human psyche to the places we call home, more and more students have become interested in conducting this kind of research. As a result, the need now arises to address a) whether this approach mixes with other approaches, b) its validity, and c) its reliability. The issue of d) potential projection onto the landscape under study has been dealt with previously[1] but will receive further consideration below.

Mixed Methods and Place Research

Terrapsychological Inquiry (TI) was originally designed as a pilot methodology for detecting and working with *ecological complexes:* recurrent patterns of environmental wounding and colonization that recur thematically generation after generation in the symptoms, dreams, folklore, relationships, and even architecture and politics of a place's occupants.[2] Because TI uses a flexibly transdisciplinary framework for organizing observations and impressions, it

317

can easily welcome techniques from other approaches. Most methodologies worship at the altar of some dominant archetypal perspective or "god": experimental (Procrustes), hermeneutics (wily Hermes), phenomenology (Aphrodite, with "meaning units" chopped out for her by Hephaestos), case study (Theseus led by Ariadne's thread), heuristic (Narcissus bent over in reflection), organic inquiry (grown in the lap of Demeter), or grounded theory (Apollo). Romanyshyn's alchemical hermeneutics (see his book *The Wounded Researcher*) foregrounds the presence of the eloquent seeker Orpheus.

Since its inception, some graduate students have used TI as it stands and others have mixed it with procedures from heuristics and hermeneutics and other qualitative approaches. Although the resulting projects turned out well and made interesting reading, they sometimes suffered from a subtle (and sometimes not so subtle) lack of coherence. This is observable in mixed methods in general. The result stands like a temple built as a collage of architectural styles devoid of an organizing motif or approach. Additionally, because the trauma of an ecological complex tends to produce powerful emotional reactions ("ecotransference") in the people caught in its field, mixed methods risk expressing that trauma unconsciously as a form of fragmentation, as when an assortment of research strategies thrown together but not consciously related to each other echoes the destruction and chaos of a gunnery range or the geographic splits dividing a badly planned community.

In most cases TI can serve as the central methodology of choice for studying deep interactions with the soul of things, beings, place, and nature and to build in tools from other approaches—including quantitative work—as needed. TI is not a fixed set of procedures: it grows and changes with every application. Nevertheless, the researcher should always bear in mind that the methodology should fit the needs of the study and not vice versa.

Validity

In social science research *validity* refers to whether the study actually did what it was supposed to. *Construct validity* means that the working conceptualizations under study are adequately operationalized. For example, in a hypothetical study on the effects of a person's self-esteem on test scores, do test scores adequately represent self-esteem, and do they really go up as self-esteem rises? *Internal validity* has to do with cause and effect: did manipulating a variable actually affect another variable? *External validity* is the degree to which results can be generalized beyond the study.

A strength of qualitative research is that it samples wide ranges of variables instead of breaking apart and focusing on only a few at a time. Although this gives it less precision and less validity narrowly defined, a much broader relevance and richness emerges, especially with relatively unexplored research topics. Another strength is that qualitative research investigates the undeniable presence and impact of the researcher. Mountains of research have proved beyond reasonable doubt that the observer influences the observed even in controlled situations. Rather than denying this or trying to eliminate it, qualitative research honors and explores the subjective dimension of research.

Quantitative definitions of validity in terms of generalizability and well-operationalized variables (measuring what they are supposed to measure) have been relentlessly criticized for thoughtlessly importing 16th Century science techniques into human research for which they are not suitable (for three out of hundreds of examples, see Giorgi, Fischer, and Eckartsberg,[3] Reason,[4] and Creswell[5]). The discussion has since moved on from how traditionally performed research recreates hierarchical power relations, alienation in the Marxist sense, Western notions of ego autonomy, psychological distancing, reductionism and determinism, masculinist ideals of objectivity, and prizing of cognitive knowing over tacit and intuitive forms of knowledge into thoughtful discussions about what constitutes valid and reliable research done with living, sensitive participants.

For TI, validity and reliability remain important criteria capable of being reimagined and reapplied from within its perspective. Similar updating attempts appear regarding four innovative methodologies: Depth Inquiry, Intuitive Inquiry, Co-operative Inquiry, and Liberation Psychology.

In describing Depth Inquiry, Coppin and Nelson indirectly address the issue of validity by outlining the philosophical commitments of depth psychology research, which include the following in relation to the psyche: it is real, both personal and more than personal, fluid and protean, and multiple, relational, and dialectical.[6] When the psyche's natural fluidity and multidimensionality attempts to study itself, its *least* useful tools are those borrowed from natural science; instead, the topic should guide the consciousness of the researcher into ever deeper avenues of inquiry. The same applies to TI.

Rosemary Anderson's Intuitive Inquiry draws on two types of validity procedures: *resonance validity* and *efficacy validity*. The first relies on the quality of emotional resonance within the participant, for whom the findings must have identifiable value and make sense of the participant's experiences. "Research can function in a manner akin to poetry in its capacity for immediate apprehension and recognition of an experience spoken by another and yet be true for oneself, as well."[7] Resonance should occur not in just one domain, but across multiple domains of experience. Resonance validity also includes a "resonance panel" of peers who evaluate the research in progress.

The second criterion, efficacy validity, has to do with whether research fosters creative jumps and insights and "inspires, delights, and prods us into insight and action."[8] Taken together, both types of validity provide a qualitative measure of whether a study adds value to human life and promotes beneficial transformations in the participant's consciousness.

For Co-operative Inquiry (also known as Collaborative Inquiry), the primary criterion for validity is *coherence*, a mutually enriching and informing influence developing between the research statements (which should also be coherent with each other), the inquirers' experience (including intersubjective agreement), their "propositional" or conceptual understanding of the topic they explore, and any actions taken as a result of the study. Coherence also refers to the strength of real-world grasp provided by the research constructs and how successfully they are applied experientially and practically.[9]

Liberation psychology research takes a critical participatory approach as its version of *action science:* research for social change. Its tests of validity include *contextual validity*, the fruitfulness of how the research effort and questions are framed and the relevancy of data collection to those involved in the research (in the case of a place studied with TI, relevancy to those who actually live there); *interpretive validity*, which increases as people come together from various social locations and levels to discuss possible meanings of dominant social narratives and to propose alternative interpretations; and *catalytic validity*: whether the research leads to creative, liberatory transformation in the individuals who participate and in the world at large.[10] To this TI might add: research that leads to transformations in the relationships of local residents to where they live.

TI can work well with all of the above (the more that are included in a place study, the higher its validity) while emphasizing additional dimensions of validity assessment unique to person/place/nature research.

The first dimension is *ecotransference resonance* exemplified by the researcher's "aha!": the deeply felt discovery of consciously or unconsciously enacting themes resonating in the place, object, animal, etc. under study. If resonance panel (in some cases a thesis or dissertation committee) and researcher pick up on similar resonant themes, this provides an indication that the researcher's detection of them is valid. Other responsibilities of the panel include the role of devil's advocate, generating possible disconfirming explanations and hypotheses, and assessing whether the researcher is projecting personal material onto the research site (see more about projection below).

In traditional research, criterion validity refers to whether one set of study results stands up against another, such as how effectively test grades match actual later performance. The consistency with which imaginal themes identified by the on-site researcher as manifestations of an ecological complex continue to resonate and develop during and after the study provides a TI version of criterion validity. Is San Diego really "defended," or do its borders, bases, outposts, and steep seaside cliffs fail somehow to line up with the researcher's constellated defensiveness, the jet patrols circling above La Jolla, or the paranoia found in local conservative politics?

As noted above, construct validity means how closely constructs like operational definitions mirror actual entities being studied. For example, do test scores really measure self-esteem? *Ecoreactivity*, the felt sense of impingement or invasion by the terrain under study, furnishes an ongoing check on construct validity by providing the researcher with dreams, ecotransference reactions, and other indicators of "fitness" between research constructs and the living presence of the research site. An example of this is how Orange County as an imaginal figure appeared in one researcher's dreams to criticize the researcher for omitting an important local motif.[11] Construct validity is further strengthened by TI's use of cycles of reflection and action similar to those employed by Collaborative Inquiry.[12]

Transformation validity refers to the depth of perceived transformation in the relationship between researcher and researched as a result of the research. This includes transformations in how the presence of the site manifests in the psychological field or relational matrix. For example, ecologically damaged sites tend to appear in initial on-site dreams as disturbed or violent personifications that gradually soften and mutate as the study continues.

Intragroup validity means that the more researchers, the better the validity, especially when the researchers have different backgrounds and typologies. So far most place studies have been done by individuals, but Craig Chalquist recently visited California's gold country with Kathryn Quick to try out a small team approach. Chalquist's Myers-Briggs typology is INFJ, whereas Quick has introverted sensation as her superior function and was familiar with the research site. Both discovered numerous examples of Norse mythology at play in Placerville, but their observations came through different channels (in Chalquist's case through extraverted feeling and sensation).[13] Typology of the researcher(s) should be kept firmly in mind.

TI also adds the criterion of *community response validity* stated in the form of two key questions: How consistently do the people who live at the research site resonate to or recognize the findings, and to what degree does the study contribute to the aliveness, sustainability, and ecological integrity of the research site? Because TI does not split advocacy from bearing witness, very often the research itself can be seen as actively valid by changing the ecoreactive "feel," the researcher's relationship to the site, and the community's ways of thinking about where and how they live there. Research should also serve as an opening in a conversation with the place about what it needs from the researcher and from its own community. The same applies to research work with entities other than places.

Reliability

Reliability refers to whether research results can be successfully replicated by other studies. Because TI research topics are complex and multifaceted, "reliability" as replicability or interjudge sameness of results is abandoned in single studies for the same reason it serves no purpose when evaluating psychotherapy: the presence of each therapist/researcher evokes different responses in the client/participant. The relational matrix constellated by each collaborative pair is unique to each. In multiple studies of the same place some form of inter-relationship could be implemented among investigators and peer reviewers.

For TI, reliability refers primarily to whether the work of different researchers combines to form a coherent, intelligible picture of the place, objects, weather, etc. under study. *Generative reliability* is the degree to which the study's clarity, resonance, and attention to detail allow other researchers to use it as a point of departure. This includes the use of poetic and evocative "wild speech" noted and used by Laura Mitchell as appropriately descriptive of the world's aliveness.[14]

Place or Projection?

A criticism sometimes made of TI and of other qualitative methodologies is that findings are merely projections of the researcher's unresolved complexes or psychic wounding.

In some cases this charge is leveled because of a cultural prejudice that the landscape could not possibly be alive, let alone capable of reacting intimately to how we treat it. We are used to thinking of subjectivity as a purely human quality, forgetting traditions like panexperientialism, panpsychism, and Naturphilosophie running all the way back to the stories and practices of "animistic" land-based people who experienced Earth and matter as sentient. Because of this we sometimes forget that the qualities of consciousness that mark us as human evolved in the natural world and still have counterparts there, like bacteria that can tell toxins from nutrients, soil fungi that communicate through neurotransmitter-like signals, and ecosystems that create new adaptive combinations. We also forget that seeing inner as separate from outer and mind apart from world is a relatively recent historical development, and one that paralleled territorial expansion and the global plundering of landscapes now regarded as dead resources.

Even so, we who investigate the forms and patterns found in place, nature, and matter do run a risk of projecting various aspects of ourselves onto the land, sea, and sky. How can we tell when such projections operate, and that patterns we see below and around us do not originate solely from within?

That a thorough self-inventory is necessary before the work starts hardly needs to be said. This should be backed up by at least one peer (an entire resonance panel would be better) who knows the researcher well and who can keep an eye out for projections and other errors of perception. Ideally this watcher, who remains outside the field, possesses some level of psychological training, experience working terrapsychologically, and a knack for knowing whether a suspected symptom of an ecological complex really is one. Does the symbolism make sense in terms of being characteristic of the place? Is it consistent with the total picture there? Do local residents confirm it intuitively? Does it cut across many domains of experience (e.g., the local geology, folklore, politics, art)? Does the ecological complex repeat predictably? As with spotting a syndrome in a psychotherapy client, single symptoms mean little unless they form meaningful, identifiable patterns of expression. Does it carry explanatory weight for local happenings? Do dreams on site seem to confirm it? Or does it primarily express the investigator's unresolved conflicts?[15]

This task is made easier by the fact that projections normally make the relationship with the place go dead. They kill the aliveness of the contact. Descriptions of the place go dry or sound stereotypical, bombastic, or absolutist. Also, critical dreams soon arrive, like the Orange County dream mentioned above, to correct the investigator's impressions. Only for theories of mind steeped too long in their own solipsism could projection, at bottom a symptom of displacement (Linda Buzzell calls it *dysplacement*[16]), be mistaken for actual relationship.

Of course, the fact that one gets triggered by ecotransference does not necessarily mean that the task of analysis should halt. Terrapsychological work can hone a talent for using personal wounds to learn more about our surroundings, especially when they suffer ecological trauma. Properly tended, our "inner" places of scarring, pollution, or barrenness can open doors into understanding and healing similar states in the terrain.

Ultimately, what a person understands and feels is not wholly inner or outer. It is both. By staying thoughtfully and heartfully within the overlap of the two, a realm of soulful interconnection and relationship emerges.

Future Pathways

It would be difficult to identify a bone taken from an archeological find without the means to compare its shape and age with other finds. A psychotherapist trying to explain why certain client behaviors point to a character disorder would scarcely sound convincing without a list of disorders to point to. Terrapsychological Inquiry needs at least two catalogs: one to describe what differentiates an ecotransference reaction from other emotional disturbances, and one providing a list of known ecological complexes. Much investigation awaits. Until it is accomplished, researchers will need to keep their suppositions tentative while recognizing that the charge of seeing patterns where none exist is common throughout the history of disbelief. Probably every significant discovery that changes how we view the world begins with the struggle to trust one's perceptions despite corrosive criticism hurled by defenders of a dying paradigm.

Meanwhile, terrapsychology as a genre continues to flourish, as this anthology testifies.

Ultimately, our understanding of place will need to move beyond single research projects to gather force as a movement capable of expanding our collective consciousness to include sane and loving contact with the living ground beneath our feet.

Endnotes

1 Chalquist, Craig. *Terrapsychology: Reengaging the Soul of Place*. Spring Journal Books, 2007.

2 In *Terrapsychology* (2007), ecological complexes were referred to as "placefield syndromes."

3 Giorgi, A., Fischer, W., and Eckartsberg, R. *Duquesne Studies in Phenomenological Psychology, Vol 1*. Duquesne U Press, 1971.

4 Reason, Peter. *Human Inquiry in Action: Developments in New Paradigm Research*. Sage, 1988.

5 Creswell, John. *Qualitative Inquiry and Research Design: Choosing Among Five Traditions*. Sage, 1997.

6 Coppin, Joseph, and Nelson, Elizabeth. *The Art of Inquiry*. Spring, 2005.

7 Anderson, Rosemary. "Intuitive Inquiry: Ways of the Heart in Research and Scholarship." Unpublished paper, 2006.

8 Anderson, 2006.

9 Reason, 1988.

10 Watkins, Mary, and Shulman, Helene. *Toward Psychologies of Liberation: Critical Theory and Practice in Psychology and the Human Sciences*. Palgrave MacMillan, 2008.

11 Chalquist, Craig. *The Tears of Llorona: A Californian Odyssey of Place, Myth, and Homecoming*. World Soul Books, 2009.

12 Yorks, Lyle, and Kasl, Elizabeth, eds. *Collaborative Inquiry as a Strategy for Adult Learning*. Jossey-Bass, 2002.

13 Chalquist, Craig. *Ventral Depth: Brewing Alchemies and Mythic Motifs of California's Great Central Valley* (in press with World Soul Books).

14 Mitchell, Laura. *The Eco-imaginal Underpinnings of Community Identity in Harmony Grove Valley: Unbinding the*

Ecological Imagination. Unpublished dissertation, Pacifica Graduate Institute, 2005.

15 In the case of Rankin's research on Petaluma, where she tracked the motif of the Phoenix, her master's committee provided a resonance panel, and Chalquist had previously visited the site. See Rankin, Sarah. *A Terrapsychological Study of the Psyche of Petaluma.* Unpublished master's thesis at Sonoma State University, 2007.

16 Buzzell, Linda, personal communication, 2009.

The Art of Nature: Alchemy, Goethe, and a New Aesthetic Consciousness

Seth T. Miller

From the author: *"This essay explores the prospect of building a new aesthetic consciousness, worked out in part with insights drawn from alchemy, into a new aesthetic method of observation first brought forth by Goethe. This mode of consciousness, which hears the 'speech' of natural elements and living things, can be developed through active practice."*

The Art of Nature

In some sense, all art begins with nature, the primal context within which consciousness—including aesthetic consciousness—evolves and transforms. Experiences of the aesthetic afforded through multimodal sensory contact with the natural world work on the individual in ways that no contrived art form can. The play of light and shadow, the shifting of shape and form, the ebb and flow of interweaving sounds, the wafting smells, the warmth or coolness of the air and ground: all these aspects and countless more coalesce into the complex experience of nature, which can radically modify our inner life, and not just temporarily.

329

When I was about eight years old wandering alone through the fields behind my house in Austin, Texas after having traveled what seemed like a slightly dangerous distance (just enough to almost feel lost, and thus to be on the edge of adventure), I came unexpectedly through some trees into an idyllic meadow covered with grass and wildflowers and complete with flitting butterflies, a tiny stream, and a delicate breeze that wafted unidentifiably sweet smells to me. That summer day the elements were aligned in just the right way, and I was awestruck by what seemed a perfect scene. The impact of the essential beauty of this event has stayed with me for my entire life. It was the moment I became awake to nature *as a being,* almost trespassing on some sacred ground—a ground that was perfect and whole in itself. This encounter marked the beginning of my capacity to experience aesthetically.

There seems to be a special relationship between consciousness and the "art" of nature. As beings that evolved in the natural world, we are ideally suited to engaging with its tonality and gesture, taking these sensations aesthetically rather than just practically. Indeed, some of the oldest art known seems clearly inspired by our connection to nature and its activities. Rather than being solely representational, Paleolithic art is evocative, mixing the human and the natural together in a dancing flow.

The modern sciences of ecology and complexity provide clear evidence that nature is not something separate from us, and that almost every aspect of human life, including "inner" life, arises within and partly from these complex interwoven connections to the outer sensory world. In quantum mechanics, it is impossible to run an experiment fully isolated and free from extraneous inputs; isolation as a criterion is no longer tenable for a scientific endeavor, which now *must* include wider "environmental" contexts to gain valid results. Qualitative research recognizes this and calls for ongoing investigation of the investigator. On yet another front, advances in cognitive science have shown that the very roots of perception and consciousness are intimately entwined with the "outer" environment through complex, multi-layered feedback loops that span more than just the brain.[1]

All of this means that the very best intellectual endeavors of humanity now converge on the idea that "out there" and "in here" are not only inseparable, but that their mutual boundary is more dynamic, fluid, and ever-changing than 19th Century rationalism would like to admit. Yet this insight is not radically new. Rather, it is new to the type of Modernity consciousness that has forgotten or downplayed its intrinsic embeddedness in the world.

Alchemy and the Art of Nature

This sense of embeddedness in nature has been embodied in a variety of traditions, not the least of which was alchemy, whose primal statement, "As Above, so Below; as Below, so Above" is an inspiring expression of this wisdom. "Nature" in alchemy stood in meaningful relationship to the human researcher, who could, through specific operations, help it reach an refined state. Yet the sought-for results were not made possible by external manipulation of outer substances alone. Inner substances—the feelings, passions, thoughts, and attention of the alchemist—also had to go through transformations. Moreover, it was not a matter of simply combining inner and outer, or of parallel but disconnected transformations occurring in each realm. Rather, the inner and outer were inextricably entwined, mutually influencing each other's unfolding in a rhythmic dance, as indicated symbolically by the Staff of Hermes, an important alchemical symbol.

The art of the alchemist was both completely unnatural (an *opus contra naturam*—a "work against nature") and a way to further nature's already significant "art" evident in the immense variety of living and nonliving forms it produces. What is important for us is that the entwining of the human and the natural held significance for the evolution of consciousness. The alchemist's consciousness *transformed* when it involved itself in the play of natural rhythms. One of the effects of this transformation led to the alchemist's ability to "read the signatures" of the natural world and skillfully utilize them for healing or for furthering the alchemical opus.

These "signatures" arise within the complex, permeable boundary between the alchemist's inner soul life and the outer world. There is something sublime and difficult to express about this relationship because of its unique character. *It is as if the substances in the outer world* speak *to the alchemist*—not in a hallucinatory or shamanic way, but through a sensitization of the alchemist's soul life that opens a space into which the world announces its movements and changes in a kind of dialogue. This speaking takes shape in the alchemist's mind through the arising of qualitative gestures, moods, and tones.

These words, commonly used when appreciating the world of the art, also describe the alchemist's side of this dialogue with nature. The defining characteristic of such feelings is that they are not "merely" subjective, but give us access to a realm *in between the subjective and objective*. Development of this skill in both the artist and the alchemist requires a continual feedback loop connecting concentrated perception of the outer world with its direct engagement through one's will. For example, where an artist might observe a scene and then mix and apply different combinations of color to a painted work, an alchemist might observe the heating of a substance in an alembic and apply techniques to increase or decrease the amount of heat according to celestial cycles aligned with inner promptings.

Alchemical knowledge was often expressed in symbolic mandalas and obtuse phraseology that obscured the kind of pristine logical relations expected by a modern mind. To fathom alchemy requires a *metaphoric* approach. On the one hand this has led to alchemy being discredited as a fanciful search for physical gold, or at best a type of proto-chemistry. On the other hand, the essential wisdom of alchemy (in terms of the development of human consciousness as discussed briefly above) has never been lost, and has continued to evolve even into the present.

Goethe's Contribution

A prominent figure behind the development of this stream is the German savant Johann Wolfgang von Goethe (1749-1832). Goethe, who is most well known as Germany's greatest literary figure, found great inspiration in alchemy, even going so far as to create a beautiful alchemical Rosicrucian allegory in his work *The Green Snake and the Beautiful Lily. Faust*, his most famous play, is packed with alchemical imagery. But despite his literary status as the "German Shakespeare," his scientific works, dealing with morphology and color, have not been valued until recently as equally important. Goethe himself believed them to be as significant as his other writings.

Goethe understood that the physical nature of the world cannot be divorced from the aesthetic; a lily, a snake, and a rainbow are aesthetic expressions as much as physical manifestations. His morphological studies of plants and animals convinced him that each individual creature is

> a small world, existing for its own sake, by its own means. Every creature is its own reason to be. All its parts have a direct effect on one another, a relationship to one another, thereby constantly renewing the circle of life; thus we are justified in considering every animal physiologically perfect. Viewed from within, no part of the animal—as so often thought—is a useless or arbitrary product of the formative impulse.[2]

Goethe saw the individual plant or animal as a *necessary whole* with a logic and consistency of its own. Perception of this whole requires more than reliance upon what is immediately and passively available to the senses: we must *actively take part* in developing and refining our sensory capacities so that they become appropriately sensitive to the complexity of the particular realm we are observing.

Goethe devoted much of his life to exploring, refining, and applying what is now known as *Goethean phenomenology*. This methodology requires that the element of *time* be re-introduced by the observer in a specific way because how a phenomenon *changes* speaks far more directly to its nature than any isolated moment, however detailed. A Goethean observer endeavors to connect with a phenomenon in as wide a variety of contexts as is feasible. Goethe called this style of working a "delicate empiricism that makes itself utterly identical with the object, thereby becoming true theory. But this enhancement of our mental powers belongs to a highly evolved age."[3]

This is an artful empiricism, aesthetically placing the observer *within* the world of the observed through what Goethe called *exact sensorial imagination*. This non-fanciful imaginative activity joins the *feeling life* of the observer directly to the observed. Goethe described this dissolution of the subject-object boundary:

> My thinking is not separate from objects; that the elements of the object, the perceptions of the object, flow into my thinking and are fully permeated by it; that my perception itself is a thinking, and my thinking a perception.[4]

If we follow Goethe here, we recognize that phenomena—particularly natural phenomena—*deserve* our attention, the free giving of which is an act of love that allows us to perceive beyond the normal habits of modernist consciousness to reach into the unknown towards the whole. But how is this accomplished?

Reading the Signatures

Goethe practiced this art in his morphological studies of the plant world.[5] An essential aspect of it involves directed but open perception towards a living form as it evolves over time. The *way* that form changes in response to environmental variations (as well as to its own complex internal ecology) is more important than the simple fact of such changes. Developing attention to such shifts builds a soul sensitivity to gesture, mood, and tone.

For example, it is possible to identify people by bearing and style of movement apart from other identifying visual features such as body type, facial characteristics, and so forth. Each person's unique way of moving embodies qualitatively coherent patterns that we can learn to perceive. The gestalt of such movement and form can simply be called one's *gesture*. When we become sensitive to another person's gesture, we can notice how it changes, then link these outer changes to shifts in the person's inner life. Reading the nuances of someone's total gesture is a reading of their "signature" that provides a gateway into aspects of their being which may otherwise be hidden.

This example helps us see how the reading of "signatures," which may seem a bit strange or even esoteric at first, is already something most of us already do, at least within limited contexts. A child with an alcoholic parent, for example, quickly becomes adept at reading changes in the parent's gesture, which then become *signs* of possible danger. Goethe and the alchemists before him show us that these "signatures" extend into every aspect of living and non-living environments overflowing with little windows and doors that invite us "into" the world in a deeper way. It is possible to learn to be sensitive to these qualitatively rich offerings from the world and what they have to "say."

The Space In Between

Something interesting happens as we build our sensitivity to the qualitative gestures of the world. A point arises where we realize that what we perceive no longer bears the stamp of the "other," impressed upon our senses by the normally operative boundary (for modern day-waking consciousness) between the inner and the outer. *What used to be "out there" starts to have the character of sensations and feelings that arise "from within."* For example, hunger, or sadness, or delight, although obviously connected to outer events, take shape from within; we identify these as "ours"—my hunger, my sadness, my delight—because of the qualitative way in which the sensations arise. When we follow through with the Goethean methodology, we sense aspects of what we normally identify as belonging strictly to the outer world as *inner*. We thus feel the qualities of an outer process *as if* it were "mine" arising from within, but retaining its own particular character, its own *language*.

This language, like all language, unfolds in a space *in between* our subjective world and the objective world around us. It is a gray area, not wholly subjective, not wholly objective, but having characteristics of both. Goethe called it the "subjective-objective" for this very reason. By working within this space, our dialogue can be enhanced without reducing nature to an objective set of facts. Real dialogue keeps the complexity complex.

Engaging like this involves an exchange: we not only "listen" to the world, but we find that something flows back from us to the world as we "speak" to it as well. We have involved ourselves in a subtle dynamic feedback loop which joins the inner and outer worlds. We tune ourselves to allow the outer world's inward aspect to become our own inner sensation. Alchemically, this means perceiving the "moods" of the *anima mundi* or "world soul" as our tuning in loops back delicately into the unfolding of the whole movement.

As a result, our perception becomes less like that of an observer standing at a distance and more a loving activity, a gift of attention flowing outward through our intention. Perception becomes *love*, and this love actively unites us with what we are present for.

Moving-Image-Building

We are complex beings—wholes—and it is unreasonable to expect that we can arbitrarily separate off parts of ourselves when we enter into observation. Even if every aspect of our inner life were conscious this would be an impossible task, but given the vast amount of continual unconscious activity, and the complexity and subtlety with which it influences observation,[6] an ideal of separation has often proved socially and ecologically dangerous, as much of modern history has shown. By contrast, Goethe continually put himself in the way of what he observed rather than attempting to stand off to the side (like most modern science does).

Goethe also knew that the human being is the most sensitive of instruments, capable of perceiving far more than any possible machine, and that the human instrument can be retuned to *enter into* the phenomena before it. In part this involves observing a specific phenomenon over time across a variety of contexts. When this is done, certain features or aspects of the phenomenon stand out in the stream of its unfolding. However,

> If I look at the created object, inquire into its creation, and follow this process back as far as I can, I will find a series of steps. Since these are not actually seen together before me, I must visualize them in my memory so that they form a certain ideal whole.[7]

Goethe takes individual moments that stand out and, rather than isolating them to determine or control particular slices of the phenomenon, he attempts to connect each slice with what surrounds it *in time*. In other words, Goethe imaginatively joins two moments of a thing's unfolding through disciplined inward picturing: "At first I will tend to think in terms of steps, but nature leaves no gaps, and thus, in the end, I will have to see this progression of uninterrupted activity as a whole."[8]

The whole is paramount, but it cannot be perceived all at once. It takes a certain activity—an *alchemical* activity, equally an *artistic* activity—to begin to form an inward picture capable of holding the complexity of the whole without reducing it to single moments or piecemeal sensations. Goethe states that "if we want to reach a living perception of nature, we must become as living and flexible as nature herself."[9] Our inwardly developed capacities must take on the gesture, tone, and mood of the outer process we are observing.

To grasp the whole we must fill in the gaps with an exact imagination borne on the back of detailed, *loving* observation of the outer, whether it be a rock, a flower, a hummingbird, or a person. This in turn yields a sort of inner time-lapse movie that morphs from state to state. More than an inner *visualization*, this moving reconstruction is filled with dynamic relations between unfolding *qualities*, carried initially through sensation, which begin to have a life of their own and take on more and more significance.

Goethe knew that it is not enough to build up sequences of moving images. To allow the living whole of a phenomenon to present itself, a space must be made for its full appearance. Tending higher-level wholeness, which he called the *urphenomenon*, required eventually *dissolving* the activity by which the particular presents itself in order to allow the subtler nature of the phenomenon to rise completely to the surface. Now we can let Goethe finish his thought from the previous quotation:

> At first I will tend to think in terms of steps, but nature leaves no gaps, and thus, in the end, I will have to see this progression of uninterrupted activity as a whole. *I can do so by dissolving the particular without destroying the impression...*[10]

This cannot be shortcut. We must do the difficult work of observing, of building up an inner moving picture that connects our observations into a coherent whole, and then dissolve the particularity of our imaginative sequence so that the larger whole can speak itself into the silent space thus created.

This process is difficult to describe. As indicated before, nothing can substitute for actually carrying out the procedure not just once, but rhythmically and repeatedly, like sketching a figure many times from different angles.

An Exercise

You are invited to view the following still images while attempting to inwardly morph each leaf shape into the next. Transformations of single leaf forms across the life cycle of a plant will keep things simple and demonstrative, but ultimately one would work with the entire plant and its surroundings.

The goal is to become familiar with exactly how the leaf unfolds in its life cycle and thereby feel something of its overall gesture. Take the sequence forward, and then reverse the sequence and "play it back" to its beginning. At first you can do this while looking at the images, try to reproduce the essential form without having the object before you. Repeat this forward/backward activity until you find a rhythm that feels less effortful and more organic.

Now for the hard part: while *still moving the gesture inwardly, let the particulars of each image dissolve*. Let the details of the leaves fade into the background as the sequence moves forward and back. Keep a soft inward focus. With practice you can gain a feeling of the moving gesture of the plant without having to inwardly picture any leaf shapes.

Once you have made an attempt at this, however faulty or incomplete, do the same with the second sequence. You may be surprised to sense a real difference in the quality of the unfolding even without clear thoughts or words. See if working through both image sequences enhances your ability to perceive the differences in gesture between the plants.

Sequence 1[11]

Sequence 2[12]

Whether you work with still images or with the plant itself, the key is to shift your focus from an outward perception to an inward perception based on the kind of exact sensorial imagination developed by Goethe. The rewards include the slow but certain development of your powers of subtle observation, an increased sensitivity to relationships between what appear initially to be separate phenomena, and a growing intimacy with your own process of knowing.

Endnotes

1 See, for example, Andy Clark's book *Supersizing the Mind* (2008).

2 Goethe, J.W. and Miller, D. *Scientific Studies*. Princeton, N.J.: Princeton University Press., 1995, p. 121.

3 Goethe and Miller, 1995, p. 307.

4 Goethe and Miller, 1995, p. 39.

5 Goethe, J.W. and Miller, G.L. *The Metamorphosis of Plants*. Cambridge, MA: MIT Press, 2009.

6 What we are capable of observing is very dependent upon the particular (often unconscious) sensitivities peculiar to a particular individual. Whether certain aspects of an outer phenomenon "appear" may depend upon whether a person is more situated towards proprioceptive, spatial, or aural stimulation, for example. It is really not a question some "objective datum" that is either perceived or not. Every "objective datum" is part of a *perceiving ecology* that can have its own inner tendencies and rules. Good teachers are aware of this fact and create opportunities to engage multiple ways of knowing and perceiving in any given "lesson."

7 Goethe and Miller, 1995, p. 75.

8 Goethe and Miller, 1995, p. 75.

9 Goethe and Miller, 1995, p. 64.

10 Goethe and Miller, 1995, p. 75.

11 Colquhoun, M., & Ewald, A. *New Eyes for Plants: A Workbook for Observing and Drawing Plants*. Lansdown, United Kingdom: Hawthorne House, 1996. Musk Mallow.

12 Talbott, S. "Can we learn to think like a plant?" http://www.natureinstitute.org/txt/st/mqual/ch09.htm Buttercup.

Resources

Colquhoun, M., & Ewald, A. *New Eyes for Plants: A Workbook for Observing and Drawing Plants*. Lansdown, United Kingdom: Hawthorne House, 1996.

Debivort. Leaf morphology disposition. 2006. http://en.wikipedia.org/wiki/File:Leaf_morphology_disposition.png

Goethe, J.W. *Goethe's Fairy Tale of the Green Snake and the Beautiful Lily*. D. MacLean, trans. Grand Rapids: Phanes Press, 1993.

Goethe, J.W. v., & Miller, D. *Scientific Studies*. Princeton, N.J.: Princeton University Press, 1995.

Goethe, J.W. v., & Miller, G.L. *The Metamorphosis of Plants*. Cambridge, MA: MIT Press, 2009.

Mandera, R., & Meyer, U. Portrait of a medicinal plant - tropaeolum majus l. - nasturtium, 1995. http://www.anthromed.org/Article.aspx?artpk=248

Steiner, R. *Man as Symphony of the Creative Word*. J. Compton-Burnett, trans. London: Rudolf Steiner Press, 1970.

Talbott, S. "Can we learn to think like a plant?" http://www.natureinstitute.org/txt/st/mqual/ch09.htm

Videos depicting how these transformations of the image might look from outside are available at http://www.spiritualalchemy.com.

Seth Miller has taught physics and other subjects in Waldorf high schools across the West, where the spirit of Goethe is alive and well. A bachelor's degree in philosophy and a master's degree in consciousness studies taught him that it is just as important to explore how we think as what we think. He is currently writing a PhD dissertation in the nascent field of transformative studies on the topic of transformation as viewed through the lenses of alchemy, anthroposophy, and cybernetic epistemology, while doing freelance web and print design.

ethicks

It is Leaping At You

this juicy green
will only last a few minutes
so love it
while it's running towards you
roll in it
until things fall out of your pockets
let it cover you with kisses
and dampen your hair
and cajole your cells into remembering
that you too
once were so full of growingness
you could barely contain it

let it slip its way
into your eyes
and fill the thirst that puddles there
in the long dark of winter
let it bake bread in your belly
and soften the arches of your feet
until you find yourself hovering
in that space between yellow and blue
until your being is draped in the gleaming
laying itself on to the hills
until the giddiness of it all
rises up in your throat
and sprouts leaves in your mouth
and your words fall away
and you start speaking
in flowers

—Catherine Baumgartner

Sandhills Listening

Wendy Sarno

Can we evolve a new land ethic for a time in which nature has few rights? If so, such an ethic will need to stand on a deeply transformed sense of nature, creature, and place. Below Wendy Sarno describes transformations that prepared her for the one she writes about in this chapter:

> *In May of 2010, I sat in a circle of people on a plateau in southern Utah. There at over 8000 feet we were surrounded by Ponderosa Pines. As we spoke together in council about our soul's journeys and what had brought us to that place, I sensed a stillness deepen among the trees. It seemed almost they bent a little and stilled the wind to hear us. I believe the land does listen to us and probably mourns much of what it overhears. I have sat with the stones in northern New Mexico and sensed the whispers of a sacred conversation. We must get very quiet. We must be very still. And when we can slow down enough to pay our much-owed attention to the places of earth, I believe we come into real relationship; and as in any relationship when we slow down and pay attention, when we speak the other's name with respect, even affection, does the other not heal and thrive and blossom?*

345

We are part of the prairie; it is part of us.—Stephen R. Jones

Not long ago I had the opportunity to visit the Sandhills of Nebraska for the first time, in the company of a geologist who had spent his career studying this landscape. Here I was touched not by trees or stones, but by grass and wind and sky.

First there is the rhythmic sound of the windmill breathing ...whoosh, woof, whoosh, woof...as it draws water up from the ground to the pool at its feet. Behind the breath of the windmill is the wind itself. Across the rolling twenty-thousand square miles of the Sandhills of Nebraska, listening is done between the wind and the grass, between the wind and the far train moving unseen beyond the dunes carrying coal east from Wyoming. A train every half hour.

Deep in the low interdunal valleys, cattle low thru the night. Listening, the land lies quiet, treeless, held in the grip of grass for this millennium. In another millennium the grass withers, the sand moves, and the listening is between the wind and the sand as the grains bounce up one side of the dune and avalanche down the other. The dune creeps slowly on sandy cat's feet, forming and unforming the Aeolian landscape, braiding and unbraiding the ancient rivers.

This night on the valley below the dunes the listening is between the wind and the tent. The flapping of nylon goes on all night under the black field of a billion stars, the Milky Way spread across the great table of sky like a spilled banquet, the meteors falling like salt. The sky over the Sandhills is utterly silent. One can listen deeply for hours and hear nothing but the wind in the grass, in the dry sunflowers, against the tent. And now and again between the gusts of wind the breathing of the windmill...whoosh, woof, whoosh, woof. Once coyotes. Then again the fingers of wind playing with this thin fabric of human presence.

The Prairie

This is the great American prairie and it is part of each of us, part of the mythos and the very soul of this country. The gently rolling hills are covered with big bluestem, sand bluestem, prairie sandreed and switchgrass, a hundred kinds of wildflowers. There are wetlands and fens with their groves of cottonwood nestled in among the hills that draw water from deep under ground. The place is wide with sky. Know yourself fortunate to walk here for a day. This land has not easily welcomed human occupation.

Once sixty million bison roamed here along with elk and grizzly bear, antelope and wolf. Not a hundred years ago the bison had been hunted to near extinction, and the wolf and bear and elk are long gone from this landscape. Men saw the wide-open spaces and came with their wagons and their plows and their domestic cattle and parceled it out. But they hadn't listened yet to what the land needed or was willing to do for them. The farms this place were never meant for failed on the fragile soil. The over-grazing herds of cattle destroyed the ancient grasses. The loose topsoil blew off in the constant wind, resulting in years of drought. The old ethic of human domination, imposing our will and our hungers with little regard for the earth was, in a short time, defeated by this place.

Today there are some who are finding a new relationship with this land, listening to the sand under the dirt, to the deep aquifers under the sand, to the grasses and the weather. Bison are being reintroduced and now number a hundred times more than humans. Those who want to cultivate human life here are learning the grazing patterns of their herds that will support the wild grass, and how the grass supports the owl and the fox, the endangered upland sandpiper and blowout panstemon; and how the grassy wetlands provide habitat for a myriad of creatures, including the curlew and the migrating flocks of Sandhill Crane. Some talk of extensive preserves to set aside vast acres of this native prairie, of bringing back elk, and, maybe in time, the wolf. Humans are beginning to understand biodiversity as we never have before, but most of us still listen with our own interests in mind. A lasting transformation will occur only when we learn to listen to the land for its own sake and to truly know ourselves as a part of it. Stephen R. Jones says:

We are part of the prairie; it is part of us. We inhale moisture given off by the transpiring grasses and breathe the oxygen they create during photosynthesis. We eat the seeds of wheat, barley, and rye, and the roots of other prairie plants. Our blood flows with the same molecules that nourish the big bluestem and cottonwood. Our collective memories radiate from the dusty savannas of central Africa and converge on the blood-soaked plains of the American West...Should we destroy what remains, we will lose much more than Indian grass, black-footed ferrets, burrowing owls, and grasshopper sparrows. We will lose an irreplaceable work of creation, a critical strand in the web of life that binds us to this planet and keeps our humanity and spirit whole. We may, in Sweet Medicine's words, "become worse than crazy."[1]

In a place like this it takes a special kind of listening to hear the stories the land has to tell, a special sensitivity to the songs of deep time. It takes one who knows how to move his hand over the delicate layers of sand to find the strata of centuries, the weathers laid down, the rains, the years of grass, the dyings of grass, the hoof prints of bison after the ice moved north. One who speaks with reverence for the paleosol, the peat, the fens with the deep water a thousand years old, the grass, the generations of grass.

This generation of cattle, these dusty roads, these miles of fence, the weathered faces of the people who draw their own lives from this place, the heartbeat of these windmills is only an eye blink in the long story of these hills. Coming as a stranger to the life here, I can barely listen below the surface, under the wind that falls off the hot sun against the sandy blowout atop the highest dune. The meadowlarks, the flying ants, a brown winged ladybug, the quick lizard and the shiny black beetles. The spread of stillness reaches somewhere around my belly and quiets me. My own breath joins the breathing of the place.

To one who grew up in the shade of oak and maple forests in northern Illinois, this wide-open prairie is a new landscape. I am touched by sun and wind and the broad brush of sky. This is a new kind of beauty, open and silent, that blows into my soul and changes me. I am brought to a fresh sensitivity to the fragile ecologies of our earth, to the complex interweaving of land and creature and weather and time. I am brought to grief for the ways humans have misunderstood our place in this delicate balance and misused the land for our own shortsighted advantage. Truly, it has not been to our advantage at all and we have lost things we can never replace.

Listening to the Land

When I stand on a slope of prairie grass feeling the whisper of wind on my skin I sense deeply the ways this land offers a spaciousness of soul and asks of me so little in return. Even so, it asks much. The land asks that I pay full attention, that I listen to its language and learn the poems it writes in sand and grass and birdcall. It asks that I listen to the seasons and the weathers and step with reverence where my foot falls.

We are, I think, each asked to bring our unique resources to bear on the healing of our world as we seek a more humble apprehension of our human place here. It is an overwhelming task in the face of climate change and what our presence is costing this planet. It is a task that requires courage and sacrifice. Answering the needs of this grassland alone won't be fast or easy. We must do what we can. At the very least we must walk out under the open sky and let the beauty we encounter break our hearts and break us open to the work we are each called to do.

I come to the land as a poet. I come with the eyes and ears of a poet to meet the poetry of our earth. It is in poems I speak of it and speak back to it. I have no illusion that my small words will change the economies of our world or save the great forests or the oceans or these seas of grass. But poems are what I have in my pouch. Poems are what I scatter as gift to this aching land.

In the morning the late moon curves over the eastern sky that lies in a blush over the hills, and below the moon hang Venus and Saturn and Regulus in Leo. The sky is utterly clear and still. To the north Ursa Major lies heavy and low over the dunes. Later, over tea, the cows come down from behind the hills and we walk together up the valley. We watch each other as we walk. They seem eager to show me the way to the sweet grasses. Then, as our paths diverge, they disappear over a roll in the hill and move deeper into the valley, at home in their spread of grass. The sun rises with the wind and shapes the dunes in shadowed hillocks covered in soft green and yellow, purple and tan, the countless shades of grass.

As we leave the valley, the listening goes on between the cows and the grass, the birds and the wind, the grass-held hills of sand and the sun. Up the road another windmill turns its tail, easily breathing in the morning wind of early October...whoosh, woof, whoosh, woof...pulling water up from the sand. Listening between wind and water, the land is shaped and reshaped.

One day the dunes will move again covering these fences, this road, the bones of cattle, the impress of human hands. Who listens then, I wonder, when the song is all between the sand and the wind, when galaxies still wheel across the silent night, still a moon hangs over the bloom of dawn?

Endnote

1 Jones, Stephen R.; *The Last Prairie, A Sandhills Journal*; University of Nebraska Press, Lincoln; 2000.

Wendy Sarno has lived in the Midwest all her life. For over forty years she has been in the St. Louis area, where she raised two children and found community and cultivated work she loves. She has been listening to people as a Spiritual Director for more than fifteen years. She leads retreats and facilitate workshops on a variety of topics designed to nourish the soul life and lead toward greater presence and wholeness. Much of her work now involves the use of writing in groups to facilitate the collecting of individual stories and aid in spiritual exploration.

Communities Living in Partnership with the Earth: The Permaculture Solution

Linda Buzzell

Until recently, permaculture, a worldwide movement toward human habitations whose operations mimic those of the natural world, has had to do without either a psychological framework for building community or any sense of Earth as sentient and responsive. Permaculturalist and psychotherapist Linda Buzzell makes a case for augmenting permaculture design with both.

Once we begin to wake up from what Steven Foster and Meredith Little call "The Big Lie,"[1] we start to realize that our bodies, minds, souls, spirits, families and communities are not separate from or superior to the rest of the natural world. Gradually we come to know in a very profound way that we humans are but a tiny part of the entirety of Nature, deeply embedded in the whole.

Then we can live as a conscious, creative expression of this huge and mysterious living organism: the unfathomably strange cosmos, our own local universe, and, even more locally, our home planet Earth, our watershed, and even the ground under our feet.

Once we come to recognize Gaia as a living being, it seems natural for us to communicate with her and listen for her replies. Being

351

a Gaian human means engaging in dialogue and even in loving partnership with her.

Our old rules about dominating Earth and treating her as an object to be exploited for human benefit no longer hold. But where can we look for alternatives?

Permaculture

The permaculture concept was developed in the mid 1970s in Australia by Bill Mollison[2] and David Holmgren.[3] Equally grounded in the science of modern ecology and ancient indigenous Australian wisdom, permaculture offers ethics and practices to help us regain our proper perspective and behavior towards the sacred earth and other beings. The word "permaculture" combines the word "permanent" with both "agriculture" and "culture," the idea being that if our species wants to continue to enjoy life on this planet, we need a sustainable way of thinking, acting and being that doesn't destroy our life support systems and those of countless other species with whom we share this home. As conditions worsen and threaten our extinction as of the second decade of the new millennium, more people are turning to the permaculture design system for guidance and inspiration.

Permaculture Ethics

Permaculture's three ethical principles provide a solid base for our lives and communities as newly awakened partners in the larger earth community. They are usually articulated as follows:

- Care for the Earth
- Care for the People
- Share the Surplus

Simple, easy to remember, and profoundly life-changing. Notice that earth care comes first, but that people care is also important.

Industrial society ignores both, trashing the earth without regard for most of its people, let alone the other sentient beings with whom we share our life support system. Even the modern environmental movement, which tries to address the first ethic, often ignores the obvious fact that human primates are also nature's children and we have been an integral part of our planet's ecology for over a million years. We need to once again behave like a responsible keystone species rather than a runaway virus in order to regain our natural place within the earth family.

Because of our destructive behavior, environmentalists often fantasize about "pristine" natural wilderness free of pesky, overpopulating humans, ignoring the fact that archeologists and anthropologists are now discovering that much of our planet's so-called wilderness areas were actually human-managed food forest until European agricultural practices disrupted them. It is said that John Muir wondered why the wonderful "wilderness" he saw when he arrived in North America seemed to degrade as years went by—ignoring the fact that many of the native peoples who carefully and intelligently tended these forests for millennia had died of European illnesses or been exterminated by the invaders.

The third ethic—sharing the surplus—scares some people. It smacks of the dreaded word "socialism." But permaculture wisely points out that excess surplus becomes pollution. So if we don't figure out how to handle surpluses—of people, fruit or manure—we drown in our own productivity and simultaneously starve other people and species of the basics of life. The ideal is to produce no more than can be absorbed by other people and the rest of nature. As many have pointed out, unchecked growth is analogous to cancer, and we must relearn how to live once more within nature's limits. If we don't, she will intervene to see that we do. Gaia is no benign "Mother Earth" when aroused.

The 12 Permaculture Principles

Many alcoholics and other addicts use the 12 Steps to overcome their destructive behavior. Permaculture too offers 12 things we must do to recover and heal from our ecocidal behavior. They are offered as guidelines to ecological design at every level, including what permaculturists call "Zone 0"—the human psyche.

1. Observe and Interact.
This is a wise first step in beginning to live as part of an animate

earth rather than as its dominator (as Riane Eisler[4] might put it). Before starting any project, whether it's a backyard garden or a new community, we need to begin by being quiet and listening. Our relationship with any aspect of living nature (including the interior wild nature in our own bodies, minds and souls) must be a dialogue, not a monologue. This is the biggest mistake we make in modern agriculture and land care, of course. We rush in and start to change things, not waiting for a full solar cycle to observe who else is already here.

If we are patient instead, we see the birds and other animals with whom we share the land, including those who inhabit the subsoil universe. We are surprised by plants that pop up here and there in their seasons and then melt back into the soil. We marvel at the majestic cycles of the sun, moon and stars and at the various flowerings and dyings that form the rhythm of life. We observe wild natural forces as they express themselves in our particular place: wind, fire, sun, rain. We also sense the "invisible" presences that whisper to us as we sit quietly on the earth, for we are not the first or last people to live here. Sometimes they visit us again in dreams. Enough observation and interaction will convince us that, indubitably, the earth and the land are alive.

Once we have begun by listening and observing, we are ready to progress to the following principles that teach us additional ways of living responsibly with our earth-parent. I'll address them in groups:

2. Catch and Store Energy.
3. Obtain a Yield.
4. Accept Self-Regulation and Feedback (which Earth supplies readily).
5. Use and Value Renewable Resources and Services.
6. Produce No Waste.

These five principles are practices many indigenous cultures teach from early childhood onwards, but we moderns must relearn them from the ground up. Their implications for land care are obvious, but it's also wise to apply them to people care and community building as well. By doing so, we start to conserve our psyche's energy as well as fossil fuel and other energy, wary of wasting it on relationships that sap life forces and offer no yield.

We are also encouraged to hear what others—whether land, animals, plants or people—have to tell us about how we behave. We value and refuse to waste the "free" services of nature that allow all people and creatures to survive (clean air, water, natural beauty). And we begin to investigate how to avoid creating cultural waste as well as biological and chemical waste.

The final six principles take us even more deeply into how to apply the permaculture ethics in everyday personal and community life:

7. Design from Patterns to Details.
8. Integrate Rather than Segregate.
9. Use Small and Slow Solutions.
10. Use and Value Diversity.
11. Use Edges and Value the Marginal.
12. Creatively Use and Respond to Change (the problem is the solution).

Again, it's easiest to see how these principles apply to land care and green building, but what about people care? The seventh principle advises us to notice nature's patterns—air current shapes, stream patterns, spirals, circles, edges—and mimic them in our own lives. What is nature's way for us as humans, we learn to ask, and how does that differ from recent cultural patterns in modern media-saturated consumer society?

It's also wise to notice the natural stages in plant, animal, human and perhaps even planetary lifespans, and to honor the progression from youth to adulthood to elderhood and beyond, as the cycle returns to its source and our bodies return to the earth and water from which they emerged, while our souls (in some belief systems) rejoin the collective Spirit permeating all things.

The eighth, tenth and eleventh steps remind us to appreciate the value of differences and include them in our designs for land, culture and psyche. Polyculture, not monoculture, is nature's way.

Designing for and welcoming many sources of support ensures resiliency in our lives and communities.

The most generative springs of creativity often await in these marginalized areas and in people we may think of as "Others." Permaculture cautions us against rejecting and discarding so-called "weeds" or "invasives" before exploring all of their gifts and encourages us to find the "yield" in every element or individual.

The ninth step is a call to slow down our lives to nature's pace and to let go of the inflated human ego that flies, like Icarus, too close to the sun, heading for a nasty fall. Eternal growth is an impossibility on Earth, for excellent reasons. Again, when we harmonize our lives and land with nature's ways, we find that a richer yield awaits us.

The twelfth step is a preparation for when nature reasserts her control over runaway human life. Rather than viewing change—even seemingly catastrophic change—as always negative, the permaculture mantra is, "The problem is the solution." My permaculture teacher, Larry Santoyo, loves to tell the story of a Texas rancher who called him to solve a problem on his cattle ranch: too many grasshoppers. Santoyo arrived, took time to "observe and interact" with the land, and pronounced: "You don't have too many grasshoppers. You have too few turkeys." Delighted, the rancher bought turkeys and watched them fatten up on the grasshoppers. A year later Santoyo received another frantic call from the rancher, who was doing very well selling his grasshopper-fed turkeys: "How can I get more grasshoppers?"[5] This story reminds us of the wisdom of reconsidering what we view as waste to see if it can be put to better use.

Grass, cattle, grasshoppers, turkeys, and even "excess" people: finding the right balance between elements can be tricky but is necessary as we try to design sustainable ecosystems. When conditions change, permaculture encourages us not to resist, but to open our eyes to the benefits of seemingly negative circumstances. For example, job loss means less cash, but also a surplus of time. How to invest that surplus in a new direction?

Permaculture's Edge: Living in Community

Applying permaculture principles to individual and communal people care is a relatively new pursuit. Until recently permaculture's primary focus was on land care and regenerating sustainable local ecosystems. Now attention is being paid to "Invisible Systems": law, the economy, etc., including increasingly critical tasks like community organization and designing for psychological well-being.

Here again we must seek the guidance of Earth and the land we live on. Gaia offers us natural templates for cooperation as well as healthy competition. And she also provides deep ecotherapy—the profound healing that results from slow, sweet connection with our planetary parent and siblings.[6]

In applying the permaculture ethics and principles to the creation of community, the word "interact" from the first principle gives us our strongest guidance. To live in healthy, harmonious community we need to interact not only with other humans, but also be in constant communication with other living beings and also the natural forces, the living land itself (above and below ground) and even the greater cosmic forces with whom we share our lives. It is wise to remember that interaction is a two way street. We modern humans love to express our own thoughts and feelings, but we also need to relearn the ancient art of slowly, patiently listening for subtle responses to our observation, attention and communication. This requires an entirely different way of living and being—one that takes time to adapt to. For most of us—even those who have practiced permaculture for some time—the idea of a living, communicating Earth takes some getting used to.

What kinds of communities might emerge if we fully practiced these 12 principles? One example is Crystal Waters, one of the oldest permaculture intentional communities. In this eco-village in Australia, two hundred residents of all ages from many cultural backgrounds live on eighty-five private one-acre lots. Two community lots owned by a co-operative of residents contain buildings for community events and for the operation of businesses. Residents are involved in a wide variety of social, cultural, environmental, and spiritual activities.

Another application of permaculture principles on the community level is the burgeoning Transition movement started by UK permaculture teacher Rob Hopkins to help towns, cities and neighborhoods build local resilience to withstand and adapt to the shocks of climate change and the end of cheap fossil fuels. Hopkins has developed a permaculture-based protocol for community change that includes emotionally uplifting building activities. Permaculture cofounder David Holmgren offers his own thoughts on building community in "Future Scenarios: How Communities Can Adapt to Peak Oil and Climate Change."[7]

The emergence of "Social Permaculture" is yet another expression of the desire to implement permaculture ethics and principles on a community scale. Co-housing consultants like Margo Adair and Bill Aal, and permaculture teachers Penny Livingston-Stark, James Stark, and teacher/ecofeminist Starhawk, train political and community activists to perceive and understand natural versus dysfunctional social patterns, move from conflict avoidance to embracing and channeling conflict constructively, and transform power dynamics by using various techniques like Appreciative Inquiry and meditation.

Patty Ceglia and Karen Stupski at the Heathcote Community in Freeland, Maryland have expanded social permaculture to include personal care ("Zone 0"), voluntary simplicity, cooperative skills, deconstruction of the "patrix" (interlocking patriarchal, racist, dominator systems), ecofeminism, and liberation psychology. Permaculturalist Jan Spencer of Eugene, Oregon is teaching community activists to utilize existing resources like neighborhood associations, Neighborhood Watch groups, and emergency preparedness initiatives to transition to greater local resilience.

As we look for tools to help us survive as members of the Earth family, the simple, nature-based ethics and principles of permaculture may offer one way forward. They are easy to learn, cross-cultural, and non-sectarian. Tested out in deserts, forests, shorelines, jungles, and urban neighborhoods, permaculture has a decades-long record of being accepted and applied in radically different cultures around the world. They work not only for local and global land and ocean care, but also for community-building, useful across so many fields: economics, psychology, sociology, law, education, security systems, medicine, and spirituality.

Endnotes

1 Foster, Steven, and Little, Meredith. *The Four Shields: The Initiatory Seasons of Human Nature.* Big Pine, CA: Lost Borders Press, 1998.

2 Mollison, Bill. *Permaculture: A Designers' Manual.* Tagari, 1977.

3 Holmgren, David. *Permaculture: Principles & Pathways Beyond Sustainability.* Hepburn, Victoria, Australia: Holmgren Design Services, 2002.

4 Eisler, Riane. *The Chalice and the Blade: Our History, Our Future.* New York: HarperCollins, 1987.

5 Larry Santoyo, personal communication, 2006.

6 Visit ecotherapyheals.com for more examples of permaculture principles redesigned for people care and mental health.

7 Holmgren, David. *Future Scenarios: How Communities Can Adapt to Peak Oil and Climate Change.* White River Junction, VT: Chelsea Green Publishing, 2009.

Resources:

Anderson, M. Kat. *Tending the Wild: Native American Knowledge and the Management of California's Natural Resources.* Berkeley, CA: University of California Press, 2006.

Buzzell, Linda and Craig Chalquist (eds.). *Ecotherapy: Healing with Nature in Mind.* San Francisco: Sierra Club Books, 2009.

Chalquist, Craig. *Terrapsychology: Reengaging the Soul of Place.* New Orleans: Spring Journal, 2007.

Hopkins, Rob. *The Transition Handbook: From Oil Dependency to Local Resilience.* Totnes, Devon, UK: Green Books Ltd, 2008.

Roszak, Theodore, Mary E. Gomes and Allen D. Kanner. *Ecopsychology: Restoring the Earth, healing the Mind.* San

Francisco: Sierra Club Books, 1995.

Websites:

Social Permaculture Workshop - http://www.heathcote.org/cms/content/social-permaculture-worskhop

Linda Buzzell, MA, MJournalism, MFT is a psychotherapist and career counselor in private practice in Santa Barbara and Los Angeles, California. A co-editor of Ecotherapy: Healing with Nature in Mind *(Sierra Club Books, 2009), she founded the International Association for Ecotherapy (http://thoughtoffering.blogs.com/ecotherapy) in 2002 and is the editor of Ecotherapy News, its quarterly journal. She teaches continuing education classes on ecopsychology, ecotherapy and "New Career Opportunities in the Emerging Sustainable Society" at Santa Barbara City College, and is Adjunct Faculty at Pacifica Graduate Institute, where she supervises first-year student "Community and Ecological Fieldwork and Research" in the Depth Psychology PhD program. With her husband Larry Saltzman, she founded the Santa Barbara Organic Garden Club in 2000. Linda and Larry are graduates of the Permaculture Design Course and members of the Santa Barbara Permaculture Guild. They are members of a Voluntary Simplicity circle and tend a small permaculture food forest in their backyard.*

Tuning In to Terra through Our Animal Kin

Karen Diane Knowles

Consorting with our planetmates may offer an antidote to the wide-spread perilous disconnection from nature. Because earth speaks to us through our animal kin, repairing nature requires a re-pairing of our bond with other animals. Learning to recognize and listen to their wisdom—through stories, symbolic acts, dream messages, and personal exchanges with animal companions—offers a transformation of consciousness toward embodied presence, and can help mend our de-natured condition. For a deeper understanding of our earth, we can ask the earthlings who still live as one with nature what this earth feels like from where they stand, fly, swim, or slither.

Philosopher Tom Regan relates the story of his medical school roommate who practiced surgical procedures on a dog. As Regan tells it,

> He described to me how he broke the poor animal's leg and then set it, only to break it again and set it again...Throughout her long, painful ordeal, the loyal animal greeted his arrival with a wag of her tail and even licked the very hands that had injured her. In the end...he was required to 'euthanize' the

361

dog...He wondered what sort of human being he was or would become.[1]

This dog's engaged and loving presence broke through the medical student's conditioned objectifying defenses; the student became aware of and psychologically troubled by the dog's suffering. Unfortunately, that is where the story (and the dog, for that matter) ends: despite thinking it cruel and unnecessary, despite his incipient tender mercy, the young man soldiered on so as not to pierce the veil of objective experimental rigor.

A microcosmic peek into a biological research lab reveals a common perceptual bias characterized by detachment and objectification. It also reveals that acting contrary to what we believe is right, true, or just makes us feel at odds with ourselves, and that this particular flavor of cognitive/emotional dissonance leaves us at odds with Nature—especially with the animal nature within us.

Discontinuity and Denial: the Cartesian Legacy

Our alienation from nature and from the animal nature within ourselves has been handed down to us; we have learned to objectify nonhuman animals (hereafter, "animals"), in order to separate and elevate ourselves.

"Animals are without feeling or awareness of any kind...they merely behave *as if* they feel pain when they are, say, kicked or stabbed."[2] These are not the out of touch ramblings of an unreflective simpleton; they are the out of touch ramblings of René Descartes, the "father of modern philosophy." In the 17th century Cartesian framework, nonhuman animals have no ontology; they are excluded from the category of *being*.

This view has been countered throughout history before, during, and after Descartes' time. Two other influential founding "fathers" offered opposing views of animals. In the 6th century BCE, Pythagoras, known as the "father of numbers," is known to have said that animals share with us the privilege of having a soul. In the 4th century BCE, Hippocrates, the "father of western medicine," asserted that the soul is the same in all living creatures, although the body of each is different. (He might be upset to know the eponymous

Hippocratic Oath is *not* generally applied to nonhuman animals). In the 18th century, following Descartes' mechanistic assertion and the spread of vivisection in its wake, Enlightenment philosopher and writer Voltaire ridiculed Descartes' conclusions by pointing out glaring violations of common sense, challenging, "Answer me, mechanist, has nature arranged all the springs of feeling in this animal in order that he should not feel? Does he have nerves to be impassive? Do not assume that nature presents this impertinent contradiction."[3]

By the 19th century, a passionate naturalist had come upon the scene speaking plainly and respectfully about animals. Charles Darwin, whose work remains the foundation of biological thought, affirmed nonhuman animals' sentient nature and reminded us of our own animal nature. Darwin put us on the continuum of Nature—where we belong—departing radically from Descartes' human-animal ontological distinction with the assertion that "there is no fundamental difference between man and the higher animals in their mental faculties."[4] Descartes' declaration that "the cries of animals in laboratories are simply the equivalent to the noise a clock makes when ticking"[5] was countered by Darwin: "The lower animals, like man, manifestly feel pleasure and pain, happiness, and misery." Moreover, "the fact that the lower animals are excited by the same emotions as ourselves is so well established, that it will not be necessary to weary the reader by many details."[6] Darwin could not have imagined that a century and a half later, the question of animal emotion would still be bandied about.

The paradigm-shifting conceptions of evolution and species continuity started the scientific community on the long road toward recognizing us in animals and them in us. As rigorous, multi-disciplinary evidence mounts, the Cartesian model that has held a four-hundred-year sway over the western view of Nature crumbles. Earth is now widely accepted as a living organism, and most scientific and philosophical scholars now agree that nonhuman animals have their own physical, mental, and emotional experience of the world. Research triumphs over Descartes' claim that animals have no interiority as our planetmates reveal themselves to be emotionally and psychologically complex beings. In a blow to speciesist vanity, we have discovered that we are not the only species to think, feel, use tools, use language, use rationality, express intentionality, dream, empathize, perform funeral rituals, engage in cultural transmission, demonstrate self-reflection, or even to exhibit post-traumatic stress disorder.

Anthropodenial

There remains the age-old debate over the legitimacy of ascribing supposed human characteristics to nonhumans: "anthropomorphism," condemned outright as a sin of conjecture or bias. "No one has yet proven that the 'Big Bang' theory is true," replies Tom Regan. "But it hardly follows from this that those who accept this theory must be in the grip of some prejudice."[7] Evolutionary biologist Marc Bekoff defends anthropomorphism's utility as a way to make other animals' worlds accessible to our human view of the world.[8] Psychologist and Jungian scholar James Hillman recognizes that without anthropomorphizing we are

> Doomed to read a horse's gambol not as its joy but as our projection, a stray dog's whining not as its desperation but as our sentimental identification with its plight, a coon's thrashing in a trap not as its fear but as our own claustrophobia and victimization.[9]

Debate notwithstanding, anthropomorphism should be used with care. The dolphin's charming "smile" should not be interpreted as perpetual happiness. Unlike humans, the facial anatomy of dolphins—the curved mouth—is fixed and does not indicate mood or health. (Like humans, they are not always enjoying themselves—especially in captivity.) Similarly, the chimpanzee's familiar toothy "grin" should not be misunderstood as gaiety; it is, rather, an indicator of fear, a common sight at institutions of captivity. Renowned primatologist Frans de Waal offers the example of an oil company's advertisement symbolizing its "green" status through a scene depicting a grizzly bear romantically overlooking a lovely landscape with his arm around his mate.[10] We would never know from this message that bears are nearsighted and do not form pair bonds.

What is more damaging than anthropomorphism is its counterpart: what Frans de Waal refers to as "anthropodenial," which he describes as "a blindness to the humanlike characteristics of other animals, or the animal-like characteristics of ourselves. Those who are in anthropodenial try to build a brick wall to separate humans from the rest of the animal kingdom."[11] According to de Waal, this wall is starting to look like Swiss cheese.

Amazingly, some hold firm to the belief that our species appeared on the planet *ex nihilo*, no thanks to evolutionary continuity. Under this false species discontinuity, human nature loses its nature while animals are de-psychologized. Recognizing this twofold rift, the emerging field of trans-species psychology "embeds humans in the continuum of nature" and strives to "release psyche from identification with solely human subjectivity."[12] Looking at nonhumans through the grounded lens of trans-species psychology bypasses the fallacies of both objectification *and* projection while expanding psychological inquiry to species other than our own.

Once anthropomorphism is accepted and anthropodenial eschewed, the way is clear for interspecies communion, and for recognizing the communicative value of animals' actions in the world. James Hillman assures us that "we can and do understand each other despite the arrogant philosophies that would preserve consciousness as an exclusively human property."[13]

Special Perceptions and Perspectives

Biologist Rupert Sheldrake affirms that bonds between humans and nonhumans can yield unconventional and advanced forms of communication. Sheldrake reports on discoveries about animal perceptiveness and communicative behavior. It has been shown that even when physically distant, animals retain their connection to their human companions; that is why animals often know, among other things, when their humans are heading home.[14]

According to Sheldrake, who has studied dynamics within the interspecies relationship, animals possess "powers of perception that go beyond the known senses."[15] Many dogs, cats, and even rabbits have saved the lives of human companions by alerting them to medical dangers before any outward signs of these have manifested.

Animals warn of impending seizures (emphatically directing the unsuspecting human to lie down), diagnose cancerous lesions (whining, sniffing, licking, and even nipping at afflicted body areas), intervene in diabetic episodes (waking up sleeping humans when blood sugar levels start to drop), and, even anticipating sudden death (changing the quality and intensity of their affection days in advance).

Sheldrake offers stories of animals bringing awareness to dangers in the external environment—again, before outward signs are detected by human senses: A "stubborn" horse refusing to ride into the path of an impending avalanche; a mild-mannered dog frantically trying to prevent his human companion from leaving for work, nearly losing his companion to a life-threatening traffic accident a few hours later; the poodle of a couple driving on a mountain road erupting in howls and pawing at the driver to warn of a precipice awaiting them around the bend...[16]

Heeding these messages saves lives—*many* lives when communication concerns large-scale planetary events, as when, based partly on the anomalous behavior of animals, the Chinese government called for the evacuation of Haicheng, a city with a population of a million people. Thanks to the predictive behavior of the animals and the trust put into those messages, hundreds of thousands were saved from becoming casualties in the 7.3 magnitude earthquake of 1973.

Animal Voices

Because animals live closer to the earth, they can be, for us, the voices of the earth. When we respect the perceptions and perspectives of animals, we glean useful information that only they seem to be privy to—information about them, about us, about our planet:

- A black bear enters a home, eats some fruit, drinks water from a fish bowl, and then steals a stuffed teddy bear. The bear left the teddy bear thrown on the lawn for the humans to find. Although we can assume the bear was hungry and thirsty, what might this bear be communicating by stealing the little stuffed bear? Has the bear lost bear cubs due to human encroachment? Is this a nonviolent protest or a simple act of grief?[17]

- During a Japanese marine show a captive dolphin "accidentally" leaps out of a tank. The dolphin lay listlessly on concrete, the other dolphins craning to see what's happened to their tankmate.[18] Dolphin suicide? It is in their nature to roam the open seas for miles and miles a day, not to circle the same crowded, noisy tank day in and day out. Was the dolphin desperate to avoid the stress of captivity?

- Repeated whale strandings off coastal waters lead researchers to confirm causal link between human-caused noise and the deaths of these sound-sensitive creatures. Necropsies show surprising evidence of "the bends"—suggestive of a desperate mass exodus from the crazy-making noise of military sonar testing.

- A Labrador retriever shoots a hunter in the back by stepping on the man's shotgun.[19]

- The simple act of not getting pregnant speaks volumes. Keepers of captive wild animals often wonder why animals often won't breed naturally, why in-vitro methods must be used, and why mothering doesn't always happen. Are these animals revealing the wisdom of avoiding having offspring while imprisoned?

- An elephant terrorizes a timber company in an arena of intense conflict between the logging industry and local rural residents. Locals say the elephant is airing their frustrations.[20] Perhaps the elephant also had his own axe to grind?

- A mother whale and calf were stranded on a sandbank. Human rescuers tried to help but were about to give up when the whale and a dolphin started verbally communicating with each other. The dolphin led the whales to safety.[21]

- When a woman had a heart attack, her pig raced out into the road to help. She laid down in the road in front of a car, then led a motorist back to the house. The doctor on scene confirmed that the pig saved the woman's life.[22]

Dream Animals

Unleash the dream messengers! Let us not imprison the animals in our dreams the way we do in waking life.

Dreams are a natural avenue for tuning in to the messages of animals. A few questions to consider about your dream visitor: Is the animal wild or tame? Neglected or healthy? What is the animal's natural home environment—sky, land, ocean? Are you interacting directly or are you viewing the animal from a distance?

In order for the dream animal to remain alive with the message he or she brings, it is important to hold in check the temptation to interpret the dream based on projection. In *Dream Animals*, James Hillman emphasizes seeing the animals as they are: "What is *their* need, *their* reason for coming into our sleep?"[23]

When we see dream animals as imaginal figures devoid of a connection to the animals themselves, we miss the point of the animal's visit, as when someone eats a hamburger while describing a sacred cow communicating to them in a dream. On the other hand, perhaps animals inhabit our dreams "to remind us of our affinity with them," or, possibly, "to guard against extinction, both theirs and ours."[24]

The Sixth Extinction

The loudest way animals communicate planetary distress to us is through their permanent silence.

Extinctions are an increasing occurrence. We are in a period referred to as the Anthropocene Era because the global problems we face are anthropogenic: caused by humans. By virtue of our activities—increased human population, climate change, habitat destruction, and species exploitation—this century will see the disappearance of half of all plant and animal species if destructive practices continue. As our planetmates are driven into oblivion, entire ecosystems upon which we depend for our life support are collapsing. According to Paul Ehrlich of the Center for Conservation Biology at Stanford University, "When we wipe out populations and species of other organisms, we're sawing off the limb that we're sitting on."[25]

This is the Sixth Extinction. The last mass extinction (sixty-five million years ago) was blamed on an asteroid. Nevertheless, like the dog on the surgical table who wags her tail in greeting for the vivisector, the earth continues to offer us what's left of her bounty as the ironies inherent in our disregard of nature's needs pile up:

- On the eve of Earth Day 2010, an oil rig infested with safety violations explodes and sinks in the Gulf of Mexico off the Louisiana, the resulting outpour of thousands of barrels of oil a day threatening humans, plants, and wildlife.

- In the Year of the Tiger 2010, every species of tiger is facing extinction. (Even those confined in public display facilities are endangered by the stress of captivity.) If current trajectories continue, these wild beauties will exist only in our memories, photographs, our cave paintings.

- Easter is the deadliest time for real bunnies. Cute and cuddly hype notwithstanding, the typical fate for rabbits given as Easter bunny "gifts" is death due to neglect, abandonment, euthanasia in overcrowded shelters before their first birthday.

- The Great Seal of the United States of America is emblazoned with the national bird, an enduring icon representing the soul of America, yet the flesh and blood inspiration nearly stopped enduring all together. The bald eagle was declared an endangered species in the mid 1960s.

- The bear on the flag of the State of California has been extinct for decades.

- Within this century it is expected that 50% of all plant and animal species will become extinct while human population rises by 50%.

Disconnection and dissonance persist individually too. A person who wears an ivory totem necklace professing a love of elephants may not even think about what happened to the elephant whose body used to own that ivory: how that slaughter left a close-knit matriarchal extended family unit disintegrated, with babies traumatized and left orphaned. For the human, a piece of ivory may symbolize connection to the earth, but for the elephant it symbolizes brutal and final separation from the earth.

In his essay "An Animal's Place," bestselling author and Berkeley scholar Michael Pollan addresses our disconnect:

> There's a schizoid quality to our relationship with animals, in which sentiment and brutality exist side by side. Half the dogs in America will receive Christmas presents this year, yet few of us pause to consider the miserable life of the pig—an animal easily as intelligent as a dog—that becomes the Christmas ham.[26]

For every pet pampered, countless equally sentient, sensitive, and psychologically complex animals are forsaken. Confined in deplorable conditions, they suffer and die not by the minute and by the millions, but by the second and by the billions. While we react in horror to reports of human kidnappings, our nonhuman kin regularly endure the anguish of extended confinement in circuses, zoos, aquaria, laboratories, puppy and kitten mills, fur farms, and factory farms.

> Man feels himself isolated in the cosmos, because he is no longer involved in nature and has lost his emotional "unconscious identity" with natural phenomena. No voices now speak to man from stones, plants, and animals, nor does he speak to them believing they can hear. His contact with nature has gone, and with it has gone the profound emotional energy that this symbolic connection supplied.[27]

Re-pairing Our Disconnection with Interspecies Communion

Marc Bekoff challenges us to ask what the animals might say to all this and what we might learn from the answer:

> While animals are unable to consent to or refuse our intrusions into their lives, it is useful to ask what they might say if they could do so. We should also ask ourselves if we would

do what we did again, given what we learned.[28]

Consorting directly with our planetmates may offer an antidote to widespread, perilous disconnection from nature. Learning to recognize and listen to animal wisdom—through stories, symbolic acts, dream messages, and personal exchanges with animal companions—opens us up to different ways of knowing and being. Engaging in dialogue with nonhuman intelligence exposes us to an epistemology of earth-centered feeling and awareness.

Nonhuman beings have an advantage over us as "they live in the 'isness of being'"[29] characterized by a feeling-based liminal awareness. When we pay attention to earth's primal intelligence, we realize we need each other and that, in many ways, we *are* each other. Casting off the human accoutrements of capitalistic priorities and self-help obsessions, we see with a soul born of the same earth as our nonhuman kin who know what this earth feels like from where they stand, fly, swim, or slither.

The convention of using our senses to look through microscopes or telescopes or stethoscopes and using our reason to interpret what we espy leaves us mind-blinded to what is readily evident through emotional and intuitive lenses. Interactions with other animals are at once earthy and spiritual; they inspire and transform us. Our growing knowledge of animal consciousness calls for a new kind of ethic, one based not just on logic or principle but on the kind of empathy that arises naturally when we interact with animals.

Endnotes

1 Randour, M. *Animal Grace: Entering a Spiritual Relationship with Our Fellow Creatures*. New World Library, 2000, p. 35.

2 Cottingham, J. "A brute to the brutes: Descartes' treatment of animals." *Philosophy*, 1987, Vol. 53, No. 206, pp. 551-559.

3 Voltaire, F., and Besterman, T. (translator). *Philosophical Dictionary*. Penguin Classics, 1984.

4 Darwin, Charles. *The Descent of Man, and Selection in Relation to Sex*. John Murray, 1871, p. 34.

5 Randour, 2000, p. 34.

6 Darwin, 1871, p. 38.

7 Birch, C., Eaken, W., and McDaniel, J., eds. *Liberating Life: Contemporary Approaches in Ecological Theology.* Orbis Books, 1990, p. 75.

8 Bekoff, Marc. *The Emotional Lives of Animals.* New World Library, 2007, p. 52.

9 Hillman, J. *Dream Animals.* San Francisco, CA: Chronicle Books, 1997, p. 22.

10 De Waal, F. B. M. "Are we in anthropodenial?" *Discover* 18 (7), 1997, pp. 50-53.

11 De Waal, 1997, pp.

12 Bradshaw, G. A., & Watkins, M. "Trans-species psychology: Theory and praxis." 2006. *Spring.* 75:69-94.

13 Hillman, 1997, p. 22.

14 Sheldrake, R. *Dogs that Know when Their Owners are Coming Home: And Other Unexplained Powers of Animals.* Three Rivers Press, 1999.

15 Sheldrake, 1999, p. 2.

16 Sheldrake, 1999.

17 "Bear Walks Into House, Chows On Fruit, Steals Teddy Bear." WCVBTV5 Boston. July 28, 2010. http:// www.thebostonchannel.com/ news/ 24424283/detail.html

18 "Shocking moment dolphin desperate to escape captivity leaps out of its own tank during marine show." MailOnline. July 9, 2010.http://www.dailymail.co.uk/news/worldnews/article-1293379/ Shocking-moment-dolphin-leaps-tank-marine-show.html

19 Burgess, Kelly. "Duck hunter gets shot in the back—by his own dog." *Los Angeles Times.* February 1, 2010. http://latimes-blogs.latimes.com/outposts/2010/02/hunter-shot-by-his-dog.html

20 Paye-Layleh, Jonathan. "'Possessed' pachyderm is livid over logging." MSNBC. July 19, 2010. http://www.msnbc.msn.com/id/ 38308045/ns/business-going_green/

21 Shears, Richard. "Hero dolphin saves stranded mother and baby whale facing death on New Zealand beach." MailOnline. March 13, 2008. http://www.dailymail.co.uk/news/article-531748/ Hero-dolphin-saves-stranded-mother-baby-whales-facing-death-

New-Zealand-beach.html

22 Fuoco, Michael. "Oinking for help." PG News. October 10, 1998. http://www.post-gazette.com/regionstate/19981010pig2.asp

23 Hillman, 1997, p. 13.

24 Hillman, 1997, p. 13.

25 Levy, Gina (Producer/Director). *The Sixth Extinction*. [Film]. 2010. Paul Ehrlich featured in trailer of documentary project. http://6thextinctiondoc.com/

26 Pollan, M. "An animal's place." *New York Times*. November 10, 2002.http://www.rawfoodinfo.com/articles/ art_ananimal-splace.html

27 Jung, C. G. *Man and His Symbols*. Random House, 1968, p. 85.

28 Bekoff, M. *Animal Passions and Beastly Virtues: Reflections on Redecorating Nature*. Temple University Press, 2005, p. 228.

29 Randour, 2000, p. 102.

Karen Diane Knowles, MA is a professional sign language interpreter and an animal advocate. Her graduate work in consciousness studies emphasized nonhuman consciousness and interspecies relations; she has also received postgraduate training in the emerging field of trans-species psychology and has designed and taught a course on animal consciousness at John F Kennedy University. As a rescue volunteer, Karen has worked with marine mammals, farmed animals, rabbits, and cats. Her life's goal is to inspire passionate curiosity and respectful regard toward our animal kin.

EarthKeeping: Dialogical Practices of Reverence for an Intimate, Sustainable Earth

Eileen Pardini

Working with a small group of men and women, Eileen Pardini explores how heart-based, dialogical expression can expand the quality of emotional and spiritual intimacy between humans and the Earth. This approach includes engaging in meaningful group discussion, exchanging of love letters with the Earth, creating sacred space to honor the Earth, and ritualizing verbal declarations of deep reverence, gratitude and reciprocity.

Silent gratitude isn't much use to anyone.—G.B. Stern

How would we dialogue with the Earth as if it were our lover, and how would such a practice affect our relationship with the Earth and with others? The inspiration for *EarthKeeping* grew out of my own poignant awakening to the Earth as a living being, the indigenous ways of my ancestors, and the universal human experience of feeling unseen, unheard, unacknowledged, unappreciated, ignored, forgotten.

If one is truly paying attention and deeply listening at this time in global history, it is difficult to ignore the tragic and alarming assault that is occurring on and to our beloved Earth and to not feel something. How do we address spiritual blindness to what is sacred, this disconnection from the Earth *and* each other, the widespread inability to see and feel the sacred? In our small group of adult strangers in a facilitated two-day workshop, the primary objective is to assess the impact of engaging in intimate dialogue with the Earth in the presence of a community of witnesses, and in a lovingly created sacred space. Intuitively conceptualized and approached, the agenda is designed to shift human consciousness from a "separate from" mindset with respect to the Earth and others to one that embraces the spiritual truth that to revere the Earth is equivalent to revering others and oneself. In their own work with small groups, Joanna Macy and Molly Brown explain that groups provide focus, duration, synergy, and momentum.[1] Additionally, Cecile Andrews believes that small groups serve as containers for creative discussion, safe experimentation, mutual support, exchange of critical feedback, and healing the breach between self and nature.[2]

Establishing a Safe Environment

To be loose, open, and comfortable in a group is to feel secure. I expected that participants would initially feel apprehensive, vulnerable, fearful, and cautious about sharing so intimately with strangers they did not know. Preventions were incorporated into the agenda to create a culture of caring throughout the two-day encounter.

From start to finish, great care is taken to ensure an environment of safety and belonging for the participants. Taking the necessary time up front to introduce facilitator background and personal connection to the topic, sharing the agenda and asking for consensus, defining group norms and directing the group to develop their own plan for working together, facilitating group introductions that immediately reveal shared commonalities, and honoring confidentiality are key to establishing a safe environment and a culture of compassion for EarthKeeping.

Dedicating the Work

Throughout the workshop, all activity is conducted around an altar constructed by the facilitator, an altar to which participants are invited to contribute when they arrive. Participants are immediately drawn to the altar upon entering the room and, without prompting, often add their own special items to the compilation. The altar serves as sacred space and assists with setting the tone for the valuable work to come.

Such an altar begins with a special cloth placed on the floor or table to frame and honor the various altar objects. Selected objects are such things as bird feathers to honor the element of air, seashells to honor the element of water, a candle to honor the element of fire, and a tree branch, stones, leaves, herbs, flowers, fruit, and/or photos of ancestors to honor the element of earth. The arrangement and intention behind the task is meaningfully carried out with great reverence.

Every module of the workshop begins with participants joining hands around the altar while the facilitator dedicates the work to the healing of the Earth and the creation of a sustainable society.[3] A sustainable society is defined as one that is compassionate, just and beautiful.[4] This opening serves to focus the group on developing, sustaining and expanding their capacity for love and compassion.

Group Discussion of Foundational Concepts

Participants are given a set time frame to discuss several concepts in the form of statements and quotations covering ideas such as the nature of quality relationships, awakening to our intimate, daily relationship with the Earth and others, connecting emotionally with the Earth and with one's own heart, healing through feeling, our sacred interconnectedness with the Earth and all sentient beings, the intelligence of the heart, the intelligence of the Earth, the concept of sustainability, and demonstrating gratitude and reverence with one's daily actions and words.

Participants are also asked to generate a list of truths or conclusions based on their discussion of these quotes. This exercise proves to be an excellent topic icebreaker and serves as preparation for more intimate work to come. The following are a few examples of truths generated by one group:

The quality of our relationships shapes the future of our planet.

We are either asleep to our intimate lives or we are awake and present.

Everything is everything. Everyone is everyone.

We must awaken to the suffering of the Earth.

The heart knows the truth and is key to our salvation.

The Earth's heart is our heart. Our heart is the Earth's heart.

We must be the voice, eyes, ears and heart of the Earth.

To heal the Earth is to heal ourselves.

There exists a sacred potential in every act and in every moment.

Ritualizing Shared Pain for the Deterioration of the Earth

Borrowing from the despair-to-empowerment work of Joanna Macy and Molly Brown, participants are then guided through a dialogical ritual called *Truth Mandala* that focuses on expressing personal pain for the alarming ecological degradation of the Earth.[5] Working with natural objects representing fear (a stone), anger (a tree branch), sorrow (dead leaves), and emptiness (a wooden bowl), participants stand in close proximity to each other and, one at a time, spontaneously select and hold each item while expressing their corresponding feeling about a particular example of ecological trauma.

Macy believes that opening up to the collective experience of planetary anguish makes room in our hearts for the world to heal, and is a measure of our shared humanity and evolutionary maturity.[6] Participants experience group intimacy as they crack open their hearts and share varying degrees of openness, emotional expression, compassion, and solidarity. One participant wrote after the workshop:

I enjoyed the Truth Mandala ritual and I really felt deep empathy for some of the things that were shared. It brought out emotions that were uncontainable at the time. I felt a sense of release and at the same time, a sense of urgency. The journal writing afterwards helped me to bring my thoughts forward and keep them in front of me.

Discussion of Gratitude, Reverence, and Reciprocity

Participants are introduced to the orienting concepts of gratitude, reverence, and reciprocity through sharing of stories, brief lectures, experiential exercises and reflection. These virtues are presented as the wellspring of all religions[7] and the heart of what virgin nature has to teach us.[8] The foundational components of EarthKeeping, akin to a spiritual practice, a philosophy, a lifestyle, are also essential for a sustainable society.

When the Japanese spiritual practice of self-reflection called *naikan*[9] is introduced, participants are asked to reflect on their favorite place in nature and write a love letter to this special site to express their deep gratitude and reverence for all that it gives to them. They are then asked to reflect on what this beloved place might have to say to them.

Journal writing and sharing of responses to these tasks engender more group intimacy and more intimacy with one's own heart and the spirit of the Earth. One participant wrote, "This was an excellent exercise to really feel the love that we hold for a special place—then to have this place respond with openness back to you, to beckon you, to welcome you."

Discussion of Sacred Space, Altar and Ritual

After this participants are introduced to the concepts and purpose of sacred space and altar, and to the components that comprise the creation of each.[10]

Sacred space is a place that by design is created to inspire and awaken one to the fact that there is sacred space all around. One common thread found in all sacred space is that it enhances one's ability to commune with its spirit or essence, from which flows a deep feeling of connectedness.

An altar is a tool of transformation that humans create quite naturally. At its simplest, an altar is a raised structure that serves as a resting place for meaningful objects, which are chosen intentionally and intuitively, while it functions as a place for contemplation or ritual. The facilitator shares a variety of illuminating visuals as examples of such indoor and outdoor ritual places.

The group's attention is then focused on the altar as participants are invited to share the objects that each has contributed to the altar and why these items hold special meaning. For example, many of the participants brought favorite flowers or herbs, special stones or shells, or personal items from ancestors that held sentimental value. The facilitator follows this sharing by introducing the concept of ritual, ritual process and the purpose of ritual.

Bill Plotkin defines ritual as a bodily enactment, in real time and space, that engages us not only verbally, cognitively, imaginatively, emotionally, and symbolically through the body by way of imagistically rich gestures.[11] Malidoma Somé describes ritual as the most ancient way of binding a community together with Spirit, as a spontaneous and public expression of emotions, as an unrehearsed and deeply moving response to Sprit, and as a genuine and pure intention focused on healing.[12] Participants are reminded of the Truth Mandala ritual they engaged in earlier, offered now as an example of sincere, unscripted expression of emotion done with the utmost humility. This show-and-tell of personal objects representing earth, air, fire, and water, combined with the witnessing by group members within a lovingly created sacred space, builds on the emotional and spiritual intimacy continuing to develop throughout the day.

Assigned Group Task

Day One concludes with a group assignment in which participants are asked to design a group ritual that incorporates the elements of gratitude, reverence, and reciprocity for and toward the Earth. The ritual cannot be rehearsed or scripted except for personally created poetry or song. Dialogue must come from the heart and the gut, in the moment. The ritual can include music, movement, singing, chanting, dancing, drumming, art, poetry, flowers, herbs, offerings, photos of ancestors, and other personal and meaningful objects. Each participant must engage in dialogue with the Earth through conversation, song, poetry, chanting, or a blessing.

For all this participants are given two weeks for planning, ninety minutes to prepare the sacred space on ritual day, and three hours to engage in the actual ritual. If needed, the facilitator is available to answer questions throughout the planning stage; otherwise the facilitator's main role is now complete. Participants are invited to share in a potluck meal at the conclusion of the day to celebrate their good work.

Group Ritual Creation

The unfolding of heartfelt expression on ritual day confirms that when humans connect their hearts with their voices in spontaneous and sincere articulation of love, gratitude, reverence, and reciprocity for the Earth, visible and invisible authentic transformation occurs. The level of transformation is greatly influenced by the community of witnesses, the unscripted and spontaneous nature of the engagement, and the level of willingness of the participants to fully connect with their hearts. A variety of emotions are displayed and felt collectively throughout the ritual as one participant sings a love song to the Earth while playing his guitar; another leads the group in becoming a grove of trees whose branches sway and touch in the wind; another facilitates spontaneous expression of desired world healing as the group stands in a close circle with their arms around each other; and another facilitates the group in giving voice and movement to each of the four elements in a spontaneous and free form dance of emotion.

Visible shifts in terms of pride, self-esteem and softening are witnessed by all when the Earth is thus held as a living spirit with heart and immeasurable worth. All of the participants leave with a deeper connection with the Earth and a newfound inspiration for how they will relate to the Earth in the future. One participant described their journey:

This has really opened my eyes to some things that I might be doing unconsciously, but not recognizing. I also think it has helped me to not focus on my small space immediately in front of me, but to look at the big picture. It's a planet you know! I have forever been changed by this experience and would like to learn a lot more. This is something I would make an investment in to better myself and the world around me for us all.

Afterword

EarthKeeping is about tuning in to what is around us: people, animals, plants, Earth. It is using all of our senses, particularly listening and observation, at a very deep level to awaken to the subtleties of our immediate surroundings. It includes interpersonal generosity, or tending to the *quality* of all of our relationships, and tending takes time. It could also be referred to as aslow communion that acknowledges what or who needs to be acknowledged, making the "other," including this one Earth that feels unseen and unheard, visible. It's about aligning our thoughts, words and deeds with what is best for the Earth, because *we are the Earth.*

To keep the Earth is to give thanks for the gift of life. EarthKeeping is about coming home to our sacred interconnectedness.

Endnotes

1 Brown, Molly & Macy, Joanna. Coming Back to Life: Practices to Reconnect Our Lives, Our World. New Society Publishers, 1998.

2 Andrews, Cecile. The Small Group as Ecotherapy Building a Culture of Connection. Buzzell, Linda & Chalquist, Craig, Eds. Ecotherapy: Healing with Nature in Mind. Sierra Club Books, 2009.

3 Brown, Molly & Macy, Joanna. Coming Back to Life: Practices to Reconnect Our Lives, Our World. New Society Publishers, 1998.

4 Fox, Matthew. Radical Prayer: Love in Action. Sounds True, 2003.

5 Brown, Molly & Macy, Joanna. Coming Back to Life: Practices to Reconnect Our Lives, Our World. New Society Publishers, 1998.

6 Macy, Joanna. The Greening of the Self. Ecotherapy: Healing with Nature in Mind. Sierra Club Books, 2009.

7 Macy, Joanna. World as Lover, World as Self. Parallax Press, 2007.

8 Versluis, Arthur. Sacred Earth: The Spiritual Landscape of Native America. Inner Traditions International, 1992.

9 Krech, Gregg. Naikan: Gratitude, Grace, and the Japanese Art of Self-Reflection. Stone Bridge Press, 2002.

10 London, Eileen & Recio, Belinda. Sacred Rituals: Connecting with Spirit through Labyrinths, Sand Paintings & Other Traditional Arts. Fair Winds Press, 2004.

11 Plotkin, Bill. Vision Questing: A Nature-Based Approach to Soul Encounter. Shaman's Drum 65, 51. 2003.

12 Somé, Malidoma Patrice. The Healing Wisdom of Africa: Finding Life Purpose Through Nature, Ritual, and Community. Jeremy P. Tarcher/Putnam, 1998.

Eileen Pardini holds a Master of Arts degree in Consciousness Studies from John F. Kennedy University, and is a Certified Mediator serving the East Bay since 1996. Dedicated to social transformation and connection, Eileen's mission is to inspire EarthKeeping, the cultivation of a more intimate, quality relationship with Earth and each other as key to the planet's healing and the creation of a sustainable, just society. Eileen currently teaches at John F. Kennedy University, and facilitates year-round workshops and retreats in team building, interpersonal communication skills, Earth intimacy practices and SoulCollage®. Visit her website at http://www.eileenpardini.com.

Toward an Ethic of Earthly Beauty:
An Interview with Rebecca Elliott

Most approaches to sustainability and transition to a petroleum-free future emphasize concrete projects and technical innovation. Rebecca Elliott believes that a deeper transformation must take place: a renewed appreciation for the beauty of the natural world.

Craig: Rebecca, you've been following the news about what's happening environmentally for some time now. You've done recent presentations on how to face up to the challenges of peak oil, and you're aware of all the talk about sustainable living. You stay informed about the latest ecological crises: climate change, toxic chemicals in our food and clothing, and so on, not only as a graduate with a degree in consciousness studies, but as a concerned mother of twins. What's missing from the public discussion about all this?

Rebecca: What's missing from the discussion is appreciating the beauty that surrounds us: the beauty provided by the natural world. Not just natural landscapes and recreation that people periodically enjoy, but a deep felt sense of the beauty that nature and being connected to nature provides in day-to-day living.

People regard "sustainability" as giving up a way of life, deprivation, sacrifice, or living in caves. I think what we fail to recognize are the nourishing life-giving forces we gain by caring for the Earth and living within its laws. I am reminded of a Native American proverb: "Only when the last tree is cut, only when the last river is polluted, only when the last fish is caught, will they realize that you can't eat money."

In permaculture design we are using our ingenuity to rebuild the environment to meet the needs of people and the earth, thereby creating a regenerative relationship. The primary focus is on utility. However, I'd like to see permaculture take into consideration concern for design that honors aesthetics. A beautiful aesthetic would invite people into its majesty. It would completely shift the perception of deprivation toward one of aspiration. Only then might people be willing to awaken from the illusion of a convenient modern lifestyle to one that truly provides health, well-being, and joy.

It is amazing how quickly the earth responds to our care. When we provide colorful flowers, then birds, beneficial insects, and bees are invited to join us. When we tend the soil, luscious gardens can bloom. In return for our tending, we are given gifts allowing us create, enjoy, and savor beauty. We can make wonderful meals, listen to the sounds of life tweeting and buzzing, and provide for our own wellness, all contributing to a lifestyle that deeply connects us to the place where we live.

Craig: It seems to me that the important points you raise come down to the problem of finding ways to transform our relationship to nature, the elements, and place, and that we can do this through an appreciative orientation. Why do you suppose that, culturally speaking, we resist the aesthetic side of life and even denigrate it? To say it in the language of mythology, what is our problem with Aphrodite, whose footsteps were said to leave green marks on the earth?

Rebecca: Nurturing and maintaining beauty in the world requires some forethought, planning, and an ability to see beyond quick gratification. It's the socially sanctioned need to get what we want right now that's diminished our ability to understand the unintended consequences of our actions. Even corporations look for return on investment in quarters, not years. Mass media has colluded in and perpetuated the fear that we are less than whole without whatever they peddle. I don't think we want to destroy the aesthetic side of life. I believe it is an unintended consequence of our behavior.

Wanting everything now has been at the expense of the source from which it came, resulting in massive pollution, environmental destruction, unfair distribution of the commons, and resource depletion. This mindset of spoiled adolescence shows limited capacity to comprehend consequences.

Or to practice patience. It is common to hear the refrain that "I don't have enough time." Nature *takes* time to seed itself, grow, die back, and replenish. Likewise, we are best served emotionally, physically, and spiritually when we take time for life. Movements have started by calling themselves Slow Food, Slow Money, and Voluntary Simplicity. Inherent in each is the expectation that it takes time to achieve what is worthwhile.

A common criticism of slowing life down and becoming more self-reliant is that it's a lot of work. This concern is legitimate, but we need to remember that *we* created these high-speed realities we face. Maybe we can create new realities incorporating more of what's most important to us. I would love to see a society in which more of us could create livelihoods out of what we were most passionate about and were good at. Imagine spending our time doing what we love.

As we witness the breakdown of the environment and the man-made systems upon which we have relied, perhaps there will come a collective maturational recognition that by living in accord with nature, and recognizing that we are part of nature, we can reimagine and recreate a world where we care for the planet, each other, and ourselves.

According to the sage Lao Tzu, "Nature does not hurry, yet everything is accomplished." Aphrodite honors these words of wisdom by encouraging people to take time, change the pace, and take notice. Several years ago I went to visit a friend who is a lifelong resident of San Francisco, California, one of the most beautiful cities in the world. We spent the afternoon catching up on what had transpired in our lives. I had asked if we could walk through Golden Gate Park, and he acknowledged that he hadn't spent much time in the park. It always seems we take for granted what is right in front of us.

We walked through the rose garden as part of our meandering. At the close of the day, to my surprise, my friend thanked me for insisting that we walk through the rose garden. As cliché as it sounds, he appreciated taking the time to smell the roses.

Craig: As you know, terrapsychology approaches nature and Earth as worthy not only of respect and appreciation, but also of dialog. How could the kind of aphroditic sensibility you describe give us a clearer sense of what nature, Earth, the land, the elements, etc. need from us?

Rebecca: Aphrodite as a nature goddess was responsible for the life, procreation, and regeneration cycles that control the entire life cycle of the planet. In order for cycles to work properly, they need to be in balance.

Nature corrects imbalances. According to myth, when Aphrodite was not properly worshipped she took revenge. We can see evidence of metaphorical "vengeance" where human activity has caused an imbalance in natural systems: coal ash levees breaking unexpectedly and sending rivers of noxious substance down a valley. Fields of locusts ravaging a monocrop. Homes regularly rebuilt in flood plains subject to annual runoff. Volcanic ash shooting so high in the sky that it paralyzes international air travel. Mutated super-weeds returning in the face of rampant herbicides. Nature answers back with the same magnitude as the offense. Industrial influence on climate change is now being answered by torrential rains, severe droughts, and rising sea levels impacting regional human survival.

What Aphrodite expects from us is based upon core human values we all have in common: empathic care and compassion. She expects reciprocity and acknowledgment that all living systems are interconnected and depend upon each other. Some may argue that greed and selfishness are basic human drives, but science is proving this to be a falsehood, as in studies that outline cooperation in nature.

Even rats flinch when fellow rats suffer. I think the world's beauty waits for us to mature beyond collective adolescence.

We can show our appreciation and maturity by turning our attention toward regenerative work in service to nature's quest to achieve balance. Restorative work could include activities like reforestation, protection of biodiversity and habitats, cleanup of polluted regions, rebuilding of agricultural soil, ocean, waterway, and wetlands protection, and climate change mitigation. In a mythological context, taking steps to restore Earth's ability to support life honors Aphrodite's divinity. In return she bestows sustenance, beauty, vibrancy, aliveness, and playfulness—all those things that inspire us to live fully in the present moment.

Craig: What is the relationship between Aphrodite and nature? Are you saying that to honor one honors the other?

Rebecca: Aphrodite has a strong relationship to and influence within nature. The myth of Aphrodite honors the archetypes of love, beauty, passion, and procreation. Her stories and symbology reveal her deep connection with nature and worship of the powers of life. These associations appear in the stories surrounding her myth.

Aphrodite's inception roots her in procreation and fertility. Hesiod tells of Cronus the Titan developing a hatred for his father Uranus the Sky. Cronos castrated his father and threw his testicles into the ocean. Aphrodite was born, mature and beautiful, out of the foam created by the sperm and blood of Uranus. Life is forever being born out of the salty water of the ocean's womb. Many symbols characterizing the beauty of nature are associated with Aphrodite, including seashells, roses, and doves. She perpetuated life through the power of desire and passion in the heart. Her footsteps fertilized the earth and caused green grass to grow.

Upon her arrival in Cyprus she was greeted by the Horae, the goddesses of the seasons, who became her attendants. Farmers particularly honored the Horae, and the relationship between them and Aphrodite influenced fertility in agriculture.

The Graces of beauty, delight, and blossom also attended

Aphrodite. Demeter tended to nurturance and growth, but Aphrodite's presence created the blooms. She is often associated with the rose and its fragrance. Natural fragrances adorned Aphrodite's sanctuary.

One of her loves was Adonis, a vegetation god. One day while hunting he was killed by a wild boar. Deeply saddened, Aphrodite sprinkled his blood with nectar, and the beautiful red springtime anemone came up from the ground.

Aphrodite's priestesses were bees called the Melissae. She had a love for the golden honeycomb. The bee represented a symbol of feminine potency because of their ability to create honey as a food source and a preservative. Female bees also pollinate flowers, creating more abundance.

Aphrodite's connections to nature reach to the interplanetary realm. Venus was the Roman name given to her, and is known as the most beautiful planet in the solar system.

Mythologically speaking, honoring nature honors Aphrodite, and honoring Aphrodite honors nature.

Craig: To mention another side of this: David Orr makes the point that a lot of the ugliness in environments built by industrial societies is not just unpleasant, but pathological. It seems from what you say that actively cultivating an aphroditic sensibility toward self, body, nature, place might work to prevent us from creating more of this health-sickening ugliness. Would you like to address this issue?

Rebecca: In his 2000 essay "Loving Children: A Design Problem," David Orr writes,

The child's sense of connection to the world can be damaged by ecologically impoverished surroundings. And it can be damaged as well by exposure to violence, poverty, and even by too much affluence. It can be destroyed, in other words, when ugliness, both human and ecological, becomes the norm. Ecological design begins with the creation of places in which the ecology of imagination and ecological attachment can flourish. These would be safe urban and rural places that included biological diversity, wildness, flowing water, trees, animals, open fields, and room to roam—places in which beauty became the standard.[1]

The sense of disconnection Orr refers to affects not only children, but all of us. Our disconnection and alienation from nature permits us to believe we have created a better way of life, dismissing obvious evidence to the contrary, such as the tolls taken on our physical, mental, and emotional health. To the extent that our inner world is pathologized, it will be reflected unconsciously in the built environments we create.

By contrast, actively cultivating an aphroditic sensibility toward self, body, nature, and place might work to prevent us from creating more ugliness. Beyond that, it also could reconnect us to the core of our humanity and soul and deeply nourish and replenish our lives.

Practices that nurture gratitude are key to finding the compass and strengths needed to navigate and persist through challenging events and emotional conflicts. Gratitude is grounded in the values of love, joy, beauty, and appreciation for the gifts all around us. Another key is the practice of curiosity. Curiosity keeps us engaged and interested in the world. It also keeps us interesting to others, facilitating deeper levels of engagement at an authentic level where the soul thrives.

As we nourish richness of soul, it follows naturally to honor our body. This is done by treating our personal health as if it were a spiritual practice we design and build into the routine of our life. Honoring our bodies shows gratitude for the physical temple that allows us to be on the earth. We honor them by receiving wholesome food, clean water, fresh air, exercise, rest, and sexual intimacy.

It is also our responsibility to limit our toxic exposure and thereby reduce the load on the bodily systems that work hard to cleanse us. With vibrant health, we exude our natural beauty as human beings and become attractors to that which nourishes us.

Our bodies have rhythms, phases, and cycles in tune with those of nature. When we feel most grounded, most at peace, and most connected, we are typically with or around nature. By deepening our connection with nature, we also cultivate our instinctual drive to protect that which we love. This keeps us from destroying and defacing the very sources of our sustenance and prevents us from creating ugliness in our environment.

An earthly ethic of protectiveness forms from practices of appreciation. An aphroditic sensibility can light a beacon over what can become a thriving world.

Endnote

1. http://www.designshare.com/Research/Orr/ Loving_Children.htm

Rebecca Elliott is an environmental life coach and holds a master's degree in Consciousness Studies from John F Kennedy University. Her bachelor's degree is in business administration (Chico State). She holds a permaculture design certification, is a trained facilitator of the US Transition Initiatives movement, and has completed biointensive farming training from one of its pioneers, John Jeavons. In addition to coaching, Rebecca gives environmental awareness presentations. She has filmed a testimonial for Deepak Chopra's "Grow Younger, Live Longer," has been interviewed by Natural Solutions magazine about eco-anxiety (and by Paige Wolf, author of an upcoming book on the subject of "green guilt"), and has contributed a chapter to the book Storied Lives: Discovering and Deepening Your Personal Myth *published by World Soul Books.*

CPSIA information can be obtained at www.ICGtesting.com
261306BV00001B/259/P